THE LAST OF THE BRAVE;

OR

RESTING PLACES OF OUR FALLEN HEROES

IN

The Crimea and at Scutari.

BY

CAPTAINS

THE HON. JOHN COLBORNE, 60TH ROYAL RIFLES, LATE 77TH REGIMENT;

AND

FREDERIC BRINE, ROYAL ENGINEERS.

———"DULCE ET DECORUM EST PRO PATRIÂ MORI."

LONDON:
ACKERMANN AND Co., 106, STRAND.
1857.

PRINTED AND BOUND IN GREAT BRITAIN BY
ANTONY ROWE LTD, EASTBOURNE

MIDDLE RAVINE.
(LOOKING TOWARDS THE CAMP.)

CONTENTS.

	PAGE
INTRODUCTION	v
ALMA	28
BALAKLAVA	37
BRITISH RIGHT ATTACK	30
CATHCART'S HILL	44
HEAD QUARTERS (British Army)	31
INGOUR	57
INKERMANN	29
KADIKOI	31
KARANI	33
KAZATCH	25
MALAKOFF	52
SCUTARI	53
YENIKALE	52
ROYAL NAVAL BRIGADE	15–23
ROYAL HORSE ARTILLERY — A. TROOP	41
C. "	"
I. "	33
CAVALRY — 1ST (King's) DRAGOON GUARDS	41
4TH (Royal Irish) "	33
6TH DRAGOON GUARDS (Carabiniers)	41
4TH (The Queen's Own Light) DRAGOONS	33
11TH (Prince Albert's Own) HUSSARS	"
13TH (Light) DRAGOONS	32
ROYAL ARTILLERY — RIGHT SIEGE TRAIN	5–28
LEFT "	21–22
E. FIELD BATTERY	27
J. (Heavy) "	34
V. " "	"
W. FIELD "	32
X. " "	36
Nos 2 Co 5TH BATN, 6 Co 2ND BATN, 8 Co 9TH BATN, &c.	28–33–34–14
ROYAL ENGINEERS & ROYAL SAPPERS & MINERS	16
GUARDS AND HIGHLANDERS (1ST DIVISION)	18–40
HIGHLAND DIVISION (KAMARA)	42
SECOND DIVISION	11–14
THIRD "	20–22
FOURTH "	11–14
LIGHT " — 1ST BRIGADE	1–6
2ND BRIGADE	7–14
ROYAL MARINES (Light Infantry)	39
LAND TRANSPORT CORPS — HEAD QUARTERS	31
2ND BATTALION	11
4TH "	"
7TH "	33
10TH "	31
ARMY WORKS CORPS	"
INFANTRY — 1ST (The Royal) REGIMENT	43
13TH (Prince Albert's) LIGHT INFANTRY	40
23RD (Royal Welch) FUSILIERS	6
34TH (Cumberland) REGIMENT	"
41ST (The Welch) "	30
44TH (East Essex) "	22
49TH (Hertfordshire) "	29
50TH (Queen's Own) "	21
71ST (Highland) LIGHT INFANTRY	52
72ND (Duke of Albany's Own) HIGHLANDERS	43
82ND (The Prince of Wales's Volunteers)	40
93RD HIGHLANDERS	43
95TH (The Derbyshire) REGIMENT	29
APPENDIX	59
INDEX	65

ERRATA.

Nos. 5, 6, 7, 13th Light Dragoons, page 32, should follow No. 3, 4th Light Dragoons, page 33.

No. 23, 1st Royals, page 43, should be No. 1.

Note, page 52.—The 71st Highland Light Infantry embarked at Kertch for Malta, 22nd June, 1856, not 1855, as stated.

INTRODUCTION.

In offering the following pages to the Public, the Compilers trust that they are not too late in attempting to excite an interest relative to the last earthly tenements of those gallant ones who, while they lived, were their country's noblest pride, and, now that they can fight her victories no more, assert a just claim to her undying remembrance. The days are gone by when numbers of enthusiastic votaries were prepared to do homage to a stone, a flower, a clod—in short, no matter how humble a relic—from the late seat of war; when, indeed, the waters of the Alma would hardly have given place to those of the Jordan, and a great nation's arms were opened wide to welcome each worn-out survivor from the arena of strife and bloodshed. Not quite two summers ago three mighty powers stood breathing defiance against one another on the shores of the Black Sea; the earth shook with their rage, and the whole world looked on amazed at the stupendous amount of intellect, science, bravery, and fortitude brought to bear on the conflict. But the struggle is over; the olive branch has been accepted, and friend and foe, now hand-in-hand as becomes those who have tested the perfection of each other's metal, unite in the pleasant interchange of national civilities and individual friendships. The sound of the horses' hoofs has died away upon those far-off plains; the familiar "huts" of the Allies may be sought for in vain; even our old friends the Tartars have emigrated to a strange land. The vines once more yield up their luscious tribute, the flowers of the field their glory, and soon a new Sebastopol of greater splendour than the former will have risen up to astonish the eyes of those whom curiosity or reminiscences may entice to the old spot. In short, few traces of our presence in the Crimea remain to this day, save those very cemeteries and monuments of which the present work humbly proposes itself to be a register.

As it is possible that a few minute particulars regarding the burial grounds may not be unacceptable to the casual reader, this opportunity is taken of affording them.

All slabs or monuments not *marked* are of the stone of the country, which is generally soft in quality, and remarkable for its dazzling whiteness, although durable—witness Sebastopol, Simpheropol, &c. Most of that made use of was procured either from the quarry in front of the Third Division camp, the wall behind the Redan, the Inkermann quarry, or the docks after they were blown up by the Allies, from whence was also procured some granite. All cemeteries were, by General Orders, enclosed and made neat, in many cases being surrounded by a dry boundary stone wall, with a small ditch outside, the earth from which was thrown against the wall within. Entrances were left in the first instance, but were blocked up previous to the departure of the army in cases where ornamental wooden gates had not been fixed; the entrance gate to the Guards' burial ground was tastefully formed of hoop iron taken from the Commissariat barrels. Of the burial grounds in general, the one most remarkable for its picturesque beauty was that of the Second Brigade, Light Division, Woronzoff Road, to which was imparted a certain foreign character from its being laid out in walks and alleys somewhat after the manner of "Père la Chaise." Cathcart's Hill might be termed an humble imitation of Kensal Green, and contains some handsome monuments, in design and execution far from inferior to many in England, as does also the graveyard of the First Brigade, Light Division. To the burial grounds of the Naval Brigade and and those of the Sailors at Balaklava and Kazatch must be assigned a touching grace peculiar to themselves. Some regiments—ex.: the 18th Royal Irish, 19th and 90th Light Infantry — erected their own monuments; in other instances these, together with all public ones, were constructed by men of the Royal Engineers, principally belonging to the 10th Company, detached from the Royal Engineers' camp to the Light Division. A map of Sebastopol and surrounding country, showing the relative positions of the various burial grounds, is published in connection with this work by Messrs. Ackermann & Co., 106, Strand, the accuracy of which may be depended upon. Inscriptions are given exactly as they appeared on the tombstones or slabs, without any corrections.

To the Comrade, the Friend, and the Relative, are finally commended these mementos of our eastern "resting places," as a tribute to departed gallantry, together with the sincere sympathy of

THE COMPILERS.

CURRAGH CAMP,
July 13*th*, 1857.

FIRST BRIGADE, LIGHT DIVISION.
(MIDDLE RAVINE.)

Victoria Redoubt

London, Published by Ackermann & Co. 106 Strand.

FIRST BRIGADE LIGHT DIVISION.

7TH, 23RD, 33RD, 34TH REGIMENTS, AND 2ND BATTALION, RIFLE BRIGADE.

NUMBER OF GRAVES—891.

(1.) (FACING INKERMANN).
I H S
THIS MONUMENT
IS ERECTED TO THE
MEMORY OF THE
OFFICERS,
NON-COMMISSIONED OFFICERS,
AND SOLDIERS OF THE
FIRST BRIGADE,
LIGHT DIVISION, BRITISH ARMY,
WHO HAVE DIED OR FALLEN
BEFORE SEBASTOPOL
BETWEEN THE 28TH SEPTEMBER,
1854, AND 30TH
JUNE, 1856.

(Left.)
2ND BATTALION RIFLE BRIGADE
7TH ROYAL FUSILIERS
23RD ROYAL WELCH FUSILIERS

(Right.)
33RD THE DUKE OF WELLINGTON'S
REGIMENT
34TH (CUMBERLAND) REGIMENT

(Rear.)
I H S
ERECTED
BY BRIGADIER
GENERAL VAN STRAUBENZEE
IN TESTIMONY OF
HEROIC FORTITUDE AND VALOR.

(2.) SACRED
To The
Memory
of
LIEUT. RICHD. BOROUGH,
2nd Battn. Rifle Brigade,
BORN 28TH MAY/38, DIED 13 NOVR/55.
Aged
17 Years
5 Months.
Oh! Death
where is thy
sting,
Oh! Grave
where is thy
Victory.

(3.) (FACING RAVINE.)
SACRED
to the
MEMORY
of the
SERJEANTS
of the
2ND BATTALION
RIFLE BRIGADE,
Who Died in the Service
of their
QUEEN and COUNTRY
during the Campaign
in the
Crimea,
1854-55,
ERECTED by their Comrade
SERJEANTS as a mark of
RESPECT.

(Left.)
KILLED.
W. BROAD,
12 May, 55.
H. MURCH,
18 June, 55.
R. BRIDGLAND,
18 June, 55.
E. BOUGHTON,
30 August, 55.
W. BLACKSTOCK,
14 September, 55.
W. SIMPSON,
20 September, 54.
J. SWALLOW,
20 September, 54.

(Right.)
KILLED.
C. HART,
4 June, 55.
R. BEECH,
2 July, 55.
W. DAWSON,
8 September, 55,
W. EVERITT,
8 September, 55.
J. CONNOR,
8 September, 55.
T. FARRELL,
8 September, 55.
W. THOROGATE
21 September, 55.

(Rear.)
DIED.
H. STEER,
9 October, 54.
A. SLADE,
14 October, 54.
J. MILLS,
4 April, 55.
H. PLUMRIDGE,
16 September, 54.
C. LOWE,
20 December, 54.
T. WILKINSON,
28 June, 55.
W. SWARBRICK,
10 August, 55.

(4.) SACRED
To The
Memory
of
LIEUT. F. G. BEAUCHAMP,
7th Royal Fusiliers,
who died in Camp before
SEBASTOPOL,
on the
2nd Octr.,
1855.

(5.) SACRED (Wood.)
TO
THE MEMORY
of
Serjeant Richard Beech,
2nd Battn Rifle Brigade,
DIED
July 2nd of WOUNDS received 18th
JUNE, 1855,
Aged 24 Years,
This Tablet is placed as a Mark
of Respect by a Comrade & Friend.

(6.) SACRED (Wood.)
TO THE
MEMORY
OF
PATRICK RINDS, BAND 34th REGT., WHO
DIED JUNE 28th 1855, AGED 26 YEARS
ERECTED BY HIS BROTHERS.

(7.) I H S (Wood.)
SACRED TO THE MEMORY OF PR. FLINN,
34th REGT WHO DEPARTED THIS LIFE 4th
JULY,
1855.

(8.) I H S (Wood.)
SACRED TO THE MEMORY
of
SERGT FREDK. SKELTON,
of
The 23rd R. W. Fusiliers,
Died
on the 24th June, 1855,
AGE 31 YEARS.

(9.) GLORIA IN EXCELSIS DEO
I H S
SACRED
TO THE MEMORY OF THE UNDERMEN-
TIONED SERJTS of H. B. M. 34th REGT
WHO FELL BEFORE SEBASTOPOL IN
THE SERVICE OF THEIR QUEEN AND
COUNTRY IN 1854-5
C. CLARKE.   J. HARRISON.   T. HULL.
W. BURNS.   R. HAWKINS.   J. DUNPHEY.
G. KING.   G. ANDERSON.
ALSO TO THOMAS, BROTHER OF
SERJT MAJOR J. MORTIMER.

Erected by the Serjeants of
the 34th Regt.

(10.) SACRED
To The
Memory
of
LIEUTENANT O. COLT
7th Royal Fusiliers
who was killed in the assault
on the
R E D A N
on the
8th Septr
1855.

(11.) SACRED
To The
Memory
of
LIEUT W. L. L. G. WRIGHT
7th Royal Fusiliers
who was killed in the assault
on the
R E D A N
on the
8th Septr
1855.

FIRST BRIGADE LIGHT DIVISION.

(12.) (FACING RAVINE).
IHS

SACRED
TO THE MEMORY OF
THE OFFICER, NON
COMMISSIONED OFFI-
CER AND PRIVATES
OF LETTER. E. COMP'Y
34TH REGT
WHO DIED IN THE SER-
VICE OF THEIR QUEEN
& COUNTRY 1854. 55
AND 56.
—o—
THIS MONUMENT IS
ERECTED BY THE OFFI-
CERS, NON-COMMIS-
SIONED OFFICERS AND
PRIVATES OF THE
ABOVE NAMED COMP'Y.
APRIL 1856.

(Left.)
PRIVATES.
W. HAWTHORNE. W. WARD
E. HERRITAGE. H. WATTS
J. HITCHENS. J. WATTS
W. LAYLAND. P. MAHONY
C. McCARTHY. C. MORLEY
J. McCARRITY. C. PALMER
W. POWER. J. RICKARD
P. SHANNON. W. SMITH
J. STANLEY. R. WHITNEY
J. MARTIN.

(Right.)
CORPL. A. SHEEKY
PRIVATES
C. ALFORD. C. ALEN
M. ALLEN. T. BARNES
J. BARRET. W. BONNER
C. BLOXHAM. E. BEVAN
E. BROWN. J. BRUTON
N. CAMM. W. COLLEGE
C. CONNERS. J. CONNER
M. CORNWALL. J. DALEY
T. EARNSHAW. P. FOX
R. HAFFEY. M. HANLEY

(Rear.)
CAPTN J. ROBINSON

(13.) SACRED
TO THE
MEMORY
of
WILLIAM PRATT
2nd Battn Rifle Brigade
WHO
Departed This Life
June the 20th
Aged 31 Years
A.D. 1855.

(14.) SACRED
To The
Memory
of
LIEUT & ADJT HOBSON
7 ROYAL FUSILIERS
who was killed in
the attack on the
"REDAN"
on the
18th June, /55.

(15.) 7TH ROYAL FUSILIERS
To their Colonel
WALTER. LACY. YEA.
who was killed on the 18 June
1855
whilst gallantly leading the
storming party against the great
REDAN
AGED 47 YEARS

(16.) IHS
IN MEMORY OF
GEORGE. O'NEIL. WILLIAM.
PRICE. ANTHONY. CUNNING.
PATRICK. RINDS, JOHN ENRIGHT.
of the Band 34th Regt
who DIED in the Service
of their Country.
—o—
Erected
by their Comrades of the
Band as a mark of Esteem
and Regard
June 1855

(17.) SACRED
To The
Memory
of
CAPT E. R. FORMAN.
2 Battn Rifle Brigade
who was killed at the
assault on the
"REDAN"
on the 18TH June 1855
AGED 33 YEARS
this stone is erected by his
Brother Officers

(18.) SACRED TO THE MEMORY OF
IHS
THE UNDERMENTIONED OFFICERS
OF THE 33rd
DUKE OF Wellington's
REGIMENT.
Who died in the Service of
their Country during the
Campaign of 1854 & 1855.
Colonel F. R. Blake, C. B
Lieut Colonel T. B. Gough.
Captain H. U. Burke.
Lieut H. A. Thistlethwayte
F. Du Pre Montagu
W. S. Worthington
H. Thorold.
V. Bennett.
L. R. Heyland.
H. Donovan.
Lieut & Adjt H. S. St V. Marsh
Paymaster, P. McGrath.

(19.) SACRED TO THE MEMORY
IHS
OF
THE OFFICERS
NON COMMISSIONED OFFICERS
DRUMMERS AND PRIVATES OF
J. No 4, OR LIEUT J. T. ROGERS COMPNY
33RD THE DUKE OF WELLINGTON'S REGT
WHO WERE KILLED AND DIED
OF WOUNDS AND SICKNESS
DURING THE CAMPAIGN OF
1854.5.

come, holy ghost, creator come,
from thy bright heavenly throne;
come take possession of our souls
and make them all thy own.

ERECTED BY THEIR COMRADES
JUNE 1856

(20.) SACRED
TO THE
Memory
of
LIEUT E. S. G. WOODFORD
2nd Battn Rifle Brigade
who died from wounds received
in the
"TRENCHES,"
on the
30TH JUNE/55
Aged
18 YEARS

(21.) (FACING RAVINE.)
IHS
SACRED
TO THE
MEMORY
of the
—o—
NON COMMISSIONED
OFFICERS DRUMMERS
AND PRIVATES
OF THE LIGHT OR
CAPTAIN
T. B. FANSHAWE'S
COMPANY 33 THE
DUKE
OF WELLINGTON'S
REGIMENT WHO
WERE KILLED AND
HAVE DIED OF
WOUNDS & SICKNESS
WHILST DEFENDING
THEIR QUEEN AND
COUNTRY IN THE
YEARS OF 1854. 55
56.

(Left.)
COPL. W. STEWART.
COPL. J. MARRA.
COPL. J. KENINGTON.
DRS J. McHUGH. J. DAY.
PRIVATES
A. BOYAD. W. BRADY
F. BOSWORTH. J. BOURDMAN
M. BOYLAND. J. BURGES
M. CAHILL. W. CRANE
W. CALCROFT. T. J. DARE
T. ELLIOTT. C. HART
W. FRANKS. J. FIRKINS
W. CUNNINGHAM. J. CUNNINGHAM
H. GREENROYDE. J. KAY
J. GRAHAM. C. HAUGH
W. HELLEWELL. P. HOGAN. P. HUGHES
J. JONES. J. JOYCE
R. KIRK. J. KELLY

(Right.)
P. LAWLESS. J. LAW.
C. LAWES. E. MARSHALL.
A. MARSHALL. W. McAREE.
D. MEAGHER. J. NEAL.
T. MONAGHAN. H. PRIOR.
O. MOUNCEY. J. QUIN.
G. RAMPLING. E. RYAN.
T. READER. D. REDFERE.
M. RUTLAND. T. TIDD.
M. READY. T. ROBINSON.
J. SLATTERY. W. SMITH.
G. SKEGGS. J. TRACEY.
W. TURNER. T. UPTON.
J. WILLISS. J. WHITTY.
W. WHITEHEAD. W. WILLIAMSON.
T. WHITMORE. W. YOUNG.
J. HODGINGS. H. TYLER.

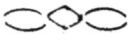

(Rear.)
THIS STONE IS EREC
TED BY THE OFFICERS
NON COMMISSIONED
OFFICERS AND MEN
OF THE LIGHT COMPY
33RD. REGT AS A MARK OF
RESPECT AND ESTEEM
FOR THEIR DEPARTED
COMRADES

WHEN RISING FROM THE BED OF DEATH
O'ERWHELMED WITH GUILT AND FEAR
WE SEE OUR MAKER FACE TO FACE
OH, HOW SHALL WE APPEAR

(22.)
SACRED
IHS
TO THE
MEMORY
of
VALENTINE BENNETT
LIEUT 33D THE DUKE
OF WELLINGTON'S REGT
who was killed in the
Attack on Sebastopol on The
18th June, 1855 Aged 27 Years
Requiescat in Pace

ERECTED By his
BROTHER
FREDERIC PHILIP BENNETT
AND
OFFICERS OF THE 33D
THE DUKE OF WELLINGTON'S
REGIMENT.

(23.)
IHS
SACRED
TO THE MEMORY OF
LIEUT LANGFORD
R. HEYLAND 33RD REGT
—O—
WHO FELL IN THE
ASSAULT
ON THE REDAN
ON THE 18TH JUNE
1855.

(24.)
SACRED
TO THE
MEMORY
OF
HANS STEPHENSON
ST VINCENT MARSH
LIEUT AND ADJUTANT
OF THE 33RD
DUKE OF WELLINGTON'S
REGT WHO WAS KILLED
IN THE TRENCHES ON
THE 24TH JUNE 1855
AGED 21 YEARS

(25.)
SACRED TO THE MEMORY
OF
THE UNDERMENTIONED MEN OF G.
No. 5. OR CAPT E. B. PRESCOTT'S COMPY
33D DUKE OF WELLINGTON'S REGT
WHO FELL BY WOUNDS OR SICKNESS
DURING THE CAMPAIGN OF 1854 & 1855
IN THE SERVICE OF THEIR COUNTRY.
SERJT J. BAILES.—J. CANAVAN.—G. METCALF.
SERJT M. McTEAUGE.—G. CLOSE.—W. MILES.
CORPL A. HAINES.—J. FULLER.—C. O'SHEA.
CORPL J. TALBOT.—J. FULTON.—W. ROWLEY.
CORPL R. WOODS.—M. FAHEY.—J. RIDDELL.
PRIVATES. H. ALSOP.—H. FUTTERS.—R SMITH.
R. BEDFORD.—J. FORSYTH.—J. SWADKINS.
W. BAILEY.—J. GALLAGHER.—R. WHITWORTH.
A. BURNS.—E. GRIFFIN.—J. WOODWARD.
J. BIRMINGHAM.—J. HALL.—E. WOOLHOUSE.
J. BARRETT.—J. HANSON.—J. FIELDING.
W. BURROWS.—J. HUTTY.—W. QUINTON.
J. BRIGHTON.—R. JOHNSTONE.—H. McKEON.
C. BETHELL.—T. HOGAN.—J. COX.
M. CARTY.—G. HUNT.—J. CLANSEY.
C. CUNNINGHAM.—J. HOYLE.—M. WALSH.
J. CORBY.—R. HARRIS.—C. THOMPSON.
H. CULVERHOUSE. - W. MULLENS.—J. TULLY.

(26.)
SACRED
TO THE
MEMORY
of
PRIVT PETER MARTEN, 7 R. F.
KILLED IN TAKING THE
QUERRIES.
—,,—
7 JUNE/55
Aged
26 YEARS

(27.)
SACRED   (Wood.)
TO
THE MEMORY OF
DRUMR JOHN A. MOORE, ROYAL FUSILIERS
who was killed in the attack on the
"REDAN"
ON THE 8th of September 1855
AGED
18
YEARS
—,,—

(28.)
SACRED
TO THE
MEMORY
OF THE
NON COMD OFFICERS
and
PRIVATES
of
B COMPANY 33 DUKE
OF WELLINGTON'S REGT
WHO FELL IN DEFENCE OF
THEIR QUEEN AND COUNTRY
DURING THE CAMPAIGN OF
1854-5
SERJTS J. CHALMERS. W. MOORE
F. KERRY., W. McLAUGHLIN
CORPLS M. WARD. P. MARTIN
DRUMR R. MORLAND
AND
71 PRIVATES

P. ELMS—J. OAKES—W. REYNOLDS
J. GREEN—T. WALKER—J. COLEMAN
W. BASSETT— BUTCHER—G. BROOKE
J. CALNAN—J. DENNY—P. HOREY
C. MASTERS—J. SPENCER—M. MORRIS
J. STEBBINGS—R. WHITTAKER—W. PENNYFEATER
S. BRANT—B. JONES—C. BIDDLE
J. DEERY—P. O'CONNOR—J. GRIFFIN
J. HERON—S. McGARRY—J. RUSSELL
T. BLANEY—W. FRANKLIN—D. GLEESON
J. GREEN—P. LEE—T. PELLING
G. ROLLINGS—D. DIVINE—S. STOKES
T. BRIDGEMAN—W. CARROLL—J. CHAPPELL
J. CUPIT—S. FALSTEAD—M. GARDINER
W. GOODACRE—T. GRIFFIN—M. HALLY
W. RUSSELL—W. SAWYER—G. SEYMOUR
S. SHORE—F. HUDDY—M. BOYLAND
T. BROOKES—A. DOWNES—J. MILLS
W. PARRY—W. RICHARDS—R. STACEY
J. HANLY—M. KANE—T. WHITEAD
J. WORRELL—J. CONNORS—G. LOWNDS
T. NASH—A. McKAY—W. BAVIN
J. BROWN—D. FOX—W. QUINTON
W. BERRY—and—H. McCANN.

(29)
SACRED
TO THE
Memory
of
DRUMR JNO. ARNOTT, 7 RL FUSILIERS
who Died on The 16 June 1855
through wounds received on the 7TH
in taking
the
"Quarries"
Aged
24 YEARS

ERECTED BY
HIS BROTHER.

(30.)
SACRED
To The
Memory
of
HOSPL SERGT EDWD S. SWYNY
33D REGT
Who Died
at
MONASTIR
TURKEY
on the
29th July 1854
Aged
25 Years
ERECTED
By
HIS BROTHER
H. W. S.

(31.)   (FACING RAVINE.)
IHS
ERECTED. TO. THE. MEMORY.
of The
NON COMSD OFFICERS & PRIVATES
OF. F. COMPANY. 33D. THE DUKE
OF WELLINGTON'S REGIMENT.
WHO DIED IN DEFENCE OF THEIR
QUEEN AND COUNTRY.
DURING THE CAMPAIGN
OF 1854-5.

SERJEANTS	CORPORALS	PRIVATES
C. BYRNE		
P. FEATHER	W. BATES	65
J. WALLACE		

CHRIST BEING RAIS'D BY POWER DIVINE
AND RESCU'D FROM THE GRAVE,
SHALL DIE NO MORE; DEATH SHALL ON HIM.
NO MORE DOMINION HAVE.
FOR THAT HE DIED 'TWAS FOR OUR SINS
HE ONCE VOUCHSAF'D TO DIE,
BUT THAT HE LIVES, HE LIVES TO GOD,
FOR ALL ETERNITY.

(Back.)
SACRED. TO. THE. MEMORY.
of the
OFFICERS OF THE SAME COMPY
Viz

H. THOROLD	V. BENNETT
WHO, WAS, KILL'D	WHO, WAS, KILL'D,
AT THE BATTLE	AT THE ATTACK
OF INKERMANN	ON THE REDAN
ON, THE 5TH NOVR	ON THE 18TH OF JUNE
1854.	1855.

(32.)
SACRED TO THE MEMORY
OF THE
NON COMMISSIONED OFFICERS
AND
PRIVATES OF THE GR COMPANY
33D DUKE OF WELLINGTON'S REGT
WHO FELL IN THE DEFENCE OF
THEIR QUEEN AND COUNTRY
DURING THE CAMPAIGN OF 1854-5
HOSPL SERJT E. SWYNEY. CR SERJT R. VINCE
SERJEANTS. T. CHECKLEY. E. HANCOCK
P. O'DONNILL J. BIRNIE. H. SIMPSON
CORPORALS
J. MURPHY. W. WEBSDALE
PRIVATES

J. O'NEILL	J. COLDWELL
W. JOHNSTON	J. DARLINGTON
A. CHAPMAN	M. COLE
J. DEMPSEY	J. BOYLAND
R. ATKINSON	J. McKAY
L. HUTCHINS	J. HARRAGAN
T. HOPKINS	T. WHITEHEAD
M. MORIARTY	G. MORRELL
J. STOTT	B. SULLIVAN
W. KNOWLES	W. CALLIGHAN
J. WHITTY	J. QUINN
W. SMITH	P. O'NEIL
C. BEEBE	W. GREENFIELD
S. ARNOLL	J. CONNORS
E. BURNS	R. ROPER
S. READ	P. CROW
W. RILEY	F. HUGHES
C. BIRGES	J. KENNEDY
W. SADDINGTON	J. HARRISON
A. DAVIS	J. WEATHERALL
P. LEONARD	J. BURNS
D. RYAN	W. McNAUGHTON
D. HURLEY	E. FINLEY
P. PAUDEN	T. FUSSEY
W. PARROCK	J. LEWIS
J. BEARD	D. McCLUSKEY
H. DOWNES	E. SIDNEY
A. McLOUGHLAN	R. STRINGFELLOW
J. SMITH	J. THOMPSON
J. KELLY	T. CAIRNS
G. CLARKE	C. WOODWARD
C. COTTON	B. ELLIOTT
J. GELASPIE	J. WYNN
M. HIGGINS	J. HICKEY
B. SHARPE	J. McSHEAN
	J. KENNEDY

ERECTED BY THEIR COMRADES

(33.) SACRED TO THE MEMORY
OF
IHS
THE OFFICERS
NON-COMMISSIONED OFFICERS
DRUMMERS AND PRIVATES OF
E. No 6, OR CAPT FITZERALD'S COMPY
33 THE DUKE OF WELLINGTON'S REGT
WHO WERE KILLED AND DIED OF
WOUNDS AND SICKNESS DURING
THE CAMPAIGN OF 1854-5.

ERECTED BY COMRADE SOLDIERS
1856.

(34.) SACRED (Wood.)
TO
THE
MEMORY
of
CR SERJT T. WILKINSON
2d Battⁿ Rifle Brigade
WHO DIED
On the 28th of June A.D. 1855
Erected By his Comrade
SERJEANTS.

(35.) SACRED
To The
Memory
of
COLR SERJT W. D. K. DOBBIE
7th Royal Fusiliers
Who was killed in Front
of
SEBASTOPOL
On The 7th June /55.

This stone is erected by the
Non Com^d Officers & Privates of
No. 2 Comp^y as a tribute to the
memory of Serj^t Dobbie

"In the midst of life we are in death:"

(36.) SACRED
TO THE
Memory
of
PRIV. MICH. MURPHY. 7. ROYAL
FUSILIERS killed in The
Trenches
on The
1 MAY /55
Aged
22 YEARS

(37.) In
Memory
of
Lieut H. M. Lawrence
34th Regt. who was killed
On The 7th June 1855, In The
Attack Upon The Quarries.
Also of
Captains J. Shiffner
J. Robinson
Lieutts F. R. Hurt
R. J. B. Clayton
and H. D. Alt
Of The Same Regt Who Fell On
The 18th June 1855 In The
Attack Upon The Redan
Erected By Their Brother
Officers As A Mark
of Esteem And Regard.

(38.) SACRED
IHS
TO THE
MEMORY
of
THE Undermentioned
OFFICERS N. C. OFFICERS
AND MEN OF. H. N° 7
Comp^y 33^D The Duke
of WELLINGTON'S
REGIMENT
Who Died in Defence of
Their Queen And Country
During the Campaign of
1854-1855

CAPTN. H. U. BURKE—SR. J. MERIAN—Corp. S. LONGSTONE
G. ANDERSON—E. LAMB—G. CRABTREE
I. BANKS—R. WEEKS—J. COTGROVE
M. BARBER—A. TYSOE—G. OSBORN
P. BOND—P. WALSH—P. LARKIN
C. BROWN—J. TOOHY—W. WINDSHEFFLE
T. BROWN—D. KEEF—J. GASCOINE
M. CARTY—W. MOOR—M. MONAGHAN
W. COBB—E. CAMP—J. MEAGHER
D. GRACE—J. MORRIS—M. JENNER
W. HIrD—L. BELL—M. DINNEEN
T. HAIGH

This is Erected by their surviving
Comrades as a mark of esteem.

(39.) SACRED (Wood)
TO
THE
MEMORY
of
SERJT G. HART
2d Battⁿ Rifle Brigade
WHO WAS KILLED
ON THE 4TH OF JUNE
A.D. 1855
Erected by his comrade
sergeants.

(40.) SACRED
TO THE
MEMORY
of
William Walker Jordan
Lieut, H.M. 34TH Regiment
Who was killed in the Trenches before
Sebastopol during A. Sortie made by the
Enemy on the night of the 22d March. 1855.
ERECTED
by his
BROTHER
OFFICERS

(41.) SACRED (Wood.)
TO
The
MEMORY
OF
SERJT W. BROAD
2nd Battⁿ Rifle Brigade
WHO WAS KILLED
ON The 12th of May
A.D. 1855
Erected by his comrade
Sergeants

(42.) SACRED (Wood.)
TO
The
MEMORY
OF
SERJT E. BOUGHTON
2nd Battⁿ Rifle Brigade
WHO WAS KILLED
On the 30th of August
A.D. 1855
Erected by his comrade
SERJEANTS

(43.) SACRED (Wood.)
TO
The
MEMORY
OF
SERGT J. MILLS
2nd Battⁿ Rifle Brigade
WHO DIED
On the 4th of April
A.D. 1855
Erected By his comrade
SERGEANTS.

(44.) SACRED TO THE MEMORY
OF
SERJT JAMES WALLACE
XXXIII. "The Duke of Wellington's"
REGIMENT
WHO DIED on the 10th Feby 1855
Aged 28 YEARS
ERECTED BY HIS BROTHER
(Foot)
A.D.
1855

(45.) IN MEMORY
OF
LIEUT NORMAN RAMSAY OF THE
34th REGT WHO DIED IN CAMP BEFORE
SEBASTOPOL ON THE 22nd JULY 1855.
ERECTED BY HIS BROTHER OFFICERS
AS A MARK OF
ESTEEM
AND
REGARD

(46.) SACRED
TO THE
MEMORY OF
DRUMR WILLIAM, DUNN
34th REG WHO DIED
FROM A WOUND REC-
EIVED IN THE TREN-
CHES BEFORE SEBA-
STOPOL ON THE 23RD
JULY 1855 AGE 21
YEARS

(47.) SACRED
—To—
—The—
Memory
—of—
LIEUT HONBLE E. FITZCLARENCE.
7th ROYAL FUSILIERS
Who died on the
23 July /55
from wounds
received during
the attack
—on the—
REDAN
on the
18 June /55

(48.) SACRED (Wood.)
TO
THE MEMORY OF
SILVESTER BURRELL
QUARTERMASTER OF
H.M.S. LEANDER
Who Was Severely Wounded
BEFORE SEBASTOPOL
On the 10th of July 1855
Aged 41 Years

Tho' boisterous Winds and Neptune's Waves;
Have toss'd us to and Fro;
In Spite of both by God's Decree
We harbour here Below
And at an anchor here We Ride
With many of the Fleet;
in hope's again for to Set Sail
Our redeemer Christ to Meet

FIRST BRIGADE LIGHT DIVISION.

(49.) Sacred To The Memory of SERJT. JOHN. McCANN 7th Royal Fusiliers Who was wounded at the taking of SEBASTOPOL on the 8th September and died from his wounds on the 11th September/55 AGED 30 YEARS.

(50.) IN MEMORY OF CAPT. THE HON. CAVENDISH BROWNE 7th Royal Fusiliers KILLED in repulsing an Attack upon the Trenches MARCH 22nd 1855

(51.) SACRED To The MEMORY —of— BUGLER. W. H. MURRAY 2nd Battn Rifle Brigade who died on the 27th Decr/55. of wounds received at the assault on the "REDAN" —on the 8th Septr/55— AGED. 21. YEARS

This stone is erected by his comrades as a mark of respect.

(52) Sacred To The Memory of LIEUT. H. S. RYDER 2nd Battn Rifle Brigade who was killed in the assault on the "REDAN" on the 8th SEPTR 1855 Aged 20 YEARS

(53.) Sacred To the Memory —of— CAP. M. M. HAMMOND. 2ND BATTN RIFLE BRIGDE Who was Killed in the assault on the "REDAN" on the 8th Sept 1855 Aged 30 YEARS

Blessed are the dead who die in the Lord Rev. xiv. 14.

(54.) SACRED (Wood.) TO THE MEMORY of THOMAS BAILEY. LATE OF H.M. 34TH REGT. OF FOOT WHO DIED OF WOUNDS RECEIVED ON THE 18th OF JUNE 1855 IN THE ATTACK ON THE REDAN AGED 34 YEARS

(55.) Sacred To The Memory of Color. Ser. J. S. WARBRICK. 2nd BATT. RIFLE BRIGDE who died on the 10th August 1855

Aged 31 YEARS.

Erected by a friend & Comrade His trust was in the Lord

PRAY FOR HIM.

(56.) Sacred To The Memory of LIEUT L. NEIL. MALCOLM 2nd Battn Rifle Brigade Who was Killed at the Battle —of— INKERMAN on the 5 Novr 1854 Aged 19. Years

(57.) IHS SACRED TO THE Memory of DRUMR. JOHN McHUGH WHO DIED ON THE 3RD MAY 1855 IN THE SERVICE OF HIS COUNTRY ERECTED BY HIS COMRADES THE BAND AND DRUMRS. of the 33RD DUKE OF WELLINGTON'S REGIMENT AS A MARK OF ESTEEM

(58.) SACRED TO THE MEMORY 33rd REGT. OF EDWARD GRIFFIN WHO DEPARTED THIS LIFE DEC. 14th A.D. 1854, AGED 21 Yrs. BLESSED ARE THE DEAD WHO DIE IN THE LORD

(59.) SACRED TO THE MEMORY 33RD REGT. OF CHARLOTTE ELIZABETH BAYFORD WHO, DEPARTED, THIS, LIFE, NOV. 9th A.D. 1855. AGED 16 MO'S SHE SLEEPS IN JESUS.

(60.) Dr. J. Kimber (Marble.) 23 R. W. F.

Died 20th June A. D. 1855.

Aged 26y. (Foot.) (Wood) J. K.

(61.) (Wood.) THIS CROSS MARKS THE GRAVE OF LIEUT. HENRY THOROLD 33rd Duke of Wellington's Regt, who fell at Inkerman aged 19 It is erected by the friendly hand of one who knew him well and loved him as a brother. Septr 24th 1855.

(Stone Slab.) SACRED TO THE MEMORY of LIEUTN H. THOROLD 33rd REGT KILLED AT INKERMAN 5th NOVEMBER 1854.

RIGHT SIEGE TRAIN, ROYAL ARTILLERY.

NUMBER OF GRAVES—80.

(1.) SACRED TO THE MEMORY OF D. A. CY. GEOE F YELLON SIEGE TRAIN DEPARTMENT R. A WHO WAS KILLED BY THE EXPLOSION 15 NOVR 1855 AGED 38 YEARS

(2.) ERECTED by His Brother CAPT JOHN. MARSHALL 92ND HIGHLRS and by his brother officers of the Royl Artillry To The MEMORY of EDWARD, PRICHARD, MARSHALL Lieutenant Royal Artillery Died November 29th 1855 Aged 17 Years & 5 Months

(3.) SACRED TO THE MEMORY OF GEORGE MURRELL OF THE ROYAL ARTILLERY DIED ON THE 6TH DAY OF AUGUST 185 AGED 37 YEARS IN FRONT OF SEBASTOPOL

(4.) Sacred To The Memory of Deputy Asst Commissary WILLM HAYTER. Siege Train Depart. who died 8th Septr 1855, of wounds received in "TRENCHES" on that day Aged 29 YEARS This stone is erected by one who knew him as a friend and loved him as a brother.

FIRST BRIGADE LIGHT DIVISION.

(5.) Sacred
To The
Memory
of
SERJT MAJOR A MORRIEN
of No. 5. Major M. G. Dixon's Co. 9th Battn
ROYAL ARTILLERY
who was killed in the trenches
on the 5th Sepr
MDCCCLV
This stone has been erected
by the Officers Non-Commd Officers
and Men of the Right Siege Train

34TH (CUMBERLAND) REGIMENT.

NUMBER OF GRAVES—18.

(1.) Sacred
TO
THE
Memory of Private
John Thornton
34 Regt
who was killed by the explosion
of a shell 26th Augt 55
AGED 34 YEARS

(On Back.)
Erected by
B. Smith

23RD (ROYAL WELCH FUSILIERS.)

NUMBER OF GRAVES—71.

(1.) SACRED
TO
THE MEMORY
of
A. KNIGHT. BAND
23rd R. W. F.
DIED 30TH DECr of DICeNTERY
1854.

(2.) SACRED *(Marble.)*
TO THE MEMORY OF
LIEUTENANT DOUGLAS DYNELEY
23rd ROYAL WELCH FUSILIERS
who Fell Mortally Wounded Before
Sevastopol in the Attack on the REDAN
September 8th 1855
Born 19th December 1831
Died 9th September, 1855

(3.) SACRED
TO THE
Memory
of
LIEUT. WILLIAM OWEN
23rd R. W. FUSILIERS
who was killed
in the trenches
On the 30th of June /55
Aged
22 YEARS
ERECTED BY HIS BROTHER OFFICERS

(4.) SACRED
TO. THE. MEMORY.
OF
JOHN. MATHEWS.
23RD ROYAL . WELCH.
.FUSILIERS.
WHO. DEPARTED.
THIS LIFE APL 17
1856.

(5.) *(Obelisk).*
(LEFT FACE TOWARDS RAVINE.)
I H S
EDWARD. S. HOLDEN
Lieutenant
XXIII R. W. FUSILIERS
mortally wounded
before the
REDAN SEBASTOPOL
8th September 1855
DIED
9th September 1855
aged 18

(RIGHT FACE TOWARDS RAVINE.)
I H S
WILLIAM
HALSTED POOLE
Captain
XXIII. R. W. FUSILIERS
mortally wounded
before the
REDAN SEBASTOPOL
8th September, 1855
DIED
24th September 1855
aged 20

(OPPOSITE LEFT FACE.)
DOUGLAS DYNELEY
Lieutenant & Adjutant
XXIII R. W. FUSILIERS
mortally wounded
before the
REDAN SEBASTOPOL
8th September 1855
DIED
9th September 1855
aged 23

(OPPOSITE RIGHT FACE.)
REGINALD. H. SOMERVILLE
Lieutenant
XXIII. R. W. FUSILIERS,
killed
before the
REDAN SEBASTOPOL
8th September 1855
aged 20

(BASE.)
(Front.)
This stone raised by
their Brother Officers of the
XXIII Royal Welsh Fusiliers
to the Memory of
those whose early and honorable death
it records
marks the place where
their remains now rest

(Back.)
ERECTED
MARCH
1856

(Right and Left.)
ЧТNТЕ МОГИЛY

ТЕР.ОЕВ5

(6.) SACRED
I H S
TO THE MEMORY OF THE
NON COMND OFFrs & SOLDIERS
OF
HER MAJTY's 23RD R. W. FUSILIERS
WHO FELL DURING THE CAMPAIGN
OF
1854. 1855 AND 1856.

(7.) SACRED *(Wood.)*
TO THE MEMORY OF EVN WILLIAMS
23rd Fusiliers 1855

(8.) SACRED TO THE MEMORY
I H S
OF
THE UNDERMENTIONED MEN OF
H. B. M. 23RD R. W. FUSILIERS
WHO DIED IN CAMP BEFORE
SEBASTOPOL IN THE YEARS. 55-6.
PTs J. CHALK. J LEWIS.
W. ROWBOTTOM. T. WEST

(9.) I H S
SACRED
TO THE
MEMORY
OF
PT JOSEPH
BAKER 23
R.W.F. WHO
DEPARTED
THIS LIFE
19TH OF MAY
1856
AGED 46 YEARS

(10.) BURIAL GROUND
OF
H. B. M.
XXIII
ROYAL WELSH FUSILIERS

(11.) SACRED
TO THE
MEMORY
of
JAS. BURTON. DM MAJOR. H.M.
23RD R. W. FUSILIERS WHO DIED
OF CHOLERA OCTR 6TH 1854
AGED
26 YEARS
This Stone
was Erected
By His Comrades
As a Small
But Sincere
TOKEN
OF RESPECT.

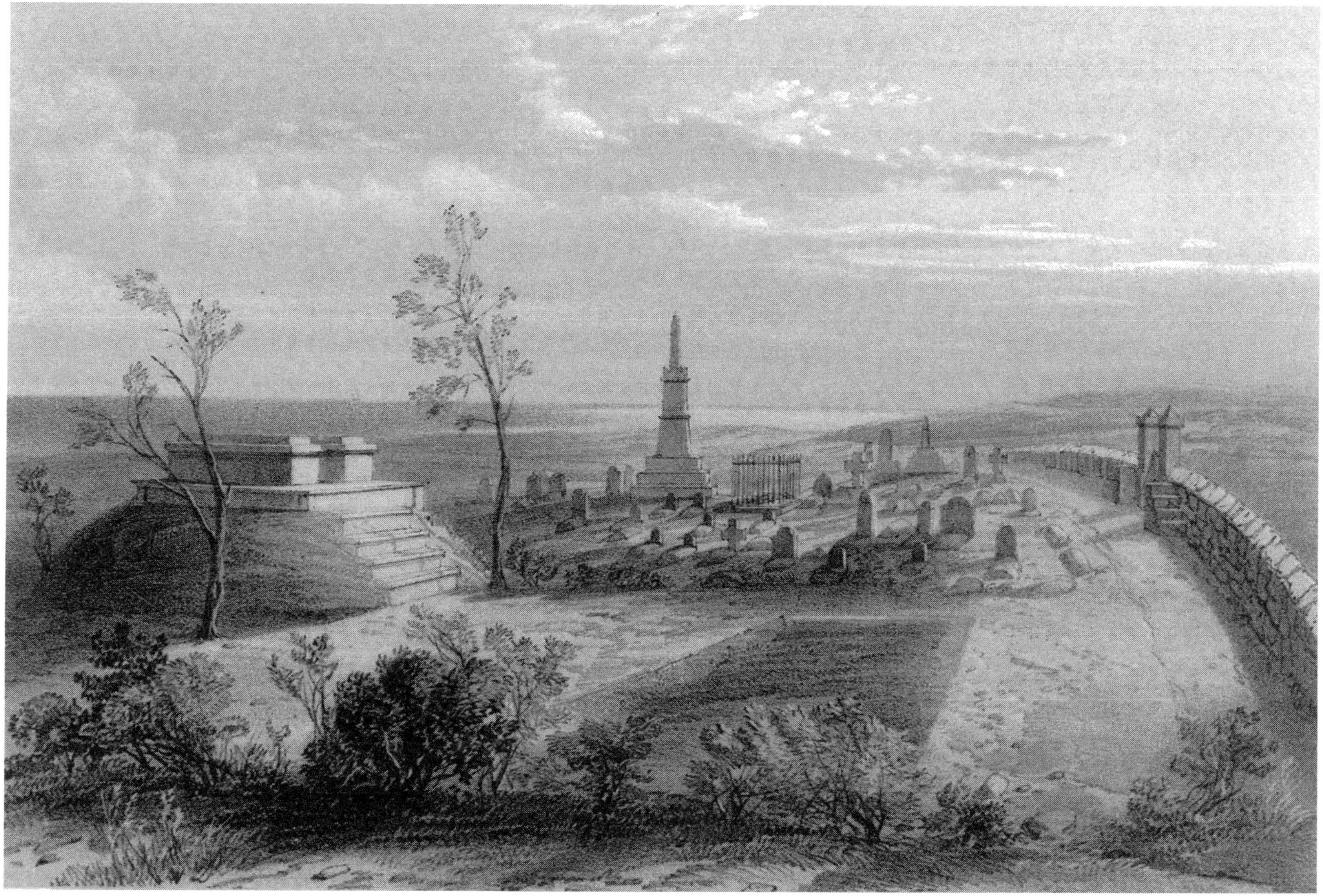

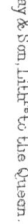

E. Walker, lith. London, Published by Ackermann & C° 106 Strand. Day & Son, Lith^{rs} to the Queen.

1 23 14 16

SECOND BRIGADE, LIGHT DIVISION.

(LOOKING TOWARDS SEBASTOPOL.)

SECOND BRIGADE LIGHT DIVISION.

19TH, 77TH, 88TH, 90TH, AND 97TH REGIMENTS.

NUMBER OF GRAVES—324.

(1.) *(Left.)*

Sacred to the Memory
✚
OF THE NON COMMISSIONED OFFICERS AND PRIVATES BELONGING TO THE 19TH REGT. WHO LOST THEIR LIVES IN THE SERVICE OF THEIR COUNTRY DURING THE CRIMEAN CAMPAIGN,
THIS STONE IS ERECTED BY THE OFFICERS OF THE REGIMENT IN ADMIRATION OF THEIR FORTITUDE AND BRAVERY

(Right.)

19th Regiment

LIEUT WARDLAW KILLED IN ACTION 20TH SEPR 1854.
ENSN STOCKWELL KILLED IN ACTION 20TH SEPR 1854.
ENS PHIPPS, DIED OF CHOLERA 25TH SEPR 1854.
CAPTN KER, KILLED IN ACTION 5TH NOVR 1854.
CAPTAIN, P, GODFREY KILLED AT THE FINAL ASSAULT OF SEBASTOPOL
LIEUT COLL T, UNETT. C.B. FELL 8TH SEPR 1855

(2.) SACRED TO THE MEMORY OF PT JOHN—HEARN 97 REGIMENT DIED 22 MARCH 1855

(3.) In Memory
I H S
of
Captn VICARS 97TH Regt Who Was Killed, in the Sortie from SEBASTOPOL on the night of the 22nd March 1855
Erected by his sorrowing Comrades

(4.) Sacred to the Memory
I H S
of
the Late Lieut And Adjutant W. Dermon 97th Regt Who was Killed By A Shell in the Trenches on The 18th August 1855

(5.) Sacred to the Memory
I H S
of
the Late Lieut Preston 97th Regt who was Killed in the trenches on the 31st August 1855

(6.) Erected
by the SERGEANTS of the 97th Regiment in commemoration of their departed comrades Who fell victims to contagion and in the exercise of their duty since their arrival in the CRIMEA NOVR 1854

(7.) SACRED TO THE MEMORY OF
THE LATE, A, W, SMITH. MUSICIAN 97TH REG. WHO WAS MORTALLY WOUNDED AT THE ASSAULT ON THE REDAN. 8 SEPT 1855
AND ALSO TO DRS P. HUGHES & D. DAWSON WHO FELL ON THE 8TH SEPT & ALSO. B. CAREY WHO DIED 23rd APRIL

(8.) SACRED
✚
TO. THE. MEMORY. OF PVTS S. FRY. S. HALL J. KIERNAN & M. KINLON NO. 5 COMPY 97TH REGT WHO. FELL. BEFORE. SEBASTOPOL 1855

ERECTED. BY. J. GRIBBIN. CORPL 97TH RT

(9.) IN MEMORY OF JOHN – LONGMORE MEDICAL STAFF AGED 22 YEARS DIED AUGUST 21ST 1855

(10.) SACRED TO THE MEMORY OF PRIT ML TOOLE. 97TH REGIMENT WHO. DIED. JUNE. 10TH 1856

(11.) SACRED TO THE MEMORY
I H S
OF THE LATE CAPTN HUTTON 97th REGT WHO FELL ON THE 8th SEPT. 1855 AT THE ASSAULT ON THE REDAN

(12.) SACRED TO THE MEMORY
I H S
OF THE LATE LIEUT & ADJT MC GREGOR 97th REGT WHO FELL ON THE 8- SEPT 1855 AT THE ASSAULT ON THE REDAN

(13.) SACRED TO THE MEMORY
OF THE LATE MAJOR WELSFORD 97TH REGT WHO FELL ON THE 8th SEPT 1855 LEADING THE LADDER PARTY AT THE ASSAULT ON THE REDAN

(14.) *(Iron Railing round Grave.)*
Sacred to the Memory
I H S
of
Lieut, Colonel the Honble H. R. Handcock 97TH Regt Who was Mortally wounded when leading the storming party of his Regt at the assault on the Redan 8th Septr —1855—

(15.) Sacred to the Memory
I H S
of
the late Lieut Goodenough 97th Regt who died of his wounds on the 20th Septr 1855 Recd a the Assault on the Redan 8 Septr 1855

(16.) IN MEMORY OF LIEUT COLL UNETT. C.B. HE FELL WHILE LEADING THE 19TH REGIMENT TO THE ASSAULT 8TH SEPTR. 1855

SECOND BRIGADE LIGHT DIVISION.

(17.)
I H S
SACRED to the MEMORY
of the
OFFICERS
Non Commissioned Officers
And Private Soldiers
of the 97th Regiment
who lost their lives
in the Service of their Country
during the Crimean Campaign
in
1854 & 1855.

(18.)
SACRED TO THE MEMORY
OF
COL^R SERG^T A. DOWDLE
77TH REG^T
WHO DIED IN CAMP
BEFORE SEBASTOPOL
5th MAY 1855
ERECTED BY HIS UNCLE
W. WILSON 77TH REG^T

(19.)
SACRED TO THE MEMORY OF
THE NON COMMISSIONED
OFFICERS AND MEN
OF THE L^T C^{MPNY} 77TH REG^T
WHO WERE KILLED DURING
THE CRIMEAN CAMPAIGN
OF 1854 " 55
THIS STONE IS ERECTED BY
THEIR SURVIVING
COMRADES

(20.)
TO
THE MEMORY
OF
P^{VT} A. MORRISSY
LIGHT COMP^Y
77 REG^T
DIED 13TH JAN^Y
1855
AGED 27 YEARS

(21.)
SACRED TO THE MEMORY
I H S
of the Sergeants of the
77th Reg^t who lost their Lives
in the Crimean Campaign
1854 & 1855

Color Serg^t J. FITZHARRIS
T. MAHER.   A. DOWDLE
Staff Serg^t R. DORMER
SERGEANTS
M. CASTIAUX   —   D. CASEY
T. DUNNE   —   R. BARNARD
W. MANN   —   J. LAUGHLIN
D. ROBERTS   —   T. RAHILLY
J. TAYLOR   —   W. TOPPS
T. RICHES   —   J. HALLENAN
C. WILLIS

This Stone is Erected by their
Surviving Comrades as a token
of Esteem & Regard

(22.)
IN MEMORY
OF THE
GRENADIERS
77TH REG^T
WHO DIED, ON THE
CRIMEA,
1854
AND 55

(23.)   (FACING ROAD.)
TO THE
OFFICERS
NON COMMISSIONED OFFICERS
AND MEN
OF THE
SECOND BRIGADE
LIGHT DIVISION
WHO FELL
1854 - 1855
R. BARNETT
90TH L. I.

(Right.)

ПАМЯТНИКЪ
ОЖИЦЕРАМЪ
И СОЛДАТАМЪ
ВТОРОЙ БРИГАДЫ
ЛЕГКОЙ ДИВИЗИИ
КОТОРЫЕ ПАЛИ
ВЪ 1854 И 1855 ГОДАХЪ

(Rear.)
REGIMENTS OF THE BRIGADE
XIX
LXXVII
LXXXVIII
XC
XCVII

(Left.)

ПОЛКИ СОСТАВЛЯЮЩІЕ

БРИГАДУ
XIX
LXXVII
LXXXVIII
XC
XCVII

(24.)
SACRED TO THE MEMORY
OF THE
NON, COMMISSIONED
OFFICERS AND MEN
OF E C^{NY} 77TH REG^T
WHO LOST THEIR LIVES
DURING THE CRIMEAN
CAMPAIGN OF 1854 " 55
THIS STONE IS ERECTED
BY THEIR SURVIVING
COMRADES.

(25.)
IN MEMORY OF
SURGEON
CHRIST^R MACARTNEY M.B
OF THE
77th Regiment
WHO DIED ON THE
11th April 1855

(26.)
SACRED
TO
THE MEMORY
OF
CAPTAIN NICHOLSON
77th REGIMENT
WHO WAS KILLED WHILST
GALLANTLY LEADING ON
HIS COMPANY IN A CHARGE
AT THE BATTLE OF INKERMANN
5TH NOVEMBER 1854

(27.)
IN
MEMORY
OF
LIEU^T ARTHUR MAINE.
77TH REGIMENT
Died November 21st
1854

(28.)
SACRED TO THE MEMORY
I H S
OF
THE OFFICERS
NON COMMISSIONED OFFICERS
AND MEN
OF THE 77TH REGIMENT
Who lost their lives in the service
of their Country during
the Campaign in the
CRIMEA
This Monument is erected by the
Officers of the Regiment
as an humble tribute of respect to
the fortitude and bravery of
their fallen Comrades

(29.)
IN MEMORY
OF
COLONEL GRAHAM EGERTON
77th Regiment
Who was Killed whilst
Commanding an attack on the
Rifle Pits
20TH APRIL 1855

(30.)
IN MEMORY OF
AUDLEY LEMPRIERE
ELDEST SON OF
REAR ADMIRAL LEMPRIERE
OF PELHAM, HAMPSHIRE
IN ENGLAND
AND CAPTAIN IN THE
77th Regiment
WHO FELL BEFORE SEBASTOPOL
WHILE ATTACKING THE
RUSSIAN RIFLE PITS
ON THE 19TH OF APRIL, 1855
Aged 20 Years.

(31.)
I H S
In MEMORY of
BREVET MAJOR
BENTINCK DUNCAN GILBY
77th Regiment
who DIED in
Camp before Sebastopol
23rd July
1855

(32.)
I H S
In MEMORY of
Lieu^t BASIL BROWNE
77th Regiment
who DIED in
Camp before Sebastopol
15th December
1855

(33.)   (Marble.)
IN MEMORY OF
CAP^{TN} EDWARD CROFTON
77th REG^T.
WHO DIED OF CHOLERA ON
THE LINE OF MARCH FROM
ALMA TO BALACLAVA
27TH SEPTEMBER
1854

(34.)
I H S
In MEMORY of
CAPTAIN PARKER
77th Regiment
who was Killed
at the Attack on the
REDAN
8th September
1855

SECOND BRIGADE LIGHT DIVISION.

(35.)
IHS
In MEMORY of
Lieut
CHARLES EARNEST KNIGHT
77th Regiment
who DIED in
Camp before Sebastopol
2nd October
1855

(36.)
IHS
In MEMORY of
CAPTAIN
William Cecil George
PECHELL
77th Regiment
who was Killed
while
Gallantly doing his Duty
in advance
of
the fifth Parallel
before
SEBASTOPOL
3rd September
1855

(37.)
IHS

In MEMORY of
Lieut ROBERT WALMSLEY
77th Regiment
Who Died
on board the Steam Ship
MEDWAY
In the Harbour
of
BALACLAVA
4th October
1854

(38.) (Wood.)
88. CONNAUGHT RANGERS
— IHS —
— SACRED —
— To The Memory of —
SERJEANT. J. SAVAGE.
Who Died. of. His
WOUNDS
RECEIVED. AT THE ASSAULT
. On the Quarries. on. the —
7th JUNE
— 1855 —
REQUIESCANT. IN. PACE.
AMEN

(39.)
IHS

In MEMORY of
COLOR SERGEANT
THOMAS MAHER
77TH REGIMENT
WHO DIED ON THE 9TH SEPR
FROM WOUNDS RECEIVED AT
THE ATTACK ON THE
REDAN
AGED 32 YEARS

(40.)
SACRED
TO THE
MEMORY OF
MAJOR EDWARD NORTON
OF THE 88TH CONNAUGHT RANGERS.
WHO DIED OF CHOLERA ON THE 20TH MAY
1855
THIS STONE
IS ERECTED
BY HIS
BROTHER
OFFICERS

(41.)
SACRED

TO THE MEMORY OF
EDWARD JOHNSON
OF H. M. 90th Lt INFy WHO
DEPARTED THIS LIFE
MARCH, 23RD 1855
AGED 22 YEARS
Blessed are the Dead
Who die in the Lord
AMEN

(42.)
IHS
SACRED
TO THE
MEMORY
OF
G. AULD
90TH REGT L. I.
DIED MAY 2
1855

(43.)
IHS

SACRED TO THE MEMORY
of
THE OFFICERS
NON COMMD OFFICERS AND MEN
of the
88TH. CONNAUGHT RANGERS
WHO LOST THEIR LIVES IN THE
CRIMEAN CAMPAIGN
of
1854 – 1855.
THIS STONE IS ERECTED BY THEIR
SURVIVING COMRADES AS A TOKEN
OF
ESTEEM AND REGARD

(44.)

THIS TOMB ENSHRINES IN ITS BOSOM THE MORTAL REMAINS
of the
REVD DENIS SHEEHAN
Catholic Chaplain to the British Forces
The 88th Connaught Rangers have had the
honor of erecting to his Sacred Memory
this Monument, for with them he lived and
with them he died 10th March 1855
Aged 31 Years
In the Battle Field he stood beside them;
In their sickness and wounds he consoled them
Many a British Soldier filled with hope
did pass to GOD, aided by the prayers and
fortified by the administration of this
HOLY PRIEST
May he rest in peace
AMEN

(45.)
SACRED
IHS
TO THE MEMORY
OF
SERJT MAJR PATK COONEY
88TH CONNAUGHT RANGERS
WHO, DIED, OF, WOUNDS RECEIVED
ON, THE, 8TH SEPTEMBER, 1855—
WHILST, ASSAULTING, THE, REDAN
AGED 26 YEARS,
REQUIESCANT. IN. PACE
AMEN

(46.)
SACRED
TO THE MEMORY
OF
LIEUTENANT H. B. PRESTON
88th (CONNAUGHT RANGERS)
WHO FELL WHILE DOING HIS DUTY
IN THE TRENCHES BEFORE SEBASTOPOL
ON THE 14TH APRIL 1855,
THIS, IS ERECTED BY HIS
BROTHER OFFICERS AS A
TESTIMONY OF SINCERE REGRET
FOR THE LOSS OF A YOUNG
AND GALLANT COMRADE
DARMANIN. MALTA.

(47.)
Sacred to the memory
of
IHS

MAJOR BAYLEY CAPTAIN CORBETT
CAPTAIN WRAY AND LIEUT WEBB
of the 88TH Connaught Rangers
who fell whilst assaulting the
Quarries on the night of the
7th of June 1855
This Monument is Erected by
their Brother Officers as a
humble but sincere testimony
of their Esteem and affection

(48.)
SACRED
TO THE MEMORY
OF
CAPTAIN HENRY WILLIAM GROGAN
88th (CONNAUGHT RANGERS)
WHO FELL WHILE GALLANTLY LEADING ON HIS
COMPANY TO THE ASSAULT ON THE REDAN
ON THE 8th SEPTEMBER 1855.
THIS MONUMENT IS ERECTED
BY HIS BROTHER OFFICERS
WHO MOURN A DEAR FRIEND
AND BRAVE COMRADE
DARMANIN-MALTA-

(49.) (Wood.)
Sacred to the Memory
of
DRIVER John Willmer
A. TROOP ROYAL HORS ARTILERY
Who departed this life the
21 day of July 1855
Aged 18 years

My race is ran my warfare is oer,
I lay me down in peace to rest,
Until the last loud trumpets sound
Shall call me home to regions blest.

SECOND BRIGADE LIGHT DIVISION.

(50.)   (FACING ROAD.)

SACRED
TO THE MEMORY OF
THE OFFICERS
NON COMMISSIONED OFFICERS
AND MEN OF HER MAJESTY'S
90TH LIGHT INFANTRY
WHO LOST THEIR LIVES WHILE
SERVING IN THE CRIMEA
DURING THE SIEGE OF
SEBASTOPOL
IN THE YEARS 1854 '55

This Monument is erected by the Non Commissioned Officers and men of the Regiment as an humble Testimonial of their esteem for the Bravery and Intrepidity of their Beloved Officers and Comrades

REQUIESCANT IN PACE.

R. BARNETT
XCTH LHT IRY

(Other Faces.)

I H S

(51.)   ✠
SACRED
TO THE MEMORY OF
CAPTAIN HENRY PRESTON.
LIEUTT. ARTHUR, D, SWIFT.
LIEUTT. HUGH F. WILMER
OF H. M. 90TH LT INFTRY
WHO WERE KILLED
AT THE ASSAULT OF
"THE REDAN"
ON THE 8TH OF SEPTBER 1855.
ALSO
CAPTN HERBERT. M. VAUGHAN.
OF H. M. 90TH LT INFTRY
WHO DIED ON 12TH SEPBER
1855
FROM WOUNDS RECEIVED
ON THE 8TH OF SAME MONTH

2ND BRIGADE LIGHT DIVISION (continued)
JUST BELOW THE 90TH. MONUMENT.
Same side of Woronzoff Ravine.

NUMBER OF GRAVES—156.

(1.)   SACRED
✠
TO THE MEMORY OF
THOMAS GOLDING
of H. M. 90th Regiment. L. I.
WHO DIED ON THE 13th MAY
1856.
AGED 20 YRS

(2.)   SACRED
TO ✠ THE
MEMORY OF
BUGLER. W, FORD. OF.
HER MAJESTY'S 90TH L. I.
WHO DIED JUNE 20TH 1855
AGED 28 YEARS.

This stone is erected by Band and Bugles as a token of their esteem and affection.

Requiescat in pace.

(3.)
H
I ✠ S
E   C

(4.)   I H S
SACRED
to the memory of
Dr MARTIN NEE
88th REGIMENT Who
DIED of WOUNDS RECEID
ON 8 of SEPTEMBER. 55.
AGED 18 YEARS

IN 77TH CAMP.

2 GRAVES.

E. Walker, lith.

London, Published by A.Ackermann, & C:o 106 Strand.

1   14   23   28   29   33   43 49   44   51   50

SECOND BRIGADE, LIGHT DIVISION.
(WORONZOFF ROAD.)
and
SECOND AND FOURTH DIVISIONS.
(WORONZOFF RAVINE.)

Day & Son, Lith.rs to the Queen.

SECOND DIVISION,

*2ND BATTALION 1ST ROYALS, 3RD, 30TH, †31ST, 41ST, 47TH, 49TH, 55TH, 62ND, & 95TH REGTS.

AND

FOURTH DIVISION,

17TH, 20TH, 21ST, 46TH, 48TH, 57TH, 63RD, & 68TH REGTS, AND 1ST BATTALION RIFLE BRIGADE.

NUMBER OF GRAVES—202.

(1.)
IHS
SACRED
TO THE MEMORY
OF
DANIEL MAHONY,
OF THE 62nd BAND
Who fell a victim to fever,
On the 19th March 1856,
Aged 30 Years.
This stone is erected by His Comrades
of the Band as a Token of Respect

(2.)
IH...S
TO THE MEMORY
of
PRIVT RICHARD BYRNES
17TH REGIMENT
WHO WAS KILLED ON THE 5 APRIL
1855
AGED 25 YEARS

(3.)
17TH REGT
SERJT
E. MATTHEWS.
DIED
28th APRIL. 1855.

(4.)
IHS
SACRED
TO
The Memory of Private
JAMES HANNON
21 R. N. B. FUSILIERS
Who Died on 20 May 1856
Errected By The Comrades
of His company.

(Foot.)
IHS

(5.)
SACRED   (Wood.)
to the
MEMORY
OF
F. J. STANLEY, LATE, HOSPITAL Sergt
30th REGT WHO DEPARTED THIS LIFE APRIL 22nd
1855, AGED, 25 YEARS.

(6.)
I.H.S
L.I
Pt W. Griffiths XXX Regt
Age 30 Years
Died May 1855

(7.)
SACRED
TO THE MEMORY
OF
CORPORAL JAMES CAMPBELL
49th REGt
WHO WAS KILLED
IN THE TRENCHES
BEFORE SEBASTOPOL
MAY 13th 1855.
AGED 23.
This monument is erected by some of his
Comrades in testimony of their admiration
of his bravery as a soldier and of his
Sincere and earnest piety as a Christian.
" Blessed are those servants whom the Lord
when he cometh shall find watching"
Luke XII 37.

SECOND & FOURTH DIVISIONS (continued).
AND
SECOND & FOURTH BATTALIONS LAND TRANSPORT CORPS.

NUMBER OF GRAVES—846.

(1.)
In   (Wood.)
Memory
of
× Pte James Gaffney ×
63rd Regiment *
Died
November *
28th
1855

(2.)
SACRED
TO THE MEMORY
of
Color Serjt JOHN MULLOY
57th Regt
Who died on the 29th of Wounds
Received on the 18th June 1855
Aged 38 Years
This Stone has been erected
by his brother Non-commissioned
Officers
As a Mark of their Esteem

(3.)
SACRED
TO
THE MEMORY OF
HENRY WHITE
17th REGT
WHO DIED OF CHOLERA
11th DECr 1855
THIS STONE IS PLACED
HERE BY HIS CAPTAIN
IN TOKEN OF HIS
FIDELITY

(4.)
IHS
TO THE MEMORY
of
PRIVATE DENIS CALAHER
17th REGIMENT
WHO DEPARTED THIS LIFE ON
THE 24th JUNE 1855
AGED 39 YEARS

(5.)
Sacred   (Wood.)
to the
MEMORY
of
Corpl George Kemp
55th Regt
Killed on duty in the Trenches
12th July 1855
Aged 32 Years

This Board is put up as a mark of
affection by his Brother
JOHN KEMP

(6.)
IHS   (Wood.)
SACRED
TO THE MEMORY OF SERJEANT
PETER McCABE. OF THE 3rd
REGT WHO DEPARTED, THIS LIFE
ON THE 23rd OF JULY, 1855, THROUGH
THE EFFECTS
OF A WOUND
RECEIVED IN
THE TRENCHES
BEFORE
SEBASTOPOL
ON THE
22nd OF JULY. 1855
AGED
37. YEARS
REQUIESCAT
IN PACE AMEN

(7.)
SACRED
to
The Memory of Hospl
Serjt MARTIN WARD
of the 68th Lt Infantry
who Departed this Life
on the 16th of Octr 1855
Aged 30 Years

This Stone was erected as a
mark of respect by his Brother
Non - Commd Officers

(8.)
17TH REGIMENT FOOT
SERJT.
THOs JAMES.
DIED 14th MAY. 1855.

(9.)
SACRED
TO
THE MEMORY OF
Private GEO. EVERED
68th Lt INFANTRY
who died 11th April 1856
Aged 31 Years.

(10.)
SACRED
to
The Memory of Serjt
George Coles
of the 68th Lt Infantry
Who departed this Life
on the 13th of March 1856
Aged 30 Years & 5 Months
This stone Was erected as a Mark
of Respect By his Brother Non
Commissnd Officers

(11.)
Sacred to the memory   (Wood.)
OF
CORPORAL
George Gower
4th Battn L. T. C.
Who departed this life
Decr 24th
1855
ALSO
HENRY JONES
of the above corps
who died decr 1st
1855

---

* Afterwards Attached to 2ND BRIGADE HIGHLAND DIVISION AT KAMARA.   † Afterwards Attached to 2ND BRIGADE FIRST DIVISION.

SECOND AND FOURTH DIVISIONS.

(12.)
SACRED TO THE MEMORY
I H S
OF
SERJT. T. ARNOLD
1st B. R. B
DIED IN CAMP
JULY 10th 1855

(13.) (Wood.)
BENEATH
this humble tablet
Lie
The Remains of
JAMES BRODIE
BAND 72nd HIGHLANDERS
who died
JUNE 19th 1855
AGED 19 YEARS

Thou weary pilgrims
Shouldst thou wend
thy way where this memento takes
thine eye, pray mark the halloed
spot, wherein doth rest the mortal
remains of one who was endeared
to his Comrades by his talent
and good nature.

This small tribute of
respect erected by his
Comrade Corpl Jms Stewart
72nd Highlanders

(14.)
I H S
SECT. TO MEMY
OF R. P. MULLALEY
17 REG OF FOOT
WHO DIED ON THE 15th
DAY OF MAY 1855
AGED 20 YEARS

(15.)
TO THE MEMORY
I H S
DANIEL HYLAHAN
BAND 17th REGIMENT
WHO DIED ON THE 15th JUNE 1855
AGED 27 YEARS
MAY HE REST IN PEACE

(16.) (Wood.)
Sacred to the Memory
OF
THOMAS MULLIGAN
4th Battn. L. T. C.
who departed this life
September 4th / 55
ALSO
RICHARD BALDWELL
who died
September 13th
1855

(17.) (Wood.)
Sacred to the memory
OF
RICHARD BRADLEY
4TH Battn L. T. C
who departed this life
January 15th 1856
ALSO
RICHARD MUSGRAVE
who died
March 24th
1856

(18.)
SACRED TO THE MEMORY OF
CR SERJT JAMES FURPHY
55TH REGT WHO DIED OF
A WOUND RECD ON THE
8TH SEPTR 1855.
Erected by his Brother N, C, Officers
as a token of their Esteem

(19.) (Wood.)
COLR SERJT
RD Cooke
Gr Co
3 REGT

(20.) (Wood.)
SACRED
TO
THE MEMORY
of
Ple ALEX STILL H M XXX Regt
Who departed this Life August 10th 1855
Occasioned by A wound received in the Trenches
Aged 30 Years
Man is like a thing of nought:
his time passeth away like a shadow. Psl. cxliv.
This memorial was erected by his loving Brother

(21.) (Wood.)
Sacred to the memory
of
Serjeant
EDWARD COLE
4th Battn L. T. C.
who departed this life
June 2nd 1855

(22.) (Wood.)
Sacred to the memory
OF
GEORGE EWELLS
4th Battn L. T. C.
who departed this life
JUNE 3rd 1855
ALSO
James Heighton
of the above battalion
September 22nd
1855

(23.) (Wood.)
Sacred to the memory
OF
ALFRED BENNETT
4t BAtt L. T. C.
who departed this life
June 15th 1855
ALSO
RICHARD GALE
who died
August 12th 1855

(24.)
SACRED
TO THE MEMORY
of
Private JAMES LEWIS
Lt Co. 57th Regt
who was Killed in The Trenches
On the 24th day of May 1855
Aged 22 Years

(25.)
Sacred
to the
MEMORY
of
George Everett,
Color Serjt of H. B. M.
55th Regt
DIED 12th JUNE 1855
Aged 27 Years

(26.)
SACRED
TO
THE MEMORY
OF
CORPL JAMES INNERDALE
OF 17th REGT
WHO DIED OF CHOLERA
ON THE 17th JUNE 1855
THIS STONE
IS ERECTED BY
COLOR SERGT SMITH
AS A TRIBUTE TO HIS
MEMORY

(27.)
SACRED
TO THE MEMORY
of
Drum Major JAMES BOYLE
57th Regt
Who died on the 4th of June 1855
Aged 28 Years

This stone has been erected
by his brother Non-commissioned
Officers
As a Mark of their Esteem

(28.)
I. H. S.
SACRED
TO THE MEMORY OF
SERJT. MARTIN MEARA
OF THE 55th REGT
WHO FELL ON THE NIGHT OF THE
7th JUNE. 1855. AT THE STORMING
OF THE REDAN. AGED 28 YEARS.

REQUIESENT IN PEACE. AMEN.

(Left Side.)
Erected by his Affectionate Brother

(29.)
SACRED
to the
MEMORY
OF
OWEN. CALLAGHAN
55TH REGt
WHO DIED
APRIL 28TH 1856
AGED 38 YEARS
REQUIESCANT IN PACE.

(30.)
TO THE
MEMORY
of
QUARTER MASTER
WILLIAM STILLWELL
THE BUFFS
Who Died 12th June 1855 in Camp
before
SEBASTOPOL
of
Cholera.

(31.)
SACRED
TO THE MEMORY OF
Pte JOSEPH WOODS 49th Regt
WHO DIED OF FEVER IN CAMP
15TH MAY 1856
AGED 27 YEARS
THIS STONE WAS ERECTED
BY HIS COMRADES AS A
TOKEN OF THEIR ESTEEM.

(32.)
SACRED
TO THE
MEMORY OF
Private Timothy Farrell
LATE OF THE
31st REGIMENT
Who Departed this Life
ON THE
13 MAY 1856
Aged 33
Erected by his Brother 97th Regt.

(33.)
TO THE
MEMORY
of
JOHN HORSLEY WHITE, ESQr
Who Died 2nd July 1855 of
Cholera while doing his duty
with the Buffs
as
Assistant
SURGEON
in
Camp before
SEBASTOPOL

SECOND AND FOURTH DIVISIONS.

(34.)
TO THE MEMORY OF
IHS
DRUMR SAML LAYLAND
H. M. 95TH REGIMENT
Who Died on the
28TH MARCH . 1856
This Tablet is Erected
by the Drum Major &
Drummers of the Regt
as a Token of their Respect

(35.) *(Wood.)*
SACRED TO
THE
MEMORY
OF
CORPL JAMES BRADY
X X X
REGT
AGED 29
YEARS

(36.)
This Monument is
Erected in Memory
of
Sergt M. Hunt Aged. 25
Corpl J. Bradley Aged. 37
Corpl E. Busby Aged. 25
Corpl J. Tansley Aged. 21
1st C.D. J. Gordon Aged. 27
died of Cholera before Sebastopol
— 1855 —
"Watch therefore for ye Know
neither the day nor the hour
wherein the son of man cometh
May 26th
1856
By the Non Comd Officers and Men of the 2nd Battn
Land Transport Corps
as a mark of their esteem

(37.)
SACRED TO
— THE —
Memory Pt T. WALLACE
of the 68th Who Died on the
27th July 1855 Aged 18.
Years

(38.)
SACRED
to
The Memory of Private
Lawrence Banks of the
68th Lt Infantry Who
Departed this Life on
the 10th of May 1856
Aged 40 Years
Erected By his Comrades

(39.)
SACRED
to
the Memory of Thos
Gibbs of 68th Lt
Infy who Died on
the 19th June 1855
Aged 22 Years

'Tis hard to part
It rends the heart
Tis hard 'tis hard to sever
Yes' 'tis bliss
To know this
We do not part 'for ever

(Left side.)
This stone was erected
by his Affectionate
Brother

(40.)
SACRED
to
The Memory of Serjt
William Kilpack
of the 68th Lt Infantry
Who Departed this Life
on the 17th of May 1855
Aged 36 Years & 5 Months
This Stone was erected as a
mark of respect by his Brother
Non Comd Officers.

(41.)
IHS
In
the MEMORY of
Color Sert Francis Taylor
The Buffs
Killed at the Attack on the
REDAN
18th June 1855
AGED
25 Years

(42.)
IHS
In MEMORY of
The
Non Commissioned Officers
and Privates of the
Buffs
Who Died or were Killed
during the Siege of Sebastopol
1855
ERECTED
by their Officers in
recognition of their
FORTITUDE
and
VALOR

(43.)
IN
MEMORY
OF
LIEUT. B. HYNDMAN
THE BUFFS
DIED 7TH OCTR 1855

(44.)
SERGT WM MURRAY
13TH P.A. LT INFANTRY
WHO DEPARTED THIS LIFE ON
THE 25TH SEPTEMBER 1855
THIS STONE WAS ERECTED
BY THE COMPANY WHICH
HE BELONGED AS TESTIMONY
OF THEIR HIGH ESTEEM.

(45.) *(Wood.)*
SACRED
TO THE MEMORY
OF
JOHN SHEEHAN
PRIVATE IN H.MS 57TH REGT
KILLED IN THE TRENCHES
BEFORE SEBASTOPOL
AGED 18 YEARS

THIS MEMORIAL IS ERECTED BY HIS FAITHFUL
COMRADE, FREDERICK CLARK, OF H.M.S 14th
REGT WHO WITH HIS LOVING BROTHER
EDWARD SHEEHAN OF H.M. 57TH REGT
DEEPLY DEPLORES HIS LOSS

Bost not thyself of to morrow
for thou knowest not what a day may bring forth
Prov. 27. 1st v

Thence shall I come when ages close
To take you home with me;
There we shall meet to part no more,
But shall together be.

(46.) *(Wood.)*
SACRED
To The
MEMORY
OF
Serjt Wm Freeman of the
46th Regt
WHO DIED ON THE 25th JANY 1856
AGED 29 YEARS
A good Soldier and Comrade Dear
A Faithful Friend lies buried here.

(47.)
(FACING RAVINE.)
THIS STONE IS ERECTED
BY THE
NON. COMMISSIONED OFFICERS
AND MEN OF THE FIFTY FIFTH
THE WESTMORELAND REGIMENT
OF FOOT IN MEMORY OF THEIR
COMRADES WHO HAVE FALLEN
DURING THE WAR
REQUIESCANT IN PACE

(Rear.)
H. B. M. 55TH REGIMENT OF FOOT

	SERJTS	DRS	R & FILE
KILLED IN ACTION	3	0	84
DIED OF WOUNDS	3	1	54
DIED OF DISEASE	9	0	223
TOTAL	15	1	361

(48.)
3rd Regt
W. Edmonds. Lt Co.
who Departed this life
On the 26 apl.—

(49.)
H. BIBBY
1st B. R. B.

(50.) *(Wood.)*
Sacred
To The
Memory
of
Pte Martin Dowd
63rd Regt
Died
30th Sepr.
1855

(51.) *(Wood.)*
SACRED
TO THE
MEMORY
OF
MICHAEL HARPER. WHO DEPARTED
THIS LIFE. 9th SEPt. THROUGH THE
EFFECT OF A WOUND RECEIVED
AT
THE STORMING
OF THE REDAN FORT
ON THE
8th Sept. 1855
AGED 18 YEARS
Requiescant in Pace
3rd REGIMENT

(52.)
SACRED
to the
MEMORY OF
SERJT W. WALDIE
57th Regt Died of Wounds
Received in the Trenches
20th Augt
1855
Aged 37
YRs 9 Monhs

SECOND AND FOURTH DIVISIONS.

(53.) [FACING RAVINE.]
SACRED
to the
MEMORY
of
269 Non - Com^d Officers
And Men
OF H. B. M^s 57th Reg^t
Who have been Killed
or died of Wounds or
disease during the
Campaign in the
CRIMEA

(Rear.)
THIS STONE
Has been erected
by the Non- Com^d
Officers And Men
of the Regiment, as
a testimony of their
esteem for their departed
COMRADES
MAY 1856

(54.)
SACRED TO THE MEMORY
I H S
SERG^T MAJOR JOHN M^CCLELLAN
the Non Commissioned
Officers
and Men of the XXX Regt.
who Fell in Action or Died
of wounds or disease in
the Crimea From Septr 14th
1854
to Feby 29th 1856

(Foot.)
I H S

(55.)
I H S
Pr J. JONEZ
XXX
1855

LIGHT, 2ND, AND 4TH DIVISIONS
(continued),
AND
ROYAL ARTILLERY
ATTACHED TO
SECOND AND FOURTH DIVISIONS.
(LEFT SIDE OF WORONZOFF RAVINE,
TOWARDS SEBASTOPOL.)

NUMBER OF GRAVES—117.

(1.)
SACRED TO THE MEMORY
OF
SERJ^T C. PESKETT
1st B^N RIFLE BRIGADE
WHO WAS
KILLED AT THE EXPLOSION
IN THE
FRENCH LINES
NOVEMBER 15TH 1855

(2.)
SACRED
To the Memory
of
Serg^t Major John Harris
and
the Sergeants of the 41 Reg^t
who fell in the Service of their
Country
during the Siege of Sebastopol
—o—
Erected by their Brother
Non Com^d. Officers
1855

(3.)
SACRED TO THE MEMORY
OF THE
NON COMMISSIONED OFFICERS
AND MEN OF THE 41ST REG^T WHO
HAVE FALLEN DURING THE CAMPAIGNS
OF 1854. 55. & 55. IN THE SERVICE
OF THEIR COUNTRY
—o—
REQUIESCANT IN PACE
AMEN.
THIS STONE IS ERECTED BY
THEIR BROTHER COMRADES
1856.

(4.)
SACRED TO THE MEMORY
of the
Non Com^{D.} Officers
and men of No. 5 Comp^y
41st REG^T
WHO FELL IN THE SERVICE OF
THEIR COUNTRY DURING
THE SEIGE OF
SEVASTOPOL
ERECT^D BY THEIR COMR^{DS}

(5.)
I H S
IN MEMORY
OF
SERJ^T DANIEL CASEY
77TH REG^T
WHO WAS KILLED
BEFORE
SEBASTOPOL
28TH JULY, 1855
"
REQUIESCANT IN PACE
AMEN.

(6.)
IN MEMORY OF
PRIV^{TE} JOHN CARTY
77th Reg^t
WHO DIED FROM HIS
WOUNDS RECEIVED AT
THE REDAN
ON THE 9TH SEP^{R.} 1855
Aged 24 Years
Requiescat in Pace

(7.)
1. B. R. B
SACRED
TO
THE MEMORY OF
WILLIAM CONOLLY
WHO DIED MAY 9TH.
1856
AGED 19
YEARS

(8.)
I H S
THIS SIMPLE TOMB WAS ERECTED BY THE
CATHOLIC SOLDIERS OF THE 2ND DIVISION
OVER THE MORTAL REMAINS OF THEIR BELOVED
CHAPLAIN THE REV^D JAMES SHEIL WHO ON
THE 8TH AUG^T 1855 DIED OF FEVER
CAUGHT IN THE DISCHARGE OF HIS DUTY.
REQUIESCAT IN PACE AMEN

(9.)
SACRED
TO
The
Memory
OF
J. S. BUSSLEY
41st REG^t
died
17th Feb^y
1856.

(10.)
I H S
SACRED
TO THE MEMORY OF
Job Trask
Royal Artillery
who died February 24th
1856
"

FOURTH DIVISION
(continued).
(RIGHT SIDE OF WORONZOFF RAVINE,
TOWARDS SEBASTOPOL.)

NUMBER OF GRAVES—3.

(1.)
I H S
SACRED
TO THE
MEMORY
OF
TH^{OS} HOLYLAND
1st Batalion Rifle Brigade
KILLED
8th September 1855

(2.)
SACRED
TO THE
MEMORY OF
P. George Weeks 1st B. R. B.
who was Killed on the 8th
of September 1855
AGED 23 YEARS
ERECTED BY HIS COMRADES

(On Wall round Graves.)
1856

FOURTH DIVISION
(continued).
NEAR LITTLE KADIKOI, OR DONYBROOK,
COMMONLY CALLED THE ENGLISH BAZAAR.

NUMBER OF GRAVES—746.

(1.) ( ) (Wood.)
i c i.
REP
OSE
Bernade
— Madame Barbance D^{ied} Le 23 Janvier 1856 —
Un-
Dépro
fondis

(2.)
SACRED (Wood.)
TO THE
MEMORY
OF
SERJ^T W SILLS
1st B. R. B
KILLED AT THE BATTLE OF INKERMAN
5th NOV. 1854

(3.)
SACRED
TO THE MEMORY OF
P^{te} EDWARD NEIL
57th Reg^t
Who died on the 8th of a
Wound Received on the
5th NOV^{R.} 1854
Aged 27 Years
—(—()—)—

(4.)
SACRED
to
the Memory
of Wm Critchley
of the 68th L. I
Who Departed
this Life on
the 9th Jan^y
1855 Aged
21 Years

SECOND AND FOURTH DIVISIONS.

(5.) (FACING SEBASTOPOL)
SACRED
TO THE
MEMORY
OF THE
Men of No 2 Co⸵.
OF
H B M XXTH REG^T
Killed and Died
while serving their
QUEEN AND COUNTRY
From Septr. 1854 to Mar. 1856

This stone is erected by
the Non Com^d. Officers and
Men of their Comp^y.
MAY 1856.

(Rear.)

KILLED IN ACTION AT
INKERMANN
5TH NOV^R 1854

P^t. T. ASHBY
 „ J. CLARKE
 „ P. FALLAN
 „ O. KELLY
 „ T. MASTERSON
 „ C. PAYNE

KILLED IN THE TRENCHES
BEFORE
SEBASTOPOL

P^t. W. HOLMES
 „ G. JAKES
 „ E. SHARPE

No. 5 Monument
(continued).
(Right.)
DIED IN CAMP BEFORE
SEBASTOPOL

P^t. S. GARWOOD
 „ W. SOUTH
 „ J. SCULLY
 „ R. GAMMAGE
 „ E. CHADWICK
 „ J. WALSH
 „ M. MACK
 „ J. SINGLETON
 „ G. GRAY
 „ P. O'NEILL
 „ F. MORRIS
 „ J. WEBB
 „ T. WOODHEAD

(Left.)
DIED IN CAMP BEFORE
SEBASTOPOL

D^r. G. BRINTON
 „ J. HOSFORD
P^t. W. WATTS
 „ W. BIRD
 „ J. VALE
 „ G. SMITH
 „ M. MEPHAM
 „ W. MARSDEN
 „ G. SYLVESTER
 „ S. WORRACKER
 „ J. BEARMAN
 „ G. CLARKE
 „ H. HALLS.
 „ T. MARSHALL.

(6.) SACRED
TO
THE MEMORY
OF 22 N. C. O AND MEN
10 COMP^Y 21 FUSILIERS
WHO FELL IN THE CRIMEA
FROM 1854 to 56
ERECTED
BY
CAP^T J. ALDRIDGE

**NEAR 3RD BUFFS CAMP,
2ND DIVISION.**
(HEAD OF WORONZOFF RAVINE.)
8 GRAVES.

---

60 Y^DS. W. OF WATERING PLACE,
BETWEEN LIGHT AND 2ND DIVISIONS.
(WORONZOFF RAVINE.)
10 GRAVES.

(1.) SACRED
TO THE MEMORY OF
HEBERDEN KARSLAKE, ESQ^r. R.N
WHO WAS KILLED IN THE TRENCHES
12TH NOV^R 1854

ROYAL ENGINEERS AND SAPPERS AND MINERS.

RIGHT ATTACK, 1ST, 2ND, 7TH, 9TH, & 10TH COS.
LEFT ATTACK, 3RD, 4TH, 8TH, & 11TH COS.

RIGHT ATTACK BURIAL GROUND NEAR WINDMILL.
(CAREENING CREEK RAVINE.)

NUMBER OF GRAVES—72.

(1.) Sacred to the Memory of
Major George Ranken
Royal Engineers
Killed in Sebastopol
On the xxviii Feby mdccclvi
Erected in token of their esteem
by his Brother Officers.

(2.) Lieutenant
Colonel
CHARLES. C. ALEXANDER
COMMANDING ROYAL ENGINEER
OCTOBER 19TH
1854

(3.) IN MEMORY OF
CAPTAIN. W. M. INGLIS
ROYAL ENGINEERS
DROWNED BY THE WRECK OF THE
PRINCE
BALAKLAVA. 14TH NOVR 1854
Blessed are the Dead that die in the Lord

(4.) ALEXANDER GORDON
OF PITLURG
CAPTAIN ROYAL ARTILLERY
KILLED
5TH JULY
1855

(5.) SACRED
TO THE
MEMORY
OF
CAPTN W. H. JESSE ROYAL ENGRS
KILLED IN THE ASSAULT ON THE
REDAN
18TH JUNE
1855

(6.) TO THE
MEMORY
OF
* LIEUTT J. H. S. CARTER R. E
KILLED IN THE TRENCHES
2ND MAY
1855

(7.) Sacred
TO THE
MEMORY OF
FREDERICK WILLIAM KING
Captain Royal Engineers
died 22nd April 1855 from a wound
received in the trenches before Sebastopol
17th April 1855

(8.) SACRED
TO THE
MEMORY OF
CAPTAIN C. ST J. CROFTON
ROYAL ENGINEERS
WHO DIED OF WOUNDS RECEIVED IN THE EXECUTION OF HIS DUTY 15TH APRIL. 1855.
ERECTED BY
HIS BROTHER
OFFICERS

(9.) ✠
SACRED
to the memory
of
EDWARD LUCE
Lieutenant
Royal Artillery
Killed Before
SEBASTOPOL
11TH APRIL 1855

(Slab.)
HERE RESTS
IN HOPE OF A BLESSED RESURRECTION
EDWARD LUCE,
LIEUTENANT, ROYAL ARTILLERY
WHO FELL IN THE DISCHARGE OF HIS DUTY
IN THE TRENCHES BEFORE SEBASTOPOL
11TH APRIL 1855
JACKSON 150 REGENT STREET LONDON

(10.) SACRED
TO THE MEMORY
OF
LIEUT. E. BAINBRIGGE
ROYAL ENGINEERS
An Officer of much promise and highly
esteemed, who was killed by the bursting
of a Shell when in the execution of his
Duty in the Trenches 4TH APRIL 1855
ERECTED
by Order of
FIELD MARSHAL
LORD RAGLAN
G.C.B.

(Back.)
RUSSIAN INSCRIPTION.

(11.) SACRED
TO THE
MEMORY
OF
A CAPTAIN A COMRADE AND A FRIEND
Captain A. D. Craigie. R.E.
WHO WAS KILLED 13TH MARCH 1855.
Erected
by the N. C. O
and men
4th Compy
R. S. & Miners

(12.) SACRED
TO THE
MEMORY
of
RODNEY A. MITCHELL
LIEUT. ROYAL ARTILLERY
KILLED BEFORE SEBASTOPOL
14TH APRIL
1855
AGED
18 YEARS

(13.) SACRED
TO THE MEMORY
OF
LIEUT. T. M. GRAVES Rl. ENGs
WHO FELL IN THE ASSAULT
ON THE REDAN 18TH JUNE 1855

(14.) Sacred
to the memory
of
T. Graves Lowry
Lieut in the Royal Engineers
Who was Killed in the assault on
the Quarries, on the 7TH June 1855
AGED 20 YEARS

(15.) Sacred
to the memory of
Lieut. James. Murray R.E
who was mortally wounded
at the assault on the Redan
XVIII June mdccclv.
Erected by his Brother
Officers
G. K. R.S.M.

(16.) SACRED
TO THE MEMORY OF
Captain. G. F. Dawson
Royal Engineers
who was killed in the
Trenches, when on duty
7th June 1855
ERECTED BY HIS BROTHER
OFFICERS

(17.) (*Wooden paling round Grave*)
IN
MEMORY
OF
CHARLES. E. G. BAYNES
Lieutenant in the Corps of
Royal Engineers, Who died May 7th 1855
of his wounds received in the trenches Apl 19
1855
This stone is Erected by his brother Officers
Who greatly loved
& respected him

---

* This Officer was killed in the Left Attack.

ROYAL ENGINEERS.
Careening Creek or Windmill Ravine

GUARDS AND HIGHLANDERS
(First Division Camp)

GUARDS AND HIGHLANDERS
(FIRST DIVISION CAMP.)

BRIGADE OF GUARDS: 3RD BATTALION GRENADIER GUARDS, 1ST BATTALION COLDSTREAM GUARDS, AND 1ST BATTALION SCOTS FUSILIER GUARDS.

HIGHLAND BRIGADE: 42ND, 72ND, 79TH AND 93RD HIGHLANDERS.

NUMBER OF GRAVES—173.

On each Pier of Gate.

(TRIA JUNCTA IN UNO)

(1.) *Front,*
(Facing Kamiesch.)
IHS
TO THE MEMORY OF
THE NON COMMISSIONED OFFICERS AND MEN
OF THE BRIGADE OF GUARDS
WHO FELL IN THE CRIMEA
THIS CROSS
WAS ERECTED BY THEIR SURVIVING
COMRADES
A.D. 1856

(Rear.)
A. D. MDCCCLVI
GRENADIER GUARDS
COLDSTREAM GUARDS
SCOTS FUSILIER GUARDS

(2.) S. KENYION 1 BATT
COLDᴹ GUAʳDS
1856.

(3.) i h s
JAMES FACEY
COLDᵐ GUARDˢ
AUGUST 5th 1855.
St JOHN XI 25-26.

(4.) SACRED TO
THE
MEMORY
OF
Dʳᴹ JOHN. GOWELL
1ˢᵀ BATTⁿ S. F. Gds.
WHO
DIED 18TH JULY
1855
AGED 19 YEARS

(5.) SAMUEL
LITTLE
6 C 3 B
G. G
AGED
26

(6.) SACRED
TO
The MEMORY Of
Cʳ SERJT Rᵀ RUSSELL
3ᴰ BATTⁿ Gʳ Gᵈˢ
DIED 29th AUGᵀ
1855

(7.) SACRED
TO
The MEMORY
of
SERJT Wᵐ HARDING
3rd BAtt Gʳ Gᵈˢ
DIED 6ᵀᴴ of AUGUST
1855

(8.) SACRED
TO THE
MEMORY
OF
CORPˡ Sᴺ STᴺNINGˢ
3 B. GRENʳ Gᴰˢ
DIED 26TH JULY 1855

(9.) SACRED
TO THE
MEMORY
of
S'EJT Jᴬˢ WARRIN
GRENʳ GUARDˢ
4ᵗʰ AUGUST
1855

(10.) W. WALTON
3ʀᴰ BATT
Gⁱᴇʳ GDˢ
1855

(11.) SACRED
TO the
MEMORY
of
* SAMᴸ GOODREM
ALSO
Wᵐ BETTS
Coldᵐ Guards
that was killed
in the
REDAN
NOVʳ 14ᵗʰ 1855

(12.) SACRED
TO THE
MEMORY
of
CORPˡ Jᴬˢ STEWART
S. F. Gᴰˢ.
1856

(13.) SACRED
To The Memory
of
J. DUNSTER
J. PATMORE
E. HITCH
3ʳᵈ Battalion
Grenadier Gᵈˢ
Killed Sep 6ᵗʰ
.1.8.5.5.

(14.) TO THE MEMORY
OF
Qʳ MASTER JOHN MᶜDONALD
72ⁿᵈ HIGHLANDERS
WHO DIED ON THE
16ᵀᴴ SEPTʳ FROM A WOUND
RECEIVED IN THE TRENCHES
BEFORE SEBASTOPOL ON
THE 8ᵀᴴ SEPTʳ 1855
AGED 35 YEARS

(15.) SACRED
TO THE
MEMORY
OF
CORPˡ J MᶜDOUGAL
RIGHT FLANK
COMPY
FIRST. BATTⁿ. S. F. Gᴰˢ
KILLED IN THE
TRENCHES BEFORE
SEBASTOPOL
22ⁿᵈ OF. AUGUST
1855
AGED 27 YEARS

(16.) SACRED
TO
THE MEMORY OF
SERJᵀ. G. BOULTON
1ˢᵗ Bⁿ Coldstream Gᵈˢ
KILLED IN THE
TRENCHES
22ⁿᵈ Augᵗ
1855

(17.) ✝
SACRED
TO
THE MEMORY OF
SERJT J. PAGE
1ˢᵀ Bⁿ Cᴹ Gᴰˢ
Died 1ˢᵗ Decʳ
1855

(18.) ✝
SACRED
TO
THE MEMORY OF
SERJᵀ W. BURROWS
1ˢᵗ Bⁿ Coldstream Gᵈˢ
Who died 1ˢᵗ Decʳ
1855

(19.) SACRED
TO THE
MEMORY
of
SAMUEL KENYON
WHO
DEPARTED THIS LIFE
25ᵗʰ NOVEᵇʳ
1855
COLDᵐ GUAᴅˢ

---

* Killed by an Explosion; joined the Storming Party as a Volunteer on the 8ᵗʰ September, 1855. See pages 352, 353, vol. ii., of "The War," by W. H. Russell.

ROYAL ENGINEERS AND SAPPERS AND MINERS.

(18.)
I H S
To the Brave
who fell at the Siege of Sebastopol

Royal Sappers and Miners

Serj^{ts} J. H. Drew. W. Wilson. Corp^{ls}
A. Ramsay. W. James. G. Luke. J. McQueen
J. Frazer. W. Swan. W. Baker. J. Maycock
J. Miller. R. Pinch. J. Evans. P. Towel
C. Bell. Pt^s R. Nicholas. D. Carswell
W. McDonald. N. Campbell. J. Clyde
R. Walsh. W. Bowman 1st Co. J. Muir
J. Lethbridge. W. Small. J. Wright
W. Collins. A. Jarratt. W. R. Collins
D. McArthur. J. Morrison. J. Hamett
A. Weir. J. Gregory. A. Rowlett 2nd Co.
S. Coles 3rd Co. J. Miller 4th Co.
J. Barnes. S. Spear. M. Mc Namara 7th Co.
J. Dilling. H. Masters 8th Co. R. Eadie
J. McRoberts. N. Gillard. W. Brine
E. Lewis 9th Co. R. Russell. J. Queen
J. McAsh. J. McNeil. J. Drummond
W. Denham 10th Co. W. Rollings 11th Co.

(*Right.*)
Died
Serving their Queen & Country
Before Sebastopol

Royal Sappers & Miners

Serj^{ts} W. Mann. G. Moore. J. Rouse
J. Harnet. H. Entwistle. Corp^{ls}
R. Power. W. Shadbolt. T. Leonard
G. Pearson. G. Diamond. P. Scott
G. Ford. J. Ryder. F. Goodall
T. Cooper. H. Pearson. W. Saunders
S. P. Worthington. W. Carmichael
W. Binness, J. Hanson. J. Gordon
W. Hardy. G. Harris. A. M^cintosh
G. Crawford.——Pt^s W. Craige.
J. Southwood. J. Bell. W. Smith.
J. McDonald. J. C. Guy. G. Jenner.
G. Bullen. W. Howard 1st Co.
J. Veitch. R. Allison. T. Ross
J. Dunham. F. Trevitt. W. Harris
H. J. Boyte. T. Prentice. T. Bates
J. Williams. H. Watts 2nd Co.

No. 18 continued.
(*Rear.*)
Died
Serving their Queen & Country
Before Sebastopol

Royal Sappers & Miners

Pt^s J. Bastion. G. Miller. W. Ferguson
R. Hopkins. W. Bradley. G. Gasson 2nd Co.
J. Tabor. W. Chapman. J. Cox. W. Thomas
J. Tollady. J. Franklyn. H. Collins.
J. Cranford. A. Jepson. H. Savery
J. Smith. W. Goddard. G. Wright. J. Hill
P. Baker. J. Cole. D. Bowey. M. J. Gumb
D. Ogg. J. Wallace. J. Weir 3rd Co——
D. Johnston. W. Rainford. T. Lumby
M. Marlow. R. Parker. H. Bristone
F. Bird. J. Porter. J. Long. J. Gould.
J. Calvar. 4th Co. C. Skinner. J. Evans
J. Chudley. A. Young. C. D. Thompson
W. Weavings. T. Allen 7th Cq. J. Rea
N. McLachlen. T. Flockhart. W. Davis
W. Brown. J. Stewart. A. Henderson
G. Butler. T. Wilson. M. Demithorne 8th Co.

(*Left.*)
Died
Serving their Queen & Country
Before Sebastopol

Royal Sappers & Miners

Pt^s G. Haskett. T. Cooper. F. Clarke
R. Layfield. J. Reynolds 8th Co.
R. Bayley. H. Hopkinson. M. George
W. Leavins. A. Anning. J. Wood
J. Patterson. 9th Co. G. Wilson
J. Shorey. G. Wood. R. Blackler
R. Blair. W. Frame. E. Springate
W. Gabriel. J. Bailey. W. Bullock
G. Cooper. R. Ferrier. G. Gill
A. Anderson. W. Ross. E. Kevill
H. Stevenson 10th Co. J. Davie
H. Collins. J. Waddle. C. Miller
P. Sinclair. H. Pollixfinn
R. Bennett. J. Deacon 11th Co

Serj^t W. Carne. Corp^{ls} J. Pendred
J. Hammond. Pt^e J. Lewis. T. Price
T. Tooeey. Drowned.
G. KEYTE, R. S. M.

(19.)
I H S
In MEMORY of
* ANDREW ANDERSON
10th Comp^y R. S. M.
DIED
24TH Feby 1855
ERECTED
by his Comrades.

ROYAL SAPPERS AND MINERS (continued),

LEFT ATTACK BURIAL GROUND, NEAR LIME KILN, IN FRONT OF CATHCART'S HILL.

NUMBER OF GRAVES—16.

(1.) IN MEMORY OF
SERJ^T W. WILSON
L^{CE} C^{PLS} C. BELL   R. PINCH
PRI^{TS} G. BULLEN   J. MORRISON
J. HEMMETT   J. GREGORY
G. GASSON   G. FOX
J. BURLING   J. PATERSON
W. BRINE   D. CARSWELL
E. LEWIS   J. DRUMMOND
H. INGLES
ROYAL SAPPERS & MINERS
1855 - 56,,

(2.) (*Front*)
IN MEMORY
OF
PTE HUGH INGLES
10TH CO R S & MINERS
WHO DIED 11TH APRIL
1856
AGED 38 YEARS

(*Rear.*)
ERECTED
BY
LIEU^T BRINE R.E
JULY 1856

ROYAL SAPPERS AND MINERS (continued),

THIRD DIVISION CAMP.

NUMBER OF GRAVES—12.

(1.) IN MEMORY OF
SERJ^{TS} W. MANN . H. ENTWISTLE
PRI^{TS} C. MILLER . J. SMITH
P. BAKER . A. JEPSON
S. COLE . J. HILL
J. WADDIE . J. DEACON
P. SINCLAIR.
ROYAL SAPPERS & MINERS
J. WESTON 50TH REG^T
WHO FELL BEFORE SEBASTOPOL
1854-55.

---

* This Soldier was decorated by His Highness Omer Pasha with the Fourth Class of the Order of Medjidie, for his distinguished gallantry in recovering the body of his Officer, Lieut. Burke, R. E., at the passing of the Danube on the 12th July, 1854.

THIRD DIVISION.

*FIRST BATTALION: 1ST ROYALS, 4TH, †9TH, 14TH, 18TH, 28TH, 38TH, 39TH, 44TH, 50TH, & 89TH REGTS.

NUMBER OF GRAVES—1334.

(1.) **SACRED**
TO THE MEMORY OF
MAJOR THE HONLE C. DALY 89 REGT.
WHO. DIED DECER 29TH 1854
AND
BT MAJOR JOHN MACDONALD 89 REGT
WHO DIED JANRY 15TH 1855
FROM EXPOSURE IN THE TRENCHES
BEFORE SEBASTOPOL
THIS TOMB IS PLACED OVER THEIR
REMAINS AS A LAST TOKEN OF ESTEEM
BY THEIR BROTHER OFFICERS

(Foot).
IHS
MAJOR THE HONORABLE
CHARLES DALY 89th REGT
DIED 29th DECEMBER
1854

(2.)
To
MONTAGU WIGLEY BELL
Lieut   28h Regt
Son of
MAJOR GENERAL BELL
Died Janr 7th 1855

✝

I SHALL RISE AGAIN.

(3.) SACRED
TO THE
MEMORY
OF
SERJT G. JENNER 50 REGT
WHO DIED
3rd JANUARY
1855

(4.) SACRED (Wood.)
to the
MEMORY
of
Jeremiah, Thompson
4th King's Own Regt
Who Died, on
the
26th August
1855
Aged 26 Years
MAY, HE, REST
IN
PEACE

(5.) SACRED
TO THE MEMORY OF
MRS BRETT WHO
DEPARTED THIS
LIFE ON THE 7TH OF
JUNE 1855 AGED 26 YRS
WAS
THIS STONE   ERECTED
BY THOM   AS BRETT
28TH   REG

(6.) (Wood.)
Sacred to the Memory of Pte
JOHN BALL
late of the 4th Regt who died on the
20th Novr 1855 Aged 30 Yrs
May he rest
in peace

(7.) Sacred
to the
MEMORY
of
CORPL THOS MARSH
6 BN R. A. DIED JUNE 1855
AGED 26 YEARS

(Foot.)
T. M.

(8.) SACRED (Wood.)
TO THE
MEMORY
OF
Pte James Smith
39th Regt Who departed
this life the 24th May 1855
AGED 27 years—
May he rest in peace
— Amen —

(9.) IHS
SACRED
TO THE
MEMORY
OF
Pte CHS BRYNE WHO DEPARTED THIS LIFE
ON THE 12TH JULY 1855 AGED 2e YEARS
THIS STONE WAS ERECTED BY THE
GRS 39TH Regt

(10.) SACRED
TO THE MEMORY OF
Dr. Stephen O'Brian
Pte John ✝ Dean
James   Wibber
who   died of their
wounds received on
the 18th of June 1855 This
stone is Erected as a token of
respect by No. 1 Coy 28th Regt

(11.) To the MEMORY of (Wood.)
Private ED. CAMMELL
aged 34 years
of the 8th Kings Rl Irish
Hussars
who Departed this life 18TH June 1855
Erected by his only Brother, D, CAMMELL
Hospital Serjeant of the same Corps

(12.) IHS (Wood.)
Drummer Dennis O'Brien
18th R. I Regt killed in the
Trenches 19th June 1855
AGE 17 Years
RequiescAnt in PACe

(13.) Sacred (Wood.)
To, the
MEMORY
of
H. M. MOONEY
14TH Regiment of Foot
WHO departed this Life
the 4th JUNE 1855
Age 21 Years

This Board was erected by his
Brother A. Mooney who deeply
deplores his loss

Blessed are the dead who die
in the Lord.

(14.) SACRED (Wood.)
✠
To the MEMORY of
Corpl T. STARKE 14 Regiment
who Died 31st May 1855
aged 27 years & 3 months

may he rest in peace — — —

(15.) IHS
ZACRED
to the MEMORY OF
DANIEL DOWNES WHO
DIED IN CAMP BEFORE
SEBASTOPOL
14 OF MAY 55
MAY HE REST
IN PEACE
AMEN
ERECTED BY
HIS COMRA
DES OF THE
39 REGt.

(16.) SACRED
TO THE
MEMORY
of
JAMES RODD Color Serjt 39th Regt.
Who was Wounded in the Trenches
before Sebastopol on the 30th March and
died on the 14th April 1855
Aged 27

(17.) SACRED (Wood.)
To The Memory of the late Serjeant John
Sutherland Killed in the Trenches
on the 13th April 1855

(18.) SACRED
TO THE
MEMORY
OF THE GRENADIERS OF
THE 28TH REGT WHO DIED
DURING THE CAMPAIGN
ON THE
CRIMEA.

---

* Afterwards attached to 2ND BRIGADE HIGHLAND DIVISION at KAMARA.   † Afterwards Attached to 2ND BRIGADE FIRST DIVISION.

GUARDS AND HIGHLANDERS.

(20.)
TO THE
MEMORY
OF
DANIEL BAKER
3RD BATT GRENADIER GUARDS
APRIL
1856

(21.)
SACRED
TO THE
MEMORY
OF
EDWARD BOYD
4th COMPY
1st BATTN S. F. GDS
WHO DIED
13 OF APRIL
1856
AGED 20
YEARS

(22.)
SACRED
TO
THE MEMORY OF
JAMES KILLICK
1ST Bn Coldstream Gds
who died May 2nd
1856

(23.)
SACRED
TO
THE MEMORY
of
ROBT MAYS ColdM GDS
Who DEPARTED THIS LIFE
29th MARCH 1856
JESUS ✳ WEPT
AND
I BLED
(Foot.)
IHS
18 56
R. MAYES

NEARER THE SEA.
(FIRST DIVISION CAMP.)

NUMBER OF GRAVES—39.

(1.)
SACRED
TO THE
MEMORY
OF LIEUTT A HILL 22nd REGT WHO DIED
JUNE 21ST 1855
THIS STONE IS ERECTED BY HIS
FRIENDS
IN THE
CRIMEA

(2.) (Wood.)
TO
THE MEMORY
OF
SERJEANT MAJOR
ANDREW RENNIE
93rd Highlanders
DIED
1ST JULY 1855
After life's fitful fever
He sleeps well
Erected
By
A Friend

(3.)
SACRED
TO
THE MEMORY OF
SERJT THOS ROBINS
1ST Bn Coldstream Gds
who died 29th June
1855

(4.)
SACRED TO THE MEMORY
OF
SERJT GEORGE MANGOR
SCOTS FUSILIER GUARDS
WHO DIED OF CHOLERA
22D JUNE 1855
ERECTED BY A FRIEND

(5.) (Wood.)
TO THE MEMORY
OF
SERGT ALEX MC KAY
79th HIGHLANDERS
DIED
20TH SEPT 1855

E. Walker, lith. London, Published by Ackermann & Co. 106 Strand, W.C. Day & Son, lith.rs to The Queen.

THIRD DIVISION.

OFFICERS' BURIAL GROUND,

IN FRONT OF QUARRY, THIRD DIVISION CAMP.

NUMBER OF GRAVES—8.

(1.)
SACRED
TO THE
MEMORY
OF
CAPTAIN FRED^K SMITH
IXTH REG^t
Died of his wounds
June 20TH 1855

(2.)
(*Front.*)
(FACING CAMP.)
IHS
HERE REST
THE REMAINS OF
CAPTAINS
BOWES—FENWICK
HON^{ble} C. W. H. AGAR
W. H. MANSFIELD
AND
F. W. T. CAULFIELD
ALL OF THE
44th REG^t
AND WHO DIED
OF WOUNDS RECEIVED
18TH JUNE 1855

(*Right.*)
ЗЛѢСЪ ПОКОЯТО ЯУБИТЫЯ
НАВОЙНѢВЪ 1855 ТОДУ, ЮНЯ
44^{ТО} ЕЯ
ВЕЛИЦЕОТВА БРИТАНСКАТО
ПОЛКА КАПИТАНЫ:
В ФЕНВЫКЪ НАЗ! ^{МВ} ТОДУОТЪ
РОЖДЕ=НИЯ
ГРАФ БК. ВГ. АКГАРЪ. НА 31 ^{МВ} ^{ІО}
Ф. В. Т. КОФИЛЛЪ. НА 29 ^{МВ} ^{ІО}
В Г МАНСВИЛЛЪ. НА 28 ^{МВ} ^{ІО}

(3.)
SACRED
TO THE
MEMORY
OF
Major Swinton Royal Art^y
WHO
DIED 2nd JANUARY 1855

(4.)
SACRED
TO THE MEMORY
OF
CAPTAIN OLDFIELD, R.A
KILLED IN THE TRENCHES
AUGUST 17TH 1855

(5.)
✝
HERE LIE THE REMAINS
OF
CAP^N EDW^D GEARY. SNOW
ROYAL, ARTILLERY
WHO WAS KILLED IN
THE TRENCHES BEFORE
SEBASTOPOL
6TH SEPTR 1855

THIRD DIVISION.

(19.) (Wood.)
SACRED TO THE
MEMORY
OF J. WALSH. PRIVATE 14TH REGT
WHO DEPARTED THIS LIFE ON THE
31st OF MAY 1855 MAY HIS SOUL
REST IN PEACE

(20.) (Wood.)
SACRED
to the
MEMORY
of William Flynn 39th Regt
who departed this life 20th March 1855
Aged 32 Years
may he rest in peace Amen

(21.)
SACRED
TO THE
MEMORY
OF
Color Serjt Richd Lovell
39th Regt
Who died of Cholera on the 27th of
June 1855 Age 29 Years
REST SOLDIER
REST THY WAR
FARE O'ER SLEEP THAT
KNOWS NO BREAK
ING DREAM OF MA-
-RTIAL FIELDS NO
MORE NIGHT OF
TOIL OR MORN
OF WAKING,
ERECTED BY
SERJEANTS

(22.) SACRED (Wood.)
To The Memory of the late Gunner &
Driver Js Birch of the Rl A Killed in
The Trenches on the 13th April 1855

THIRD DIVISION
(continued.)
NEARER KAMIESCH.

NUMBER OF GRAVES—38.

(1.) SACRED (Wood.)
TO THE
MEMORY
OF
MICHAEL CASH
late of H. M. 18th Royal Irish Band
Who Departed This Life
5th December 1855
ERECTED
BY HIS COMPANIONS

(2.)
SACRED
TO THE
MEMORY OF
PT. ―――
LIGHT COMPANY
50TH QUEEN'S OWN REGT
Who Departed This Life

THIS STONE IS ERECTED BY
HIS COMRADES AS A TESTIMONY
OF REGARD.

(3.)
ENSIGN
EDWARD DICKSON RICARD
18TH ROYAL IRISH REGT
DIED
5TH MAY 1856
THIS STONE IS ERECTED BY
HIS BROTHER OFFICERS

(4.) IHS (Wood.)
Sacred to the Memory
of Private James McFadden
38th Regiment who departed
this life on the 30th Jany
1856
This was Erected
by his Comrades
of No. 3 Company

THIRD DIVISION
(continued)
IN 50TH CAMP.

NUMBER OF GRAVES—4.

(1.)
Sacred
TO THE
MEMORY
OF
Qr Mr SERGt T. CLIFFORD
50th Regiment
KILLED ON THE 13TH APRIL 1855
THIS STONE WAS ERECTED AS A TOKEN OF
REGARD BY HIS
BROTHER SERGEANTS

(2.)
SACRED
TO THE
MEMORY
OF
MAJOR MOLLER 50th REGT
WHO WAS MORTALLY WOUNDED
21ST AND DIED 22nd DECEMBER
1854

(3.)
SACRED
to the memory of
Lieutenant
Walpole. G. Dashwood
50th Regiment
Killed at the Battle of
Inkermann 5th NOVr
1854
Erected in token of their
regard by his Brother officers.

(4.) LIEUT W. W. BOND
50th Regt
DIED 8TH DECR 1854

THIRD DIVISION
(continued).
IN CENTRE OF RAVINE, BETWEEN
CATHCART'S HILL AND CAMP OF
4TH KING'S OWN REGT.

ONE GRAVE.

SACRED TO THE MEMORY OF
PTE HENRY EWEN
4TH K. O. REGIMENT
WHO WAS KILLED AT
GREEN HILL
17TH OCT 1854

THIRD DIVISION
(continued),
NEAR LAND TRANSPORT CAMP
(Third Division).

NUMBER OF GRAVES { 14 / 50 / *49 / 5 / 17 } 135

(*1.)

IN MEMORY OF
Qr Mr Saml SPENCE
28TH REGT
DIED 7 NOV. 1854

LEFT SIEGE TRAIN
ROYAL ARTILLERY
(THIRD DIVISION CAMP).

NUMBER OF GRAVES—38.

(1.) SACRED (Wood.)
TO THE
MEMORY OF
WM HAZARD who was killed in
ACTION JUNE 9th 1855 Aged 26 Yrs

(2.) SACRED (Wood.)
To the Memory of the late Company Serjt
GEO. Farist R.A. Killed in the Trenches on the 10th
of April
1855

(3.)
IN MEMORY
OF
CAPTAIN WILLIAM K. ALIX
1st ROYAL REGIMENT
AND AIDE-DE-CAMP
TO LIEUTt GENERAL
SIR DE LACY EVANS, K.C.B.
WHO WAS KILLED AT THE
BATTLE OF INKERMANN
5th NOVEMBER 1854
THIS TABLET IS ERECTED
BY HIS BROTHER AIDES-DE-CAMP
AS A TOKEN OF THEIR HIGH ESTEEM

DARMANIN. MALTA. SC.

(4.)
IN
MEMORY
OF
SPENCER PHILIP JOHN CHILDERS
CAPTAIN ROYAL ARTILLERY
Who was Killed in the Trenches
before
SEBASTOPOL
OCTR 21ST
1854.

(5.)
UNDER THIS STONE
LIES THE
Right Arm
OF
Lt Colonel C. S. Henry
R. H. A.
17th August 1855

(6.)
SACRED TO THE MEMORY OF
WILLM D. GUILLE
CAPTAIN ROYAL
ARTILLERY
WHO DIED
28TH OCTR 1854

(7.)
SACRED TO THE MEMORY OF
IHS

LIEUT D. G. MACLACHLAN
ROYAL ARTILLERY
DIED NOVEMBER 28TH 1854
AGED 19 YEARS.

EAST OF LEFT SIEGE TRAIN.

2 GRAVES.

OFFICERS' BURIAL GROUND.
(Third Division Camp.)

ROYAL NAVAL BRIGADE.
NEAR THIRD DIVISION CAMP.

NUMBER OF GRAVES—91.

(1.) *(Wood.)*

SACRED
To
The Memory of
The following Seamen belonging to
Her Majesty's Ship Queen
Who departed this life whilst serving with the
Royal Naval Brigade
before Sevastopol

Thomas Bush   Leading Seaman
Alfred Burcher — Ord^y
John. McConochie. Sailmakers' Crew
James, Symons. Shipwright
William, Channon, Ord^y
John, Douglas — Ord^y
John A. Whitfield. A.B.
William W. Harris — Ord^y

(2.) SACRED *(Wood.)*
To
The Memory
(OF)
Thos Prince.
John. Reed.
W^m. Davidson
E^d. Quin

That fell in the Execution
of their Duty . on the 18th
June 1855

ALSO

Ja^s Murphey.
Ja^s Ennis.
Mic^l Kearns.

That fell in the Storming
Party the same Day
Much Lamented by their
Shipmates
(OF)
H. M. S. RODNEY

(3.) SACRED *(Wood.)*
to
The MEMORY of

J. Glanville St Mr Killed 9 Ap^{rl} 1855 age 28
S. Turner A.B.   D^o 11 — —   25
J. Woodford. O.S.   D^o 14 — —   23
D. Logan. G^r.R.M.A. D^o 6 June — 27
  at Greenhill Batt^{ry} N° 2
J. Lane. G^r.R.M.A. Died 7 Novr 1854 — 30
W. Wheeler Q^r M^r   D^o 8 — —   31
Mr R. Morris Mate D^o 24 — —   22
J. Callinane. O.S. D^o 16 Jan^{ry} 1855 — 22
C. Brooks. A.B.   D^o 2 May —   27
S. Swift. B^N M^t D^o 12 — —   36
S. Short. C^{pns} C^k D^o 6 July — 63
R. Fullerton. L. S^{tr} D^o 28 — —   53
P. Donaghue G.F.T. D^o 5 AU^{gst} 23

This board is Erected by the Ships
Comp^y of H.M.S Wasp as a Token of
Respect to their Departed Ship Mates

(4.) *(Wood.)*

SACRED
To The
MEMORY
OF
The Following Seamen belonging to
H.M.S. QUEEN
who departed this Life whilst serving
In the ROYAL NAVAL BRIGADE Before
SEVASTOPOL

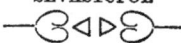

GEORGE SULLIVAN	FRANCIS EDDY
GEORGE EAMES	JOHN SYMONS
ROBERT LAVRICK	HENRY. JOHN. BAZING
JOSEPH BURROWS	THOMAS. CORBELLY
WILLIAM. GOOD	THOMAS. PHILLIPS
THOMAS. DUGON	STEPHEN. WELSH
JOHN. DAVISON	JOHN. BLEWIT
NICHOLAS. MEDLIN.	JOHN MEDLIN
WILLIAM SOULSBY	JAMES COFFIN
JOHN TRIM	PATRICK MAHONEY
THOMAS BRYANT	ROBERT JOHNS
WILLIAM HARVEY	JOHN LANAHAN
WILLIAM JONES	THOMAS CLARK
BENJAMIN TAYLOR.	HENRY CHESTER
HENRY HILL	FREDERICK DRIVER
W^M M^CDONALD	

(5.) ◁ SACRED ▷
TO
THE MEMORY
OF LIEU^T. T. O. KIDD. R.N
KILLED IN ACTION
BEFORE SEBASTOPOL
JUNE 18TH 1855
AGED 24 YEARS

(6.) *(Wood.)*

SACRED
TO The Memory of
EDWARD COLLINS
who departed this life
JAN^y 7th 1855
AGED 23 YEARS

(7.)

IHS

IN
MEMORY OF
LACON USSHER HAMMET
COMMANDER, R.N OF H.M.S "ALBION"
BORN JULY 5TH 1820
HE WAS KILLED IN THE TRENCHES
BEFORE SEBASTOPOL, AUGST 17TH 1855
WHILST SERVING WITH THE NAVAL
BRIGADE AND IN COMMAND OF THE
BATTERIES OF ITS RIGHT ATTACK

ЧЕСТЬ ХРАБРЫМЪ

(8.) SACRED *(Wood.)*
TO
THE MEMORY
OF
GEORGE CASS
SEAMAN, BELONGING TO
H. M. SHIP LEANDER
WHO WAS KILLED, ON
THE 18TH DAY OF JUNE, 1855
IN THE STORMING PARTY
BEFORE THE REDAN
SEBASTOPOL
AGED 22 YEARS

Now while I feel this mortal strife
Oh be my sins forgiven
Then death shall prove the gate of ife
The grave my road to heaven

(9.) *(Wood.)*

SACRED
TO
THE MEMORY OF
THOMAS PASCOE. A.B
on board of
H. M. S. "Leander"
who was killed before Sebastopol
on the 9th of June 1855.
Aged 21 Years

(10.) *(Wood.)*

SACRED
to
THE MEMORY
OF JOHN ARNOLD
Seaman of H. M. S. Leander
Who Was Killed 8th of June
1855
Aged 24 Years

(11.) SACRED *(Wood.)*
TO
THE MEMORY OF. J. M. COLLINS
WHO WAS KILLED IN ACTION THE
8TH OF SEPT^R 1855 AGED 24

UNTO THEE O LORD O I LIFT
UP MY SOUL

(12.) *(Marble.)*

REQUIESCAT IN PACE
Sacred
to the Memory of
LIEU^T. E. H. HUGHES D'AETH R.N.
Late First Lieutenant of H.M.S. Sidon
who after having served seven months
on shore in the Naval Brigade
died of Cholera Augt 7th 1855 Aged 34 years

This Stone is erected by the Captain
and Officers of H.B.M.S. Sidon
in testimony of their esteem and regard

(13.) *(Slab.)* *(Marble.)*

TO THE MEMORY OF
LIEUTENANT
W. H. DOUGLAS, R.N.
KILLED 11TH APRIL 1855
WHILE IN BATTERY
WITH THE R.N. BRIGADE
AT THE SIEGE OF
SEBASTOPOL

ROYAL NAVAL BRIGADE.

(14.) (Head.) (Marble.)

Поменіе
Nokoúнбіхъ.

Sacred
to the memory of
Lieut^{nt} Samuel Twyford
Royal Navy
who was killed by the fire
from the Russian Trenches
whilst serving
with the Naval Brigade
April 9th 1855

(Foot.) (Stone.)

SACRED
TO THE MEMORY
OF
LIEU^T SAMUEL TWYFORD, R.N.
OF H.M.S. LONDON
WHO WAS KILLED WHEN
IS THE ESECUTION OF HIS DUTY
ON THE 9TH APRIL 1855

ЕНТА
ВЪ ЗНАКЪ ПАМЯТЬ
ФЛОТСКА́СО ЛЕ́ИТШН
САМУ́ИЛА ТАЛФРАА́
ВОЕННАГО СУДНА ЛОНДОНЪ
КОТШРЫЙ БЫЛЪ УБЫТЪ
ВЪ ВРАЖЕАИЩ 9^{гp} АПРЪИЛ

(15.) (Front.) (Marble.)

IN MEMORY
OF
HENRY JOHN SPALDING R.N
MATE OF H.M.S. LONDON
KILLED IN THE TRENCHES BEFORE
SEBASTOPOL
ON THE 21ST of JANUARY 1855

(Back.)

ТИТЕМАГИЛА ХРАБРЫХЪ
ВОЙНОВЪ

(16.) SACRED (Wood.)
TO THE MEMORY
of
ROBERT GARDENER
of
H.M.S. LONDON WHO
was
KILLED in the TRENCHES
BEFORE SEBASTOPOL
April 9th 1855
A Ged 25 Years
May he rest in peace

(17.) SACRED (Wood)
TO
THE
MEMORY OF WILLIAM
BARRY WHO WAS KILLED
IN ACTION BEFORE
SEBASTOPOL AUGst 17 1855
AGED 23 SEAMAN OF
H.M.S. ALBION

HIM THAT COMETH
TO ME I WILL IN NO
WISE CAST OUT

(18.) SACRED (Wood.)
TO
THE
MEMORY OF
JAMES PINHORN
LATE GUNNERS MATE
OF H.M.S. ALBION WHO
DEPARTED THIS LIFE
MAY 6th 1855 AGED 32

(19.) SACRED (Wood.)
TO
THE MEMORY OF
W^M HUBANK AGED 43
W^M JONES AGED 28
EW^D MASTERS AGED 30
WHO DEPARTED THIS LIFE IN THE
YEAR 1854
AND LIKEWISE TO THE MEMORY OF
S^{IDY} SMITH AGED 40
SA^{ML} WALLACE AGED 20
J^{HN} WOODS AGED 38
WHO WAS KILLED IN ACTION
THIS TABLET IS ERECTED BY THEIR
SHIPMATES OF H. M. S ALBION
SERVING IN THE R. N. BRIGADE
AS A TOKEN OF THEIR RESPECT

LORD INCREASE OUR FAITH
LUKE XVII. 5.
[M S]

(20.) IN (Wood.)
MEMORY
of
W. MILLER
H. M. S "Albion"
Aged 32 Years
Killed at the
Greenhill Batt^y
April 9th 1855

(21.) 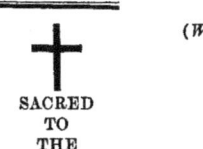 (Wood.)

SACRED
TO
THE
MEMORY. OF. WILLIAM. HAYNES
SEAMAN. OF. H. M. S. ALBION. WHO. DEPARTED
THIS. LIFE. DEC^R 17th 1854 AGED. 38.

THE. LORD. GAVE. AND. THE. LORD,
HAVE. TAKEN. AWAY. BLESSED. BE. THE
NAME. OF. THE. LORD.

(22.)  (Wood.)
SACRED
TO THE MEMORY
OF
JOHN MULLET. A B
of
H. M. S "Leander"
who departed this life
on the 21st of April, in
the Year of our Lord
1855. Aged 23
Years

(23.) SACRED (Wood.)
TO, THE,
MEMORY, OF,
CHARLES GARTON
SEAMAN, OF,
H. M. S. LEANDER,
Who died, 21st of, may,
1855
AGED 33 YEARS

(24.) H
✝
I   S

SACRED To The MEMORY
OF JOHN, TOBIN
SEAMAN OF H. M. S LEAN^{DER}
WHO DIED OF HIS WOUND
ON, THE 24 OF JUNE
1855
AGED 21 YEARS
MAY HE REST IN PEACE
AMEN
I, am Anchored here below
with many of the fleet
but once Again we will
Set sail our Admiral
Christ to meet.

NEAR NAVAL BRIGADE BURIAL GROUND.

8 GRAVES.

NAVAL BRIGADE
(continued),

IN REAR OF 21 GUN BATTERY,
RIGHT ATTACK.

NUMBER OF GRAVES—66.

(1.) SACRED (Wood.)
TO
THE
MEMORY
OF
JOHN THURLBECK
WHO DEPARTED THIS
LIFE JUNE 7TH 1855
AGED 23.

(2.) (Broken.) (Wood.)
IN
MEMORY
of
RLES M^C LEAN
Aged 23
H. M. S "LEANDER"
Was Killed at the 21
Battery on the
10th of April
1855

(3.) ✝ (Marble)

SACRED
TO THE MEMORY OF MANY
BRITISH ARTILLERYMEN, SEAMEN
& SAPPERS WHO WERE KILLED
NEAR THIS SPOT
AND BURIED HERE DURING
THE SIEGE OF
SEBASTOPOL
A.D. 1854 AND 1855

KAZATCH.

(4.) ✠ *(Wood.)*

SACRED
TO THE MEMORY of
Jonathan Thomas Green
Seaman H.M.S. Leander
Who was Killed
Before Sebastopol
On the 16th of April 1855
Aged O Years
Doom'd o'er the Watery Waste to Roam
He Often braved the tempest Strife
Until a Cannon ball
Had caused his fall
And hurried him to eternal life

(5.)

SACRED
to
THE MEMORY
of
Peter King Royal Marines
H. M. S. Gladiator
who was Drowned in the Harbour
of Sebastopol on the 10th of June
1856
Aged 21 Years
Erected by his Ship Mates

NEAR LATE PICQUET HOUSE

(WORONZOFF ROAD.)

(1.) Sacred *(Wood.)*

TO
THE MEMORY
OF
EDWARD CHURCHILL
and
WILLIAM LATIMAN
Killed Before Sebastopol 17th Oct.r 1854
and
JAMES RADMORE
Killed on the 18th of June 1855
SEAMEN OF H. M. S. DIAMOND

He hath taken us away
From the battle that was
Rageing against us

SAILORS' BURIAL GROUND, KAZATCH.

NUMBER OF GRAVES—106.

(1.)

SACRED
TO THE
MEMORY
OF
RALPH
HENDERSON
MASTER
OF THE
BRITISH QUEEN
of
No SHIELDS
DIED, MAY 14TH 1856
AGED
30 YEARS

(2.) SACRED TO THE MEMORY *(Wood.)*

OF A
✠
SOLDIER
OF The 88th Connaught
Rangers who having
Served Through the Whole
of the
Crimean Campaign
Was Killed By Accident
On Board The Belleisle
On The 9th of June 1856
The Day of His
Embarkation For
ENGLAND

(3.) IHS *(Marble.)*

TO
THE MEMORY
OF
CAPTN. PETER CHRISTIE. R.N.
PRINCIPAL AGENT FOR TRANSPORTS
IN THE BLACK SEA
WHO DIED ON BOARD
THE "GERTRUDE"
IN KASSATCH BAY
ON THE 1ST MAY 1855
AGED 58 YEARS

St. JOHN Ch. xi. v. 25. 26
1st THESSALON. Ch iv. v. 13. 14

(4.) Hier ruhet' *(Wood.)*
Heinrich Sumfleth
ges-den 10ben Nov. 1855
au Bord der
Hammonia

(5.) ✠

IN MEMORY OF
JOHN. S. GAYNOR
Lieutenant in H. M. 47th Reg.t
Who died
On the 27th of August 1855
Aged 25 Years

(6.) SACRED

TO
THE MEMORY
OF
WILLM BAILING
BOY 2nd CLASS OF
H. M. S. STROMBOLI
WHO DEPARTED
THIS LIFE ON THE
15TH APRIL 1856
AGED 15 YEARS
AND 6 MONTHS

(7.)

SACRED
TO
THE MEMORY
OF
† JOHN LINDEN SERGT
OF THE R. M. A WHO WAS
KILLED IN THE EXECUTION
OF HIS DUTY ON THE
12TH APRIL 1856
AGED 31 YEARS

This Tombstone is Erected
by the Officers and men
of H. M. S. Stromboli by whom
he was much respected

(8.) Sacred to the Memory *(Wood.)*

Of
FRANCIS RITCHIE
Chief Officer S. S. ETNA
WHO DIED 14TH Sepr 1855
Aged 35 years

(9.) *(Wood.)*

TO
THE
MEMORY
OF
WILLIAM — BRAMMAM
WHO
DIED SEPTR 29th
1855
AGED 14 YEARS
FROM A FALL FROM THE
MIZEN CROSS TREES
OF THE BARQUE
ADMRL. MOORSOM OF
"HULL"

(10.) SACRED *(Wood.)*

TO THE
MEMORY
OF
DANL BONNER
WHO DIED
AUGUST 20th 1855

(11.) SACRED *(Wood.)*

To the
MEMORY
of
J. W. DUKE
late Seaman
of the
Can*t*idate Steam Ship
who
departed
This life June 25th
1855
Aged 36 Yrs

(12.) SACRED *(Wood.)*

TO
THE MEMORY
OF
FRANCIS. BISHOP
ORDINARY. SEAMAN
Who was Killed by a fall from the main top of
H. M. S MEGÆRA
AUGUST 9th 1855
AGED 19 YEARS
and
6 months

---

* Private Patrick Callaghan.   † Shot through error by a French Guard over the Battery at Point, between the harbours of Kazatch and Kamiesch.

KAZATCH.

(13.) *(Marble.)*
SACRED
TO
THE MEMORY OF
DUNCAN RITCHIE
4TH ENGINEER
S. S. CITY OF MANCHESTER
WHO DIED AUGST 15TH 1855
AGED 28 YEARS

THIS TABLET HAS BEEN ERECTED
BY HIS BROTHER OFFICERS
AS A
TRIBUTE OF RESPECT.

---

(14) *(Wood.)*
SACRED
TO
THE
MEMORY of
JOHN ORMOND
Who was drowned in Kazatch Bay
on the 7th of Jany 1856

(15.) *(Wood.)*
SACRED
TO THE MEMORY OF
SAMUEL HENRY
of Barbadoes
late Cook of the Ship "Sumroo"
of Liverpool
DIED 9th June 1855
Aged 27 Years

(16.) *(Wood.)*
SACRED   JW   MEMORY
Of
ST m WILLINGTON
MASTER
OF
BRIG WASP
DIED June 24 1855 Age 28

(17.) *(Wood.)*
SACRED
TO THE
MEMORY
of
ALEXANDER FRAZER
O.S
S. S "CITY OF BALTIMORE"
DIED 5TH DECR 1855
AGED 30

(18.) *(Wood.)*
SACRED
TO THE MEMORY
Of
GEORGE. W. LUCAS
late Cook of the Transport
TRUE BRITON
who departed this life
July 31st 1855 Aged 36 yrs
OF CHOLERA
After an illness of only 6 Hours
THIS TABLET
is Erected as a Token of
Respect by his Shipmates

(19.) *(Wood.)*
SACRED
TO
THE MEMORY
of
LIEUT. A. F. YOUNG
H.M.S LEOPARD
DEPARTED THIS LIFE
JUNE 30TH 1855
AGED 26 YEARS

(20.) *(Wood.)*
SACRED
TO THE
MEMORY OF
DAVID MILLER
SEAMEN OF THE
STEPHEN HUNTLY
OF SUNDERLAND
WHO DEPARTED
THIS LIFE
JULY 5TH 1855
AGED 34 YEARS

(21.) *(Wood.)*
SACRED
TO THE
MEMORY OF
CHARLES RAY
A Seaman of
H. M. S. RODNEY
Who Died 13th Sepr 1855
Aged 22 Years

(22.) *(Wood.)*
SACRED
TO THE MEMORY
of
CHARLES CANE
Late of Her M.S.S. CURLEW
WHO DEPARTED THIS LIFE
THE 8TH DAY OF AUGUST / 55
AGED 30 YEARS

(23.) *(Wood.)*
SACRED
in
MEMORY
of
JOHN RAE
SEAmen of the
BARque Cairo
WHO DIED. On the
26 of JULY Aged
23 YEARS
MAY HE REST IN
PEACE

(24.)
SACRED
.TO. The. Memory. Of
CAPtn Hy AIR,
Steam Ship. Candidate.
DIED. MAY 1ST
AGED. 1855 30 YRS

(25.) *(Wood.)*
SACRED
TO THE
MEMORY
of
WILLIAM. ADAMS
AGED 47
WHO DIED JUNE 9th 1855
LATE STEWARD OF THE
S. S. Eglington of Leith
In respect of him, his Ship
mates has Erected this Tablet
C. M. G. R.

(26.) *(Wood.)*
SACRED
TO
THE MEMORY
OF
J. W. PURCELL
SEAMAN
OF THE
LADY McNAGHTEN
WHO DEPARTED THIS LIFE
JULY 26TH 1855
AGED 34 YRS

(27.) *(Wood.)*
SACRED
TO
THE MEMORY
of
SAMUEL. ISBISTER
SEAMAN
H. M. S LEOPARD
DEPARTED, THIS LIFE
JUNE 30TH 1855
AGED 55 YEARS

(28.) *(Wood.)*
SEARD
TO
MEMORY
OF
CHAS. CARR
BEN PLE HULL
AGED 22 WHO
DIED JULY 8 1855
SEAMAN TO LEAF
LIES SHIS MATE
WM BELL

(29.) *(Wood.)*
TO
SACRED
THE
MEMORY OF
W. C. BELL
WHO
DIED JULY 5. 1855
CARPENTER. BRIG
EAMONT—SHIELDS
AGED. 22

(30.) *(Wood.)*
SACRED
To The
MEMORY
of
WM FORTUNE
MASTER
RARQUE. ALICE ANN
No SHIELDS
WHO
DEPARTED
THIS LIFE
APRIL 29TH 1855
AGED 29
YEARS
Erected
Robt Meldram

(31.) *(Wood.)*
✝
SACRED
TO THE
MEMORY
of
Private, Fredk Gruite
3328, 6th Company
7th Rl Fusiliers
Who deptd this life 7th Feby
1856
Aged 22 Years

This Tablet has been Erected
by his Brother Comrades as
A
Tribute of Respect

T. Walker, lith.

London, Published by Ackermann & Co. 106, Strand, W.C.

Day & Son, Lith.rs to The Queen

NAVAL BRIGADE.

ROYAL ARTILLERY.

(32.)
SACRED
To The Memory of CPtn
JAMES Harris of The
Barque Blackness AGed 29
Who Died on The 7th June
1855

(33.)
SACRED TO THE MEMORY
OF
BENJAMIN PURDY
MASTER
OF
THE TRANSPORT No 173
"BLACK BOY"
OF SUNDERLAND
WHO DEPARTED THIS LIFE
IN KAZATCH BAY
ON THE 27TH JUNE
1855
AGED 52 YEARS

(34.) SACRED (Wood.)
TO THE MEMORY
of
SAMUEL. S. NICKELS
late Master of the Barque
TILLA and ISIE
of
SALCOMBE
Died 8th August 1855
Aged 54
Years

NEAR ENGLISH Rl NAVAL YARD (KAZATCH.)

(1.) SACRED (Wood.)
TO The memory of John
Goggin late of H.M.S.
Snake who was found
drowned July 13th 1855. aged
19 years.

FRENCH CEMETERY,
BETWEEN THE HARBOURS OF KAZATCH AND KAMIESCH.

NUMBER OF GRAVES—443.

(1.)
SACRED
TO THE
MEMORY OF
Robert Simpson
MASTER OF THE
ODESSA PACKET
DIED MAY 3rd
1855
AGED 61 YEARS

(2.) SACRED (Wood.)
TO
THE MEMORY
Of
C. W. D. COVERDALE
Seaman on board of the
WATER SPRITE of WHITBY
DIED 11th JUNE 1855
AGED XX YEARS

IN THE MIDST
OF LIFE
WE ARE IN DEATH

(3.) IN MEMORY (Wood.)
OF
HENRY. REDMAN
late Seaman
on board, the
RADIUS
Of Sunderland
Died June 13th 1855
Aged 51
Years

(4.) (Wood.)
✝
SACRED
TO THE
MEMORY
OF
WILLIAM DOOLAN
SEAMAN OF
THE
BARQUE LOCHLIBO
DIED JANUARY 14 1856
AGED 24 YEARS

(5.) SACRED (Wood.)
To
THE MEMORY
of
JOHN SMITH
DIED OCTOBER 24th
1855

(6.) SACRED (Wood.)
TO
THE
MEMORY
of
ALEXANDER FALCONER
S.S. NEW YORK
5th JUNE 1855

(7.) SACRED (Wood.)
TO THE
MEMORY OF
WILLIAM ESPLIN
WHO
DIED JUNE THE 9th 1855 AGED
17 YEARS
IN THE MIDST OF LIFE
WE ARE IN DEATH.

E FIELD BATTERY, Rl ARTILLERY
LITTLE KAMIESCH, WORONZOFF ROAD.

NUMBER OF GRAVES—21.

(1.)
SACRED TO THE
MEMORY
of
Gunr Chas Fox
DIEd 2nd July. 1855
Gunr J. McElwee. Killed in
the trenches 9th June 1855
Gunr L. Shane. Died
13th May 1855

(2.)
✠
IHS
SACRED
to the memory
of
Gunr
J. Costello
Died
27th May
1855

(3.) SACRED (Wood.)
to the
memory of
Gunr P. Kennedy, Died
30th May 55.
Gunr W. Gale, died, 3rd June 55.
Gunr L. Bentley, died
17th June 1855.

(4.) SACRED (Wood.)
to the memory
of
Bernard Faron
E Field Batty
R.A
Killed in the Trenches 9th June 1855
Aged 20 Years
deeply regretted by his
Comrades.

(5.) (Front.)
✝

E. Sturgeon 25th Sept 54   J. Tweedale 23th Sept. 54
A. Hatfield 7th Dec. 54   D. Christie 27th Novr 54
J. Dimmock 24th —,—   D. Garrett 7th Decr 54
H. Russell, 7th Jany 55.   W. Fiddler 20th — 54
W. Saunders 31st —   W. Channing 5th Feby 55
J. Durston 17th Apr. 55.   R. Pirt 20th Novr 55

(Right.)
KILLED at Inkermann 5th Novr 1854
Serjt A Gunsted
Gunr W. Brown

(Left.)
Killed at Alma 20th Sept 1854
Lieut R. Cockerell
Corpl W. Mortlock
Shoes Smith S. Beck

(Rear.)
H
SACRED
to the
MEMORY
I of S
the men of E Field Battery. No. 1 Co 3Rd Battn
Rl Artillery
who died or were killed in the Crimean
Campaign of 1854 - 5

E. FIELD BATTERY (continued).

NUMBER OF GRAVES—3.

(1.)
(Front.)
SACRED
to
the
MEMORY
of
Gunners
R. Pirt. Died 20th
Novr 1854
and
D. Christie Died 27th Novr 1854

(Rear.)
E
FIELD BATTERY
R.A

(2.)
Cigit un Français
mort dans l'hopital Anglais
l'hiver 1854

NEAR WINDMILL
(HEAD OF CAREENING CREEK RAVINE.)

NUMBER OF GRAVES—147.

(1.) ASST SURGN H. BECKWITH
49TH REGIMENT
DIED OF CHOLERA
ON THE 17TH OCTR 1854

ПАМЯТНИКЪ
Медику Хирургу 49го полка
Бекв и ту
скончался 17го октября 1854го

(2.) Sacred (*Wood.*)
TO
The
MEMORY
OF
SERGT A. SLADE
2nd Battn Rifle Brigade
WHO DIED
On the 14th of October
A.D. 1854
Erected By his comrade
SERGEANTS

(3.) Sacred (*Wood.*)
To
The
MEMORY
OF
SERGT H. STEER
2nd Battn Rifle Brigade
WHO DIED
On the 9th of October
A.D. 1854
Erected by his comrade
SERJEANTS

(4.) SACRED
TO THE
MEMORY
OF
NON COMD OFFICERS
&
GUNNERS & DRIVERS
OF THE RIGHT SIEGE TRAIN
ROYAL ARTILLERY
WHO ARE INTERRED HERE

(5.) ERECTED
TO
THE
MEMORY
OF
SERGt A. ARGO
No 5 Co 9B. Rl ARy
WHO
DIED 29 APRIL 1855
AGED 29 YEARS

OPPOSITE ROYAL ENGINEERS BURIAL GROUND
(NEAR WINDMILL)

NUMBER OF GRAVES—127.

On Gate—"97th"

(1.) SACRED (*Wood.*)
TO THE
MEMORY
OF
GUNNER AND DRIVER
RODERICK REID
OF No. 5. COMPANY 9th
BATTALION, ROYAL
ARTILLERY WHO
WAS KILLED ON
THE 17TH JUNE 1855
WHEN SERVING IN THE
TRENCHES BEFORE
SEBASTOPOL

(2.)

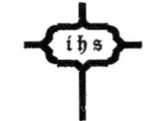

Thy will be done

SACRED
TO THE MEMORY
OF
JOHN MORRIS SAVAGE
ESQUIRE
CAPTAIN ROYAL ARTILLERY,
WHO DIED WHILST SERVING
WITH
THE ALLIED ARMIES
BEFORE
SEBASTOPOL
ON THE XXII DAY OF JUNE
MDCCCLV.
AGED XXVI

THIS MEMORIAL IS
ERECTED BY
HIS SORROWING WIFE

(3.) (*Wood.*)
SACRED TO
The Memory OF
William Vigars
Civil Collormaker
WHO DIED OF Cholera
ON THE 27th OF JUNE
1855, Aged 28 Years

(4.) (*Just Outside Gate.*)
IN
MEMORY
OF
JOHN SIBBELDS
Sa Fr Gds
WHO FELL IN THE BATTLE OF
INKERMANN
Novr 5TH 1854

The seven Officers of the Coldstream Guards killed at Inkermann were originally interred in this Burial Ground, but their remains were, after the fall of Sebastopol, removed to Cathcart's Hill.

LEFT OF "ROYAL ENGINEERS"
(LOOKING TOWARDS KAMIESCH).

3 GRAVES.

(1.) IHS

SACRED
to the
MEMORY
of
GUNNERS & DRIVERS
of the
RESVE AMMN BRIGDE LIGT DIVN
No 2 Co 5TH BATN ROYL ARTY
VIZ
JOHN. ARCHER . DIED 20 OcT ⎫
JAMES. HOSKINGS. Do. 22 Do. ⎬ 1855
ROBERT. SHARP . Do. 16 NoR ⎭
IN THE SERVICE OF THEIR COUNTRY.

ABOVE "ROYAL ENGINEERS"
(NEAR 34TH CAMP).

3 GRAVES.

ALMA.

NEAR BÜRLIUK,
226 YARDS NORTH OF RIVER,
AND
157 YARDS WEST OF BRIDGE.

(1.)* SACRED (*Wood.*)
to the
MEMORY
of
LIEUT R. H. COCKERELL
ROYAL ARTILLERY
Killed
at
THE ALMA
SEPT 20th
1854

OUTSIDE SEMICIRCULAR EARTHWORK,
544 YARDS SOUTH OF RIVER,
AND
73 YARDS FROM LEFT OF WORK.

(2.)† (*Wood.*)

E. F. DU PRE Montagu
AND
MEN 33 REGT
1854

16 YARDS IN ADVANCE OF WORK,
AND
22 YARDS RIGHT OF No. 2.

(*Front.*)

(3.)*

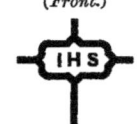

During the Attack on these heights
20th September 1854
H B M XXIII R. W. Fusiliers
lost their Commanding Officer
Lieutenant Colonel
Harry George Chester
Captains
Arthur. W. Williams Wynn
Francis Edward Evans
John Charles Conolly
Lieutenants
Fredk P. R. Delme Radcliffe
Sir William. N. Young BART
Henry Anstruther
And
Joseph Butler
All Killed on the Field
Also
Lieutenant and Adjutant
Augustus Applewhaite
Mortally Wounded
And died 22nd September 1854
This Stone
is Sacred to their
Memory

(*Rear.*)

The Regiment also lost
Sergeant Major H. Jones
Color Sergeant R. Hitchcock
Sergeant F. Edmonds
1 Drummer and
40 Privates
Killed on the Field

A great portion of the killed at Alma were buried inside this Russian Battery.

* Erected in 1856.
† Erected immediately after the Battle of the Alma.

INKERMANN.

OBELISK ON FIELD OF BATTLE.

(Front.)
(Side facing English Camp.)

IN MEMORY
OF THE
ENGLISH FRENCH & RUSSIANS
WHO FELL IN THE BATTLE OF
INKERMANN
5TH NOVEMBER 1854

(Right.)

(Left.)
ERECTED
BY THE
BRITISH ARMY
A.D. 1856

(Rear.)
ВЪ ПАМЯТЬ
АНГЛИЧАНАМЪ, ФРАНЦУЗАМЪ И РУССКИМЪ
КОТОРЫЕ ПАЛИ ПРИ
ИНКЕРМАНСКОМЪ СРАЖЕНІИ
24го ОКТЯБРЯ
5го НОЯБРЯ   1854

NEAR FRENCH CAMP OF THE 49TH REGT.

NUMBER OF GRAVES—31.

(1.)   Major T. N. DALTON
FELL AT THE BATTLE OF
INKERMAN
WHILE IN COMMAND OF
H. B. Ms 49TH REGT OF FOOT

памятникъ
Командующему 49му полкомъ Маіору
Долтону
убитъ сего Мая 5го Ноября 1854 го

(2.)   MAJOR. C. T. POWELL
49TH REGIMENT
KILLED IN THE TRENCHES
BEFORE SEBASTOPOL
ON THE 28TH OCTR 1854

памятникъ
Маіору 49го полка
Говелло
убитъ въ траншеяхъ 28го Октября 1854 го

(3.)   LIEUT AND ADJT
A. S. ARMSTRONG
FELL AT THE BATTLE OF
INKERMAN
5TH NOVR 1854

памятникъ
Поручику Армстронгу
убитъ сего 5го Ноября 1854 го

(4.)   SACRED TO THE MEMORY   *(Wood.)*
OF
MORRIS. DUNFORD H. M. 62
REGT. WHO FELL A VICTIM TO
FEVER ON THE 6TH APRIL 1855
WHILE SERVING IN THE CAMP
AIGN WITH HIS REGIMENT
BEFORE SEBASTOPOL
AGED 24 YEARS 9 MONTHS
WE MOURN HIM AS A FRIEND AND
BROTHER
ERECTED BY HIS BROTHER
SERGT. DUNFORD AS A HUMBLE AND
SINCERE TOKEN OF RESPECT AND
DEEP REGRET

(5.)   HERE LIES   *(Wood.)*
IN HOPES OF A GLORIOUS
RESURECTION
THE MORTAL REMAINS OF
SERJT. JOHN CONNORS
OF. H. M. 62ND REGIMENT
who fell a victim to fever
whilst serving in the Cam
paign with his regiment
before Sebastopol
on the 5th of April 1855
Aged 28 Years

WE MOURN HIM AS A FRIEND
& BROTHER
ERECTED BY HIS BROTHER
MICHAEL CONNORS 62ND BAND
AS A HUMBLE BUT SINCERE
TOKEN OF AFFECTION & DEEP
REGRET

NEAR INKERMANN QUARRY.

(1.)   SACRED TO THE MEMORY
OF
COLr SERJt G. GARNER
1st B. R. B
KILLED AT THE BATTLE OF INKERMANN
NOVer 5th 1854

IN QUARRY.

2 SMALL GRAVEYARDS.

79 YDS. SOUTH OF 2-GUN BATTERY

2 SMALL GRAVEYARDS.

(1.)   SACRED   *(Wood.)*
to the memory of the N.C.Officers & privates
of the Scots Fusilier Guards Who fell at the
battle of INKERMANN 5th NOVr 1854
Erected by their comrades
June 1856

NEAR OBELISK.

5 GRAVEYARDS.

(1.)   IHS   *(Wood.)*
SACRED
TO THE
MEMORY
of
PTE MR JOHNSON of H.M. 30TH REGT
WHO DEPARTED THIS LIFE ON THE 26TH FEBY
IN THE YEAR OF OUR LORD 1855 AGED 24 years
I have fought
A good fight
I have finished
my course   ii. TIM
———×———
BY H. CORE

(1.)   *Front*
(Facing Obelisk.)

TO THE MEMORY OF
THE FOLLOWING OFFICERS
OF
H.M. 95TH REGIMENT
Captn G. J. DOWDALL
Captn J. G. EDDINGTON
Lieut. R. G. POLHILL
Lieut. E. W. EDDINGTON
Lieut. J. C. G. KINGSLEY
KILLED AT ALMA

Lt. Col. J. G. CHAMPION
Lieut. BRAYBROOKE
C. R. R. Attached
DIED OF WOUNDS

CAPTAIN. L. FRASER
KILLED in TRENCHES

CAPTAIN. F. H. DYMOCK
KILLED IN ASIA

Bt. MAJOR. T. DAVIS
SURGEON W. BROWN
SURGON SMITH
Staff Asst Surgn H. HARRISON
DIED OF DISEASE

(Rear.)

SACRED TO THE MEMORY OF THE
IHS

Non. Commissioned Officers
and Men of the
95th The Derbyshire Regt
who lost their lives in
the Crimean Campaign
1854-5 & 6
Killed in Action 80
Died of Wounds 164
Died of Disease 447

(2.)

SACRED
to
MEMORY
OF
Sergt J. THOMAS
DIED
14th Febry 18—

OVERLOOKING THE TCHERNAYA

RIGHT OF INKERMANN.

SIX GRAVEYARDS.

NUMBER OF GRAVES { 1*, 4†, 28, 27, 41‡, 2 } 153

(1*.)   SACRED
TO THE
MEMORY
OF
JOHN SCHRODER
BAND
1st BATTn RIFLE Bde
KILLED, AT, THE, BATTLE
OF INKERMAN
NOVEMBER 5th 1854
AGED 25 YEARS

BRITISH RIGHT ATTACK.

(1†.)

✝

SACRED
TO
The Memory
of Private
Thomas Lillies
41st Regt
Who was Killed
5th Novr
. 1854 .

(2.)

✝

41ST REGIMENT

Sacred to the Memory
of
Lieut Colonel Carpenter
Captain Richards
Lieut Swaby   Lieut Taylor
and
Lieut Stirling
who fell at the BATTLE of
INKERMANN
on the 5th Novr 1854

ALSO
of
Assistt Surgn Jas Lamont
who Died on the 5th January
1855

(3.)

✝

SACRED
TO
the MEMORY of
Sergt. Major JOHN SPENCE
41st Regt.
who was killed at the
BATTLE OF INKERMANN
on the 5th Novr. 1854
AGED
28 YEARS.

(4.)

SACRED TO THE MEMORY

✝

of the
Non Commissioned Officers
and Men of the 41st Regt who have
Fallen during the Campaigns
of 1854 . 55 & 56 . in the Service
of their Country.

REQUIESCANT IN PACE
.AMEN.
This Stone is Erected By
their Surviving Comrades
.1856.

(1‡.)   (Head.)   (Wood.)
TO THE
memory
OF
MArgreT
STArrETT
LATE WIFE
of James STArrETT. PT 95th RegT who LANDED on The Crimea
on The 14th SEPT 1854. This womin TRAVLED wiTh The RegT
Through the Campeign. UNTILL Such Time As iT Was
PLEASED GOD. TO CALL her To himSELF ouT of
This WOrLD To the next BEing in ThE 23rd Year
of HEr
Age.
(Foot.)   (Stone.)

WOMAN ♀ ENGLISH

✝

---

*BRITISH RIGHT ATTACK.

OBELISK,
62 YARDS IN ADVANCE OF THE "REDAN"
(Front.)
(SIDE FACING SEBASTOPOL)
IN MEMORY
OF
THOSE WHO FELL
IN THE TRENCHES
AND ASSAUTS UPON THE
REDAN
1855

(Right.)
ERECTED
BY THE
BRITISH ARMY
A.D. 1856

(Left.)

✝

(Rear.)
(SIDE FACING TRENCHES.)
ВЪ ПАМЯТЬ
ТѢМЪ КОТОРЫЕ ПАЛИ ВЪ
ТРАНШЕЯХЪ
И ПРИ АТТАКАХЪ НА
РЕДАНЪ

ТРЕТІЙ БАСТІОНЪ
1855

REAR OF EGERTON'S RIFLE PIT

(Surrounded by a Stone Wall.)

(1.)

✝

ERECTED

BY WILLIAM & JAMES WEIR
47TH REGt
TO THE MEMORY OF THEIR
BELOVED BROTHER ROBERT
WHO WAS KILLED IN THE
TRENCHES BEFORE SEBASTOPOL
ON THE 12TH JULY 1855
AGED 31 YEARS

ALSO
SEAGt JOHN KEEFE OF THE
SAME REGt WHO WAS KILLED
AT THE SAME TIME & PLACE

Blessed Are Those Servants Whom
The Lord When He Cometh
Shall Find Watching. Luke xii. 37

REAR OF 21 GUN BATTERY.

(1.)

SACRED TO THE MEMORY
OF
Sergt ROBT MC COY
55TH Regiment
Who Fell at the Assault
on the Quarries on the
Evening of the 7th June
1855
ERECTED
by his Affectionate
Brother
John MC Coy
Colr Sert 40TH Regiment

---

* The greater number of the Killed in the Assault of the 18th of June, 1855, were buried in the Quarries; those of the 8th September mostly in the Ditch of the Redan.

HEAD QUARTERS.
(British Army.)

HEAD QUARTERS BRITISH ARMY.

NUMBER OF GRAVES—32.

(1.)   ✝   (*Marble.*)

MAJOR GENERAL
JAMES BUCKNALL BUCKNALL ESTCOURT
ADJUTANT GENERAL
OF THE BRITISH ARMY IN THE EAST
BORN JULY 12TH 1802
DIED JUNE 24TH 1855
HE THAT SHALL ENDURE UNTO THE END
THE SAME SHALL BE SAVED
MATH XXIV CHAP XIII VERSE

ГЕНЕРАЛЪ · ЭСКОРТЪ

(*Round Bevelled Edge of Tomb.*)

ВДОВА ПО УМЕРШЕМЪ ГЕНЕРАЛЪ
ПОКОРНѢЙШЕ ПРОСИТЬ ИМѢТЬ
ВНИМАНІЕ НА БРЕННЫЕ
ОСТАТКИ СУПРУГА ЕЯ
ЗДѢСЬ ПОЧИВАЮЩІЕ

(2.)   SACRED
TO THE MEMORY OF
C. R. CATTLEY Esq
WHO DIED OF CHOLERA
ON THE 10TH OF JULY 1855
WHILST SERVING ON THE STAFF
OF THE LATE FIELD MARSHAL
LORD RAGLAN

INSIDE FARMHOUSE.

IN THIS ROOM
DIED
F. M. LORD RAGLAN, G.C.B.
COMMANDER-IN-CHIEF
OF THE BRITISH ARMY
IN THE CRIMEA
ON THE 28TH JUNE 1855

ВЪ ЭТОЙ КОМНАТѢ
СКОНЧАЛСЯ
ФЕЛЬДЪ МАРШАЛЪ ЛОРДЪ РАГЛАНЪ GCB
ГЛАВНОКОМАНДУЮЩІЙ
АНГЛІЙСКОЙ АРМІИ
ВЪ КРЫМУ
1 ІЮНЯ 1855

IN RAVINE, NEAR WELL, UNDER THE WILLOW TREE.

(RIGHT OF BURIAL GROUND.)

TO
THE MEMORY OF
FIELD MARSHAL
LORD RAGLAN. G.C.B
COMMANDER IN CHIEF OF THE
BRITISH ARMY
IN THE
CRIMEA
DIED
28TH JUNE. 1855.

10TH BATTN LAND TRANSPORT CORPS.

(NEAR COL DE BALACLAVA.)

NUMBER OF GRAVES—21.

(1.)   (*Monument.*)   (*Wood.*)

Sacred
TO
THE MEMORY
OF
SERJT MAJOR. RICHD BROWNE
AND
THE MEN OF THE
10th BATTALION
LAND TRANSPORT CORPS.
British Army
BURIED HERE

JUNE 1856

(*Over Wooden Entrance Gate.*)
THE CEMETERY
OF THE 10TH BATTN
L. T. C.

NEAR OMAR PASHA'S REDOUBT.

NUMBER OF GRAVES—19.

(1.)   (*Stone Wall round Grave*).

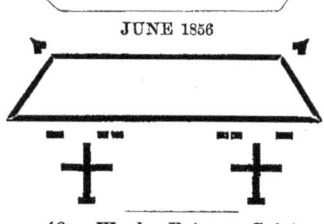

Sacred to the Memory of
Colonel Balfour Ogilvie
who died July xii. mdccclv
This Stone was Erected as a
mark of respect by his
Brother Officers

NEAR CONVALESCENT HOSPITAL,

MONASTERY OF ST. GEORGE.

NUMBER OF GRAVES—23.

LAND TRANSPORT CORPS,

NEAR MRS. SEACOLE'S.

NUMBER OF GRAVES { *99 / 77 } 176

(1.*)   ✠   (*Wood*)

SACRED TO THE
MEMORY
OF
PRVT THOS. EAGAN
XXXTH REGT
Departead This Life
February 17TH 1856
AGED 27 YEARS
Deeply Lamented By
His Comrades

(2.)

SACRED
To the Memory of
George Fredk Hunt
Late Qr Mr Sergeant of the 14th Battn of
the Land Transport Corps Son of G
Hunt Esqr of Crieve & Magistrate
for the County of Monaghan, He
died on the 23. March 1856 Aged
25 Years

This was erected by Captain
W. P. Collingwood 21st Fusiliers Commanding the Battn as a testimony
of his esteem and regard

(3.)   (*Monument.*)
(SIDE FACING ROAD.)
SACRED
TO
THE MEMORY OF
THE MEN OF THE
BRITISH
LAND TRANSPORT
CORPS
WHO DIED
IN THE CRIMEA
1855—1856

KADIKOI.

LEFT OF MAIN ROAD, GOING TOWARDS BALAKLAVA.
About halfway between Stationary Engine and Kadikoi.

†NUMBER OF GRAVES—185.

(1.)   (*Wood.*)
TO
THE
MEMORY OF
G. WILLIAS
AGED
27

(2.) (*Black Wooden Paling Round Grave.*)
ELIZABETH DRAKE
NURSE
Died August 9th
1855

(3.)   SACRED   (*Wood.*)
to the
Memory
of
 SMITH ALLEN. A. Trp.
R. H. A DEPARTED this Life
JULY
12th 1855
Aged
23
YEARS

(4.)   Sacred   (*Wood.*)
to the
Memory
of
George James
Who
Departed his life
on the
22nd June A.D. 1855
On board the
P & O. S. S. Rajah
Aged 23 Years

† Most of the Army Works Corps were buried here.

KADIKOI.

(5.) *(Wood.)*
SACRED
TO THE MEMORY
of
WILLIAM BLORE
of the 12 Co. Carp.
DIED MAY 1856
Aged 42 yr

(6.) *(Wood.)*
IN MEMORY
OF
EDWARD ELLIOTT
HAMMERMAN OF
H. M. Floating Factory
CHASSEUR
Died 12th Decr 1855 Aged 24 yrs
In the midst of life
We are in death

(7.) C. B. *(Wood.)*

(8.)
TO
THE MEMORY OF
ROBERT FINCH
WHO DIED 26 OF DECr 1855
AGED 48 YEARS
ALSO
JOHN MITCHELL
Who DIED ON THE ABOVE date
AGED 35 YEARS
ALSO
CHARLES WADE
WHO DIED 4th OF APRIL 1856
AGED 36 YEARS

(9.) *(Monument.)*
(SIDE FACING ROAD.)
SACRED
TO
THE MEMORY OF
THE MEN
OF THE
ARMY WORKS CORPS
WHO DIED
IN THE CRIMEA
1855 - 56.

(10.) SACRED *(Wood.)*
to the
Memory of
Mr JOHN SAWELL
of the
BRITISH ARMY POST OFFICE
Who Died at Balaklava
MAY 30TH 1855

(11.) Sacred *(Wood.)*
To The Memory
OF
THOMAS. J. GODMAN
WHO DIED
14TH MAY 1855
Aged Thirty-seven

(12.) *(Front.)*
(SIDE FACING ROAD.)
ARMATA SARDA
ALLA MENDRIA
DEL
CAVRE SMARTINO di Sicambino
SOTTE NEL 7o
REGGTO FANTRIA
MORTO IN CRIMEA
1855

(Rear.)
SERVIZIO, RELIGIOSO
ASTENGO, FONTANA

(13.)
ARMATA
SARDA
1856

(14.) *(Front.)*
(SIDE FACING ROAD.)
ARMATA SARDA
CORPO D'INTENDENZA
MILITAIRE
FRASCHINI, B BE CHIO MORINO
ROVEDA, IUZ
BERRONE, SIMDNINO
1855 E 1856

(Right.)
GIUSTZIA MILRE
CASTELLI
CHIAPELLO
CHIESA

(Left.)
SUSSZE MILRE
PAGGI
MOLINERI
RUNZA
TRE SPIDI

(Rear.)
UFFICIALI
DEI
VARI, CORPI
GOLZIO, AMORETTI
BAROLO, BERTAUD
BRIGNONE, VIALARDI
BIESTA, GONFORTI
COURTOIS, ODDONE
PALESTINO, ROSSI

(15.) *Wood.*
A. TOSETTO ADOLEO
CAPITAIN
NEI BERSALIER DELL' ARMATA SARDA
NATOLI 20 FEBBRAIO 1820 MORTOLI 25 MAGGIO 1855
IL FRATELLO DOLENTE POSE !!!

W. FIELD BATTERY, ROYAL ARTILLERY.

RIGHT OF KADIKOI GOING TOWARDS BALAKLAVA.

NUMBER OF GRAVES—30.

(1.)
SACRED
To the Memory of the N. C. Officers & Men
Of W. FIELD BATTERY
ROYAL ARTILLERY

Gunr JAs OWENS	Corpl H. McCOOLE
R. ELLIOTT	Bomr J. STEVENSON
THOs LOACH	Cr Mr C. TAPSCOTT
W. SHERRID	Gunr PETr ROSS
C. GODDING	J. ROBERTS
EDWD SMITH	J. BAXTER
T. WADDLE	T. COLEMAN
J. HODSKIN	J. STEWART
J. JACKSIN	A. RATTERY

Also 10 Men No 1 Compy 1st Battalion
Also 4 Men No. 6. Compy 8th Battalion

RIGHT OF ROAD MADE IN 1854-5.
GOING TOWARDS STATIONARY ENGINE,
(NEAR KADIKOI.)

2 GRAVES.

13TH LIGHT DRAGOONS
(GOING TOWARDS KARANI)

NUMBER OF GRAVES—38.

(1.) I H S *(Wood.)*
SACRED
to the MEMORY of
MICHAEL CREEVY
Who Died August 23
1855

(2.) *(Wood.)*
Sacred
To
The Memory
of
MARY PAMPLIN
13th Lt Dragoons
Died 13th Dcbr 1855
AGED 13 Months

(3.) *(Wood.)*
I S f
J. WHEELAN
DIED JUNE 27TH 1855
AGED 29 YEARS

(4.) *(Fallen down)* *(Wood.)*
SACRED
TO
the Memory of
Mr C. M. Foster
late
Quarter Master of the
13th Light Dragoons
who
Departed this life at
Camp near Balaklava
25th January 1855
Aged
40 Years & 5 Months

(5.) TO
THE MEMORY
OF
I. B. JONES
IV. L. D.
WHO DIED
25th MARCH
1855

(6.) SACRED *(Wood.)*
to the Memory of
TROOP SERJT MAJOR
J. THORP
4th Lt DRAGOONS
DIED WHILE SERVING
IN THE CRIMEA
REQUIESCAT IN PACE

(7.) IN
MEMORY
OF
CAPTAIN
*JOHN MARSHALL
4th Lt Dragoons
Died
30th SEPt
1855

---

* This Officer died at the Monastery of St. George.

KADIKOI.

11TH (P. A. O.) HUSSARS
(BETWEEN KADIKOI AND KARANI.)

NUMBER OF GRAVES—24.

OVER GATE.
(*Front and Rear.*)

ELEVENTH (Prince Albert's Own) HUSSARS

(1.)   SACRED   (*Wood.*)
TO THE MEMORY OF
THE MEN OF THE 11TH HUSSARS
WHO DIED
IN THE YEARS 1855 & 1856

Prts. W. TAYLOR.	Jany 18th	Prts. G. Priestly.	Aust. 24th
T. SAWBRIDGE	28th	A. Fleming	26th
J. STrutt	Feby. 1st	G. Robinson	26th
J. Massey	Mrch. 14th	G. Ellis	27th
T. ELLIS.	June 16th	E. HOAR	Octr. 7th
E. WILCOX	25th	G. KEATES	19th
G. Wiffey	July 5th	G. Smith	Decr. 11th
Corpl. E. MAllAllen	8th	F. Owen	Mch. 22nd '56
Prts. H. Pryor	Aust. 18th	V. Bishton	Apl. 2nd
W. Pearce	23rd	R. Friston	23rd
J. HALL	24th	W. Baker	July 5th '55

M. C. Ancell. Asnt Srgn   Agst 10th
E. Hudson. Srgnt   Jany 31st } 1855
E. Seabrook. Corpl   May 24th

(2.)   ✝   (*Wood.*)

SACRED
To
THE MEMORY
OF
SERGT EDWD HUDSON
11th (P. A. O.) Hussars
Who departd this Life
JANy 31st 1855 AGED 32
YEARS

(3.)   Sacred   (*Wood.*)
TO THE MEMORY
OF
WILLIAM BAKER
PRIVTE 11th (P. A. O.) HUSSARS
WHO DIED
JULY 5TH 1855
AGED 39 YEARS

(4.)   ✝   (*Wood.*)

SACRED
TO
THE MEMORY
OF
Cpl Edwd Seabrook
11th (P A O) Hussars
WHO Departed this
Life MAY 24th 1855
AGED 29 YEARS

(5.)   Sacred   (*Wood.*)
TO THE MEMORY
OF
MALCOLM CURRIE ANGELL
ASSNT SURGN 11TH (P.A.O) HUSSARS
Who Died
AUGUST 10th 1855
AGED 25 YEARS

7TH BATTN LAND TRANSPORT CORPS.
(BETWEEN KADIKOI AND KARANI).

NUMBER OF GRAVES—19.

(1.)   SACRED   (*Wood.*)
To the Memory
Of The
Non COMMISIOND OFFICERS & PRIVATES
BELONGING TO THE 7TH BATTALION
LAND TRANSPORT CORPS
WHO DIED
IN THE CRIMEA

Plant, plant wild flowers around their bed
Your Brothers numbering with the dead
A sacred duty 'Tis you owe
To all mankind—to friend—to foe—
Gather, gather from yon dell
the snowdrops crocus and blue bell
Unsparing strew them o'er each grave
the dead but marks the truly brave

G. Gullum	Age 22	Died Decr 20th 1855
J. Irwin	— 21	— ,, —
M. Popjoy	— 21	— 26 —
G. Fraser	— 44	— 29 —
T. Bird	— 38	Jany 3 1856
H. Blackburn	—	— 7 —
J. McKenzie	— 36	— 19 —
T. Croker	26	Feb. 9 —
T. Wenham	20	— 19 —
C. Bacon	21	— 21 —
J. Green	21	— 22 —
M. Burns	20	— 23 —
J. Young	28	Mar. 2 —
A. Williams	19	— 15 —
G. Locket	20	— 21 —
J. Beard	26	— 20 —
J. Russell	26	Apr. 18 —

(2.)   IN   (*Wood.*)
MEMORY
of
A. WILLIAMS
Trumpeter 7 Battalion. L. T. C
DIED 15 MARCH
1856
Aged 20
years

(3.)   SACRED To The MEMORY   (*Wood.*)
of
Dr T. O. MITCHELL
WHO DIED
Decr 29th 1855

4TH (QUEEN'S OWN) LIGHT DRAGOONS.
(BETWEEN KADIKOI AND KARANI).

NUMBER OF GRAVES—23.

(1.)   TO THE
MEMORY
of
W. HAYWOOD
IV. L. D

(2.)   IN
MEMORY
OF
CHS HAMPSHIRE
IV. L. D
WHO DIED
ON THE 3rd FEBy 1855
AGED 39 YEARS

(3.)   TO
THE MEMORY
OF
JOHN HUNTLY
IV. L. D
WHO DIED ON
THE 9th JANy
1855

ON SIDE OF HILL, ABOVE CAMP OF 11TH HUSSARS,
(OVERLOOKING KADIKOI.)

NUMBER OF GRAVES { 51 / 14 / 5 / 17 / *28 } 115.

(1.*)   SACRED TO THE MEMORY
of
GUNNERS & DRIVERS
JOHN DURMOT
And
HENRY CHAPMAN
LATE
of No. 6 Co. 2N Battalion
ROYAL ARTILLERY
WHO DEPARTED THIS LIFE
NOV. 27·· 1855 & FEB. 13·· 1856
CRIMEA

KARANI.

4TH (ROYAL IRISH) DRAGOON GUARDS.

NUMBER OF GRAVES { 26 / *11 } 37.

(1*.)   SACRED   (*Wood.*)
TO THE
NC OFFICERS AND MEN
OF THE 4TH DRAGOON
GUARDS WHO DIED
WHILE SERVING IN THE
CRIMEA.

I TROOP ROYAL HORSE ARTILLERY.

NUMBER OF GRAVES—19.

(1.)   Sacred   (*Wood.*)
to the Memory
of
JH CLEMENTS
of I Troop R. H. Ay
who departed this life
October 3rd 1855 Aged 23 Years

(2.)   SACRED   (*Wood.*)
to the Memory of
Dr ROBT BARROW
DIED 27th AUGst
1855
AGED 20 YEARS

(3.)   SACRED   (*Wood.*)
to the Memory
OF
Tr BENJ BRISTOL
DIED 8TH AUGst 1855
AGED 19 YEARS

KARANI.

(4.) SACRED (Wood.)
to the Memory of
Gr THOMAS. JOY
DIED 7th JULY 1855
AGED 38 YEARS

(5.) Sacred (Wood.)
TO THE
MEMORY
of
WILLIAM BOWIE
WHO
DIED
21ST JUNE
1855

(6.) SACRED (Wood.)
TO THE
Memory of
ALEXr McBAIN
DIED 15TH JUNE 1855
AGED 22 YEARS

(7.) SACRED (Wood.)
to the Memory of
JOHN TUCKER
DIED 9TH JUNE 1855
AGED 21 YEARS

(8.) TO THE (Wood.)
Memory
OF
DR GE HUNTLEY
R. H. A
DIED 6TH JUNE 1855
AGED 18 years

(9.) SACRED (Wood.)
to the Memory of
EMANL YOUNG
DIED 21ST AUGST 1855
AGED 25. YEARS
REQUIESCAT IN PACE —

(10.) SACRED (Wood.)
TO THE
Memory
OF
GR JAS STANFORD
DIED 10TH JANY 1856
AGED 28 years

(11.) SACRED (Wood.)
to the Memory of
Dr RD SMITH
DIED 3rd APRIL
1856
AGED 28 YEARS

(12.) SACRED (Wood.)
TO THE MEMORY OF
B. HOPKINS. ROYAL H
ORSE ARTILLERY
DEPARTED THIS
LIFE 11TH OF APRIL 1856
A BROTHER IS NOW DEAD A
LUMP OF LIFELESS CLAY HE
SHALL NO MORE BE SEEN
UNTO THE LAST GREAT
DAY HIS STAY WAS VERY
SHORT IN THE DARK VALE
OF WOE HE KNEW HIS
SAVOUR CALLE WITH COYFU
HE. FTEW

(13.)
THE MEMORY OF
THE NON-COMMISSIONED
OFFICERS AND MEN
OF I TROOP
ROYAL HORSE ARTILLERY
WHO HAVE DIED
IN THE CRIMEA

ROYAL ARTILLERY.

NUMBER OF GRAVES—5.

(1.) (Wood).
SACRED
TO THE
MEMORY
OF
GUNNER AND DRIVER
DUNCAN McKAY
No. 8 Co. 9th BATTN
ROYAL ARTILLERY
WHO DIED 12. MAY
1856

(2.) (Wood.)
SACRED
TO THE
MEMORY
OF
GUNNER AND DRIVER
JOHN GREEN
No. 8 Co. 9th BATTN
ROYAL ARTILLERY
WHO DIED 12 MAY
1856

(3.) SACRED
TO THE
MEMORY OF
GUNR JOHN FITTEN
Q Field Battery
ROYAL ARTILLERY
Died 2nd January
1856

(4.) (Wood.)
SACRED
TO THE
MEMORY
OF
GUNNER AND DRIVER
GEORGE TRILL
No. 8 Co. 9th BATTN
ROYAL ARTILLERY
WHO DIED 26 DECEMBER
1855

(5.) (Wood.)
SACRED
TO THE
MEMORY
OF
GUNNER AND DRIVER
JOHN BOSLEY
OF
No. 8. Co. 9th BATTN
ROYAL ARTILLERY
WHO DIED 18. DECEMBER
1855

J & V HEAVY FIELD BATTERIES, ROYAL ARTILLERY.

NUMBER OF GRAVES—38.

(1.) SACRED
To The
MEMORY
OF
WHEELER
G. MASON. J. BATTy R. A
Died Jany 1856 Aged 25

(2.) SACRED
to the
MEMORY
OF
GUNNER
C. SENDALL. J. BATTy R. A
Died August. 1855 Aged 19

(3.) SACRED
to the
MEMORY
OF
GUNNER
W. GRIMWOOD. J. BATTy R. A
Died August. 1855 Aged 20

(4.) SACRED
to the
MEMORY
OF
SHOEING SMITH
J. DUKE. J. BATTy R. A
Died August 1855 Aged 23

(5.) SACRED
to the
MEMORY
OF
SHOEING SMITH
F. CULLEY. J. BATTy R. A
Died July 1855 Aged 20

(6.) SACRED
to the
MEMORY
OF
GUNNER
T. DAVIS. J. BATTy R. A
Died July 1855 Aged 25

(7.) SACRED
to the
MEMORY
OF
GUNNER
H. HALE. J. BATTy R. A
Died June 1855 Aged 20

(8.) SACRED
to the
MEMORY
OF
GUNNERS
E. PERRY and C. BUTCHER
Died June 1855. J. BATTy R. A

KARANI.

(9.)
✚
SACRED
to the
MEMORY
OF
GUNNER
W. GILLETT. J. BATTy R. A
Died June 1855 Aged. 19.

(10.)
✚
SACRED
to the
MEMORY
OF
GUNNER
T. WEYMARK. J. BATTy R. A
Died June 1855 Aged. 21.

(11.)
✚
SACRED
to the
MEMORY
OF
GUNNER
C. RICHARDS. J. BATTy R. A
Died June 1855 Aged 22

(12.)
✚
SACRED
to the
MEMORY
OF
SERJEANT
H. McKAY J. BATTy R.A
Died June 1855 Aged 25.

(13.)
✚
SACRED
to the
MEMORY
OF
GUNNER
J. COOK. J BATTy R.A.
Died May 1855 Aged 31

(14.)
✚
Sacred
to the
MEMORY
OF GUNNER
JOHN GIMBLETT
V. BATTERY
R. A.
1855

(15.)
✚
Sacred
to the
MEMORY
OF GUNNERS
ROBt GRAHAM and ML GORTIER
V BATTy R. A
1855

(16.)
✚
Sacred
to the
MEMORY
OF GUNNERS
HENRY RAGGS and JASr THORN
V BATy R. A
1855

(17.)
✚
Sacred
to the
MEMORY
OF GUNNER
JAMES STEVENS
V. BATTy R. A
1855

(18.)
✚
Sacred
to the
MEMORY
OF WHEELER
JAMES . WRIGHT
V BATy R. A
1855

(19.)
✚
Sacred
to the
MEMORY
OF GUNNER
GEORGE BREARY
V. BATy R. A
1855

(20.)
✚
Sacred
to the
MEMORY
OF GUNNER
ROBERT. CRANE
V. BATy R. A
1855

(21.)
✚
Sacred
to the
MEMORY
OF GUNNER
WILLIAM THOMPSON
V. BATy R. A
1855

(22.)
✚
Sacred
to the
MEMORY
of
GUNNER
HENRY BROWN
V. BATy R. A
1855

(23.)
✚
Sacred
to the
MEMORY
of
GUNNERS
ROBt DRAPER and JONs BROWN
V. BATy R. A
1855

(24.)
✚
Sacred
to the
MEMORY
of
GUNNER
WILLM BROOM
V BATy R. A

(25.)
✚
Sacred
to the
MEMORY
of
JOHN. BROWNETT
V. BATTy R. A
1855

(26.)
✚
Sacred
to the
MEMORY
of
GUNNER
EDWARD FULLER
V. BATy R. A

(27.)
✚
Sacred
to the
MEMORY
of
GUNNER
HENRY WARD
V. BATy R. A
1855

(28.)
✚
Sacred
to the
MEMORY
of
GUNNER
JOHN SOUTH
V. BATy R. A
1855

(29.)
✚
Sacred
to the
MEMORY
of
GUNNER
FRANCIS GYWTHERS
V. BATy R. A
1855

(30.)
✚
Sacred
to the
MEMORY
of
GUNNER
HENRY FAULKNER
V. BATy R. A
1855

(31.)
✚
Sacred
to the
MEMORY
OF BOMBARDIER
THOMAS FLEMING
V. BATTERY R. A
died 22nd June 1855

KARANI.

(32.)
Sacred to the MEMORY of Shoeing Smith JAMES HAW V. BATʏ R. A

(33.)
Sacred to the MEMORY of GUNNER SAMUEL BARDWELL V. BATʏ R. A 1855

(34.)
Sacred to the Memory of GUNNER GEORGE LAMBERT V. BATʏ R. A 1855

(35.)
Sacred to the MEMORY of GUNNER WALTER PANK V. BATʏ R. A 1856

(36.)
Sacred to the MEMORY of SERJEANT EDWARD WALSH V BATTERY R. A died 13 March 1856 aged 40 years

(37.)
Sacred to the MEMORY of ACTɢ SERJEANT MAJOR C. T. MOSS R. A died 23 April 1856 aged 38 years

X FIELD BATTERY, ROYAL ARTILLERY.

NUMBER OF GRAVES—13.

(1.) Sacred to the Memory of Shoeing Smith ISAAC BIRD X Battery Royal Artillery 1855 Aged 24 Years

(2.) Sacred to the Memory of Gunner ALEXANDER ELRICK X Battery Royal Artillery 1855 Aged 23 Years

(3.) Sacred to the Memory of Gunner WILLIAM MUMFORD X Battery Royal Artillery 1855 Aged 19 Years

(4.) Sacred to the Memory of Gunner JOHN MULGREW X Battery Royal Artillery 1855 Aged 21 Years

(5.) Sacred to the Memory of Gunner STEPHEN GODDEN X Battery Royal Artillery 1855 Aged 25 Years

(6.) Sacred to the Memory of Gunner JAMES GARRETT X Battery Royal Artillery 1855 Aged 23 Years

(7.) Sacred to the Memory of Shoeing Smith WILLIAM GREEN X Battery Royal Artillery 1855 Aged 27 Years
(*Top.*)
These Stones are Erected by the Kind Consideration of Captain A. F. CONNELL R. A. The Commanding Officer of the Deceased Soldiers

(8.) Sacred to the Memory of Gunner ISAAC PIHER X Battery Royal Artillery 1855 Aged 19 Years

(9.) Sacred to the Memory of Gunner HENRY EXCELL X Battery Royal Artillery 1855 Aged 21 Years

(10.) Sacred to the Memory of Gunner WILLIAM GRIGG of X Battery Royal Artillery 1855 Aged 20 Years

(11.) Sacred to the Memory of Gunner JAMES VANSTON X Battery Royal Artillery 1855 Aged 24 Years

(12.) Sacred to the Memory of Gunner ROBERT Mc GAGHY X Battery Royal Artillery 1855 Aged 24 Years

(13.) Sacred to the Memory of Gunner HENRY GOODS Y Battery Royal Artillery 1855 Aged 24 Years

BALAKLAVA HEIGHTS.

BALAKLAVA.

SAILORS' BURIAL GROUND,
(ABOVE COSSACK BAY, BALAKLAVA HARBOUR.)

NUMBER OF GRAVES—61.

(1.) *(Wood.)*
SACRED
TO
THE MEMORY
OF
THOMAS JONES
Seaman of
H.M.S Leander
Who
Departed this life on
the 5th of Octr 1855
Aged 20 Years

(2.) *(Wood.)*
SACRED
To the Memory of
George Roto
Who died 22^d Augt 1855
Aged 22 Years

(3.) *(Wood.)*
SACRED
TO
THE MEMORY
OF
FORBES MICHIE
Late Commander of the Transport
MINDEN
Who Departed this Life AugST 19TH 1855
AGED 49 YEARS
Deeply lamented by all who knew him

(4.)
HERE RESTETH
THE BODY OF
JOHN NICHOLLS
SECOND SON OF
RICHARD NICHOLS
OF TREGLISSON
IN THE COUNTY OF
CORNWALL
DEPUTY ORDNANCE STOREKEPER
TO THE ARMY IN THE CRIMEA
WHO DIED IN THE FAITH OF CHRIST
NOVEMBER 3rd 1855
AGED 33
THIS MEMORIAL IS ERECTED BY HIS
AFFECTIONATE WIDOW.
"BLESSED ARE THE DEAD WHICH DIE IN
THE LORD FROM HENCEFORTH: YEA,
SAITH THE SPIRIT, FOR THEY REST FROM
THEIR LABOURS AND THEIR WORKS DO
FOLLOW THEM."

(5.) *(Wood.)*
IN
MEMORY
of
TH^{OS} AUSTIN
Who Died
At
BALAKLAVA
Novr 12Th
MDCCCLV

(6.) (Front.) *(Wood.)*

HIER RUHETINGOTT
Captain I. E Fäcks
v^n STRATSUND
𝔉𝔄𝔑𝔈𝔑𝔖𝔖𝔈𝔑
gest: den 21st April
1856

(Back.)
HIER. HATERDEN
GRUNDGEFUN,
DEN. WO. SEINAN
KER SIECHER
HELT

(7.) *(Wood.)*
SACRED
TO
THE MEMORY OF
EDWARD WILSON
ROYAL MARINE.
Of H.M.S. "Leander"
who departed this life
on the 17th of August 1855
Aged 28 Years

(8.) *(Wood.)*
SACRED
TO
THE MEMORY
OF
RICHARD HUTCHINSON
Late Master
of the Ship Duke of Bedford
Who departed this life
Nov^{br} 11th 1855
Aged 37 Years
HIGHLY RESPECTED BY ALL WHO KNEW HIM

(9.) *(Wood.)*
I.H.S
SACRED
TO THE
MEMORY OF
MARY TAULE, LATE
RICHARDSON NEW
CASTLE—WIFE OF
ANDERS TAULE
CAPT BARQUE
IRENE STATHELLE
WHO DIED OF
CHOLERA ON THE
5TH AUGUST 1855
AGED 24 YEARS

(10.) *(Wood.)*
SACRED
To the Memory of
WILLIAM MONK
who departed this life
AugST 6TH 1855.
Aged 22 YEARS

(11.) *(Wood.)*
SACRED
To The Memory of
ALEXANDER WEST
CAPTAIN. HOLD H.M.S. DIAMOND
who departed this life
AUGST 2nd 1855
AGED 32 YEARS

(12.) *(Wood.)*
SACRED
TO
THE MEMORY OF
ROBERT EMPTAGE
Able Seaman of H.M.S. "Leander"
Who was drowned
In Balaklava Harbour
On the 11th of November 1855. Aged
33 YEARS

Return and come to God:
Cast all your sins away;
Seek ye the Saviour's cleansing blood
Repent, believe, obey.

(13.)
THY WILL BE DONE
SACRED TO THE MEMORY
OF
ASSISTANT COMMISSARY GENERAL
HENRY LAMBERT BAYLEY
WHO DIED AT
BALACLAVA IN THE CRIMEA
ON THE 24 JULY 1855
AGED 34 YEARS

(14.) *(Wood.)*
SACRED
TO
THE MEMORY OF
CAPTAIN JOSEPH SMITH
late of the Bark N. H. Wolfe of
New York who Died of Cholera
on the 29TH Day of November 1855
Aged 39 Years

Oh how fast our fleeting days
Bears us down life's rapid stream
Lord to heaven our wishes raise
All on earth is but a dream
Rest in peace

(15.)
Sacred
TO THE
MEMORY
OF
CAPT^N ARTHUR JOHN LAYARD
38TH REG^T
WHO DIED AT BALACLAVA
ON THE 7TH AUGUST 1855.

Erected by his
Brother Officers
as a Mark of
their Esteem

(16.) *(Wood.)*

SACRED
To the
Memory of
JOHN THOMPSON
Late Master of the Brig "Peace"
Who Died
June 6TH 1855
Aged 39 Years

(17.) *(Wood.)*
Sacred
TO THE MEMORY OF
EDWARD TURNER
Seaman On board H.M.S. Leander
Who departed this life
6th of June 1855
Aged 19 Years

Oh how fast our fleeting days
Bear us down life's rapid stream!
Loud to heaven our wishes raise;
All on earth is but a dream

(18.) *(Wood.)*
SACRED
TO THE MEMORY, OF
NICHOLAS SMITH
Seaman on board of
H. M. S. LEANDER
Who departed this life
May 4th 1855
Aged 41

BALAKLAVA.

(19.) (Head.)

SACRED
TO
THE MEMORY OF
W, H. STOWE
WHO DIED JUNE 22nd
1855

*(Slab.)
TO THE MEMORY OF
THE BENEVOLENT & PATRIOTIC
DISTRIBUTOR OF THE "TIMES" FUND
W. H. STOWE
WHO LEFT HIS HOME AND COUNTRY
TO SUCCOUR THE SUFFERING
SOLDIERS IN THE EAST
AND AFTER A SHORT RESIDENCE
IN THE CRIMEA FELL A VICTIM
TO THE CLIMATE DYING AT
BALAKLAVA
22ND JUNE 1855

(20.) (Porphyry.)

SACRED TO THE MEMORY
OF
EDWARD BOXER, C.B.
REAR-ADMIRAL OF THE WHITE SQUADRON OF H.B.M. FLEET
WHO DIED AT BALACLAVA
IN THE BLACK SEA
ON THE 5TH OF JUNE 1855.

THIS STONE HAS BEEN PLACED
OVER HIS REMAINS
BY SOME OF HIS BROTHER OFFICERS
WHO VALUED HIM AS A THOROUGH SEAMAN
A MOST ZEALOUS OFFICER
AND A KIND HEARTED MAN

(21.)

IN MEMORY OF
GEORGE GYNGELL
Missionary to the
Crimean Railway
Expedition
Who died July 8th 1855
aged 36 years

(22.) (Wood.)

IN
MEMORY OF
WILLIAM WILLIAMS
LATE FIREMAN ON BOARD
S. S. "CLEOPATRA"
WHO DIED
OCTOBER 17th 1855
AGED 20 YEARS

(23.) (Wood.)

SACRED
TO THE MEMORY OF
SIDNEY BOXER, Esqre R. N
who departed this life
June 1st 1855

(24.) (Wood.)

SACRED
TO THE
MEMORY
OF
CAPTN Ge W. PEARSON
OF THE
STEAM TRANSPORT
UNION.
WHO DIED AT BALYa
JUNE 12TH 1855.
IN THE 49TH YEAR OF HIS AGE
REST IN PEACE

* Placed 11th July 1856.

(25.) (Wood.)

SACRED
TO
THE MEMORY OF
MICHAEL. P. SAMBELL Esqre
NAVAL INSTRUCTOR
H. M. S. LEANDER
Who departed this life
on the 21st of June 1855
Aged 49 Years

REQUIESCAT IN PACE

(26.) (Wood.)

To The
MEMORY
OF
W. P. HOOPER
MASTER MARINER
DIED JUNE 1st 1855
AGED 36 YRS

(27.) (Wood.)

SACRED
TO
THE MEMORY OF
THOMAS BURT, R, M
OF
Her Majesty's Ship Leander
Who Departed this life
on the 8th Day of July
1855 Aged 29 Years

When in the solemn hour of death
I bow to thy decree
Be this the prayer of my last breath
Good Lord remember me

(28.) (Wood.)

SACRED
TO
THE MEMORY OF
EDWARD JACKSON
Seaman
H. M. S LEANDER
Who Departed this life on
The 4th of Decr. A.D. 1855
Aged 49 years
REQUIESCAT IN PACE

(29.) (Wood.)

E. J
Octr 18th 1855

NEAR SANATORIUM, OR CASTLE HOSPITAL
(BALAKLAVA HEIGHTS).

NUMBER OF GRAVES—6.

(1.)

SACRED
TO THE
MEMORY
of
1ST Class Staff Surgeon
Nicholas O'Connor M. D
Died June 7th 1856
ERECTED
by his
BROTHER
OFFICERS

(2.)

SACRED
To The
MEMORY
of
Capt. W. Johnston
41st Regt
who Died of Fever
10th of Octr
1855

(3.)

SACRED
TO THE MEMORY OF
CHRISTOPHER H. BASSANO Esqr
STAFF SURGEON 2nd CLASS
DIED FEBRY 1ST 1856
AGED 31 YEARS

RIGHT OF PREVIOUS BURIAL GROUND.

1 GRAVEYARD.

(1.) (Wood.)

SACRED
TO THE MEMORY
OF
Frederick Spratt
PRIVATE ROYAL MARINES
LATE OF
H. M. S BELLEROPHON
WHO DEPARTED THIS LIFE
On the 21st of April 1855
AT THE AGE OF 36 YEARS

Here Lies An Old Soldier Whom all Must applaud
He Fought Many Battles Both at home and Abroad
But the Fiercest Engagement He Ever Was In
Was the Battle Of Self in the Conquest of Sin

(2.)

IN
MEMORY
OF
F. Henty, Esq.
Purveyor's department
who died June 22nd 1855
AGED 20 YEARS

(3.) (Wood.)

SACRED
To The Memory of
WILLIAM COLLINS R.E
who departed this life
July 23rd 1855
AGED 23 YEARS

(4.)

IN MEMORY OF
† JOHN GOODALL
DROWNED IN THE PRINCE
NOVR 14th 1854
PASSED FROM DEATH UNTO LIFE

ABOVE LAST BURIAL GROUND.

A LARGE MARBLE CROSS
(18 Feet in Height),
ERECTED
IN JULY 1856
BY ORDER OF
MISS FLORENCE NIGHTINGALE
(It came from Constantinople, and had no
Inscription on it.)

RIGHT OF NIGHTINGALE CROSS.

5 GRAVES.

† Captain of the "Prince."

BALAKLAVA.   39

ROYAL MARINES (LIGHT INFANTRY).
(ABOVE NIGHTINGALE CROSS).

NUMBER OF GRAVES—12.

(1.) (Monument.) (Marble.)
(FACING BALAKLAVA.)
IN MEMORY
OF
LIEUTENANTS. S. J. RICHARDS
A. T. S. CUTLER
D. W. CURRY
C. T. WITHAM
F. L. DOWSE
AND THE
NON-COMMISSIONED OFFICERS
DRUMMERS AND
PRIVATES WHO DIED WHILST SERVING
IN THE
BRIGADE OF ROYAL MARINES
IN THE CRIMEA DURING THE CAMPAIGN
OF
1854 & 1855

(2.) SACRED (Wood.)
TO MEMORY
OF
Color Serg^t Thomas Benson who
departed This Life on the 12th of March
1856
AGED 31 years
May his soul rest in
— PEACE —
— AMEN —

BALAKLAVA HEIGHTS.

2 LARGE ENGLISH GRAVEYARDS
AND
2 SARDINIAN GRAVEYARDS.

ABOVE GREEK CHURCH
(BALAKLAVA).

1 GRAVE.

(1.) Sacred
To the Memory of
Captn H. M. Patton
Royal Artillery
Died 27 Septr 1854

[Russian inscription]

FRONT OF GENERAL HOSPITAL
(BALAKLAVA).

NUMBER OF GRAVES { *10 / +2 } 12.

(*1.) SACRED
TO THE MEMORY OF
THE LATE ASSISTANT SURGEON
W. RENWICK 14th REG^T OF FOOT
AGED 23 YEARS
WHO DIED OF FEVER AT BALAKLAVA
2nd MARCH 1855.
THIS STONE IS ERECTED BY HIS BROTHER
OFFICERS, AS A TRIBUTE OF REGARD

(2.) ✠
IN MEMORY OF
The Rev^d
G$^–$ MOCKLER
Chaplain to the 3rd Divis^n
of the British Army Who
Died
SEPT^R 29th 1854
Aged 39 Years

(3.) IN MEMORY OF
ELLIS JACKSON
SECOND SON OF
WILLIAM AND MARY JACKSON
OF MIRFIELD, YORKSHIRE ENGLAND
PURSER OF H. M. S. T. ALICE JACKSON
WHO DIED OCT^R 18TH 1855
IN THE GENERAL HOSPITAL AT BALAKLAVA
AGED 25 YEARS

He was beloved and respected
by all who knew him

(4.) SACRED
to
the Memory of
CHILLEY PINE ESQ^R
Staff Surgeon of the first class
Late of the 4th Dragoon Guards
Who died March 6th 1855
This Stone
is Erected by the Officers of
the Above Corps in token
of Their Respect and
ESTEEM

(5.) ORATE
PRO ANIMÂ
R. D. JOANNIS WHEBLE
SACERDOTIS
OBIIT DIE 3^A NOVEMBRIS 1854
R. I. P

(6.) I H S
✠
SACRED TO THE MEMORY
of
CAPTAIN H. U. BURKE
33rd DUKE OF WELLINGTON'S
REGIMENT
Who Died at Balaclava
18th Jany 1855
Aged 30 Years

(7.) SACRED
to the Memory of
FRANCIS SMITH
Surgeon 95th Regiment
Who died Feby 9th 1855
AT BALAKLAVA

(8.) THY WILL BE DONE
SACRED
TO THE MEMORY OF
HENRY CHARLES DAWSON
LIEUTENANT
INNISKILLING DRAGOONS
WHO DIED AT
BALAKLAVA
OCTOBER 5th 1854
AGED 19 YEARS

(†1.) ✠
IN MEMORY
of
W. A. ANDERSON
SURGEON of the 41st Reg^t
WHO DIED
JANUARY 3rd 1855

(2.) SACRED
To The memory of
JOHN ARTHUR
FREEMAN Esq
late Captain 2nd Dragoons
Scots Greys
Who departed this life
29th September 1854
Aged 26 Years

ON SIDE OF HILL ABOVE GENERAL HOSPITAL.

2 GRAVES.

(1.) SACRED (Marble.)
TO THE
MEMORY
of
SISTER MARY ELIZABETH BUTLER
SISTER OF MERCY
WHO DIED OF FEVER
AT
BALAKLAVA
FEBR^Y 23^D
1856
MAY SHE REST
IN PEACE
AMEN
This Cross
was erected
by the
M. S. Corps
in the
Hospital
at the
time of her
death

(2.) ERECTED (Marble.)
BY THE
SOLDIERS
of the 89th REG^T
IN MEMORY OF
SISTER WINIFRED SPRY
SISTER OF MERCY
WHO DIED
OF
CHOLERA
AT
BALAKLAVA
OCT^r 20th 1855

MAY
SHE REST
IN PEACE
AMEN

NEAR CAMP OF ARMY WORKS CORPS.
(BETWEEN BALAKLAVA AND KADIKOI.)

40 GRAVES.

BALAKLAVA.

GUARDS, 13TH, & 82ND, REGTS.
(ON TOP OF HILL OVERLOOKING KADIKOI.)

NUMBER OF GRAVES—174.

(Over Entrance Gate.)
THIS
BURIAL GROUND WAS ENCLOSED BY
H. B. M. 82ND REGIMENT
1856.

(1.) 82ND REGT (*Wood.*)
PRINCE OF WALES
VOLUNTEERS
SACRED
TO THE
MEMORY OF
PRIVATE JAMES PEARSON
WHO DIED ON THE 16TH DECEMBER, 1855

(2.) 82nd REGT (*Wood.*)
P. W. V
IN
MEMORY
OF
PTE WILLIAM STREET
No 4 COMPANY
DIED 12TH JANY
1856

(3.) SACRED (*Wood.*)
to the
MEMORY
of
Pte THOMAS RODDLE
82nd Regt
WHO
DIED
at
BALAKLAVA
28th JAN
1856

(4.) Sacred (*Wood.*)
to the
Memory
of
Privte MICHl FLANAGAN
Who
DIED
at
BALAKLAVA
5th Decr
1855

(5.) SACRED (*Wood.*)
to the
MEMORY
of
Pte GEORGE NORMAN
82nd Regt.
Who
DIED
at
BALAKLAVA
1st Decr
1855

(6.) SACRED (*Wood.*)
to the
MEMORY
of
Pte CHARLES CHESTERTON
82nd Regt
WHO
DIED
at
BALAKLAVA
1st Octr
1855

(7.) (*Wood.*)
82nd Regt.
P. W. V.
IN
MEMORY
OF
PTE HENRY STREET
No. 4 COMPANY
DIED 8TH NOVR
1855

(8.) (*Wood.*)
82nd Regt.
P. W. V
IN
MEMORY
OF
PTE JOHN KEATING
No. 4 COMPANY
DIED 30TH OCTR
1855

(9.) 82ND REGT (*Wood.*)
PRINCE OF WALES
VOLUNTEERS
SACRED
TO THE
MEMORY OF
CORPORAL A. SOMMERVILLE
WHO DEPARTED THIS LIFE ON THE
26TH DAY OF DECEMBER 1855

(10.) 82ND REGT (*Wood.*)
PRINCE OF WALES
VOLUNTEERS
SACRED
TO THE
MEMORY OF
PRIVATE THOMAS KERR
WHO DEPARTED THIS LIFE ON THE
24TH OCTR 1855
Much lamented by his comrades.

(11.) 82ND REGT (*Wood*).
PRINCE OF WALES VOLUNTEERS
SACRED
TO THE
MEMORY OF
ROBERT SQUIRES
Of No 6 Company
who departed this life on the 23rd
October 1855

Much lamented by all who knew him

(12.) (*Wood.*)
82nd REGT.
P. W. V.
IN
MEMORY
OF
PTE JAMES DEACON
No 4 COMPANY
DIED 26TH OCTR
1855

(13.) 82ND REGT (*Wood.*)
P. W. V
IN
MEMORY
OF
PTE JOHN TURNER
No. 5. COMPANY
DIED
25TH
SEPTR
1855

(14.) 82nd (*Wood.*)
Regt
P. W. V
Pte John Samson
Light Compy
Died 15th Septr 1855

(15.) (*Wood.*)
82nd Regt
P. W. V
IN
Memory
of
Pte Michael Scott
No 4 Company
Died 9th Septr
1855

(16.) Pt George West (*Wood.*)
13th Regt. Died 28th July/55

(17.) (*Wood.*)
P. W. V
82ND
DANIEL COUGHLAN
LIGHT COMPANY
DIED 24TH OCTR 1855

(18.) Pt Henry Fuller (*Wood.*)
13th Regt. Died 14th July/55

(19.) Pt Thos. Netherway (*Wood.*)
13th Regt. Died 30th July/55

(20.) (*Wood.*)
82ND
P. W. V
THOMAS BAYLISS
LIGHT COMPANY
DIED 30TH MARCH 1856

BALAKLAVA.

(21.) SACRED (Wood.)
to the
MEMORY
of
L ce Corp l JOSEPH SMITH
82nd Regt.
WHO
DIED
at
BALAKLAVA
21st Oct r
1855

(22.) (Wood.)
82nd REG T
P. W. V
IN
MEMORY
OF
P TE WILLIAM SMITH
NO. 4 COMPANY
DIED 16 TH NOV R
1855

(23.) Corp l Joseph Hoey (Wood.)
13th Regt. Died 15th July/55

(24.) P t John Bennett (Wood.)
13th Regt. Died 16th July /55

(25.) P t Timothy Ryan (Wood.)
13th Regt. Died 27th July /55

(26.) P t Rob t Jemison (Wood.)
13th Regt. Died 15th July /55

(27.) P t Henry Bejent (Wood.)
13th Regt. Died 16th July /55

(28.) P t Denis Doyle (Wood.)
13th Regt. Died 17th July /55

(29.) P t W m Hughes (Wood.)
13th Regt. Died 16th July /55

(30.) P t Noris Gale (Wood.)
13th Regt. Died 24th August /55

(31.) P t William Lewis (Wood.)
13th Regt. Died 29th July /55

(32.) P t Rob t Hawkins (Wood.)
13th Regt. Died 15th August /55

(33.) P t Tho s Everson (Wood.)
13th Regt. Died 31st July /55

(34.) P t M Artin Spillan (Wood.)
13th. Died 27 Aug /55

(35.) Bugler Alfred Baker (Wood.)
13th Regt. Died 10th Aug st /55

(36.) P t James Cahill (Wood.)
13th Regt. Died 15th July /55

(37.) Bugler Charles Mills (Wood.)
13th Regt. Died 24th July /55

(38.) P t Thos. Fegan (Wood.)
13th Regt. Died 17th July /55

(39.) ✝
TO THE MEMORY
OF
GEORGE SAWYERS
WHO DEPARTED
THIS LIFE IN THE
34th YEAR OF HIS AGE
LOOKING FORWARD
TO A JOYFUL
RESURRECTION
WHO DIED JAN 31st 1856
A.W.C. C.B.

(40.) P t Rich d Doherty (Wood.)
13th Regt. Died 13th July /55

(41.) P t Thos. Callaghan (Wood.)
13th Regt. Died 12th July /55

(42.) SACRED
TO THE MEMORY OF
PRIVATE WILLIAM FILBY
H.M. 82 ND REGIMENT
WHO DIED ON BALAKLAVA
HEIGHTS ON THE 5 TH OF NOVEMBER
1855 AGED 36 YEARS
THIS TABLET IS ERECTED
BY HIS CAPTAIN, THE
NON COMMISSIONED OFFICERS
AND MEN OF THE
Grenadier Company
as a Small Tribute of their
Esteem and Respect

(43.) Bugl r W m Nash (Wood.)
13th Died 13th July/55

(44.) P t W m Rose (Wood.)
13th Died 7 August /55

(45.) P t Edward Rivers (Wood.)
13th Regt. Died 13th July/55

(46.) P r Alfred Clarke (Wood.)
13th Regt. Died 24th July/ 55

ON RIDGE BETWEEN LIGHT AND HEAVY CAVALRY CHARGES,
25 TH OCTOBER, 1854.

OBELISK.
(Front.)
(Side facing Balaklava.)
IN MEMORY
OF
THOSE WHO FELL IN THE BATTLE OF
BALAKLAVA
25 TH OCTOBER 1854

(Right.)
✝

(Left.)
ERECTED
BY THE
BRITISH ARMY
A.D. 1856

(Rear.)
(Side facing the Tchernaya.)

ВЪ ПАМЯТЬ
ТѢМЪ КОТОРЫЕ ПАЛИ ВЪ
БАЛАКЛАВСКОМЪ СРАЖЕНІИ
13 го ОКТЯБРЯ 1854.

SITE OF HEAVY CAVALRY CHARGE,
25 TH OCTOBER 1854

NUMBER OF GRAVES—30.

(1.) MONUMENT.
(Front.)
(Side facing Balaklava.)
✝
SACRED
TO
The Memory
of
The Non
Commissioned
Officers &
Men of A Troop
R. H. Artillery
WHO DIED
in the Crimea
during the War
of 1855 and 1856

(Right.)
Also of
the 1st or
Kings Dragoons
and
6th or Carabineers
Who Died in
the Crimea
during the War
of 1855 and 1856

(Left.)
ERECTED
1856

(2.) SACRED (Wood.)
to the
Memory
OF DRIVER C. HUBBARD A Tr p
R. H. A. Died on the 29 of JULY
1855
AGED
20
YEARS
◆
what
i
say unto
all
Watch
and
PRAY

A AND C TROOPS ROYAL HORSE ARTILLERY,
(JUST OUTSIDE BALAKLAVA, TOWARDS KAMARA.)

NUMBER OF GRAVES—21.

(1.) ♣ (Wood.)
SACRED
to the
MEMORY
of
CORP L. A. ANDERSON
A TROOP R. H. A
Died MAY 27th 1856
AGED
29
YEARS

(2.) SACRED (Wood.)
to the
Memory
OF
GUN R. J. GUEHRIDGE A TROOP
R. H. A
Died MAY 3rd 1856 Aged
22
years

HIGHLAND DIVISION, KAMARA.

(3.) Sacred (Wood.)
To the
Memory
OF SAMUEL BULL A TROOP
R. H. A
Who
Died
Decr 22nd
1855

(4.) Sacred (Wood.)
To the
Memory
OF GUNNER THOMAS FREER
A Troop
R. H. A

(5.) ♣ (Wood.)
SACRED
to the
MEMORY
OF
G^r. A. THOMPSON C. TROOP
R. H. A
Died July 11th 1855 AGED 22 Y^{rs}
at home
abroad
in Peace
in War
thy God
shall
thee defend
Conduct
thee. thro'
life's
Pilgrimage
Safe to
thy journey
S. END
♣

(6.) †
SAC RED
To The Memory of
THE NON.COM^{SD} OFFICERS & MEN
OF
A & C TROOPS. R. H. ARTILLERY
WHO DIED IN THE CRIMEA
DURING THE WAR
OF
1854 – 1855 & 1856

(7.) SACRED (Wood.)
❀
to the
MEMORY
OF
Gunner Wm WRIGHTON
C. TROOP R. H. A. Departed
this
life
MAY
30th 1855
AGED
27
YEARS

JUST ABOVE PREVIOUS BURIAL GROUND.

2 GRAVES.

(1.) Sacred
To The
Memory
of
LIEUTENANT. P. H. DYKE
2nd Battⁿ Rifle Brigade
who died at Balaklava
on the
19 April
1855

Aged
19 YEARS

(2.) SACRED
TO THE
MEMORY
of
CAPTAIN CHARLES THOMAS KING
32ND REGIMENT
WHO DIED MAY 27TH 1855

HIGHLAND DIVISION, KAMARA.

HIGHLAND OR 1ST BRIGADE: 42ND, 79TH, 92ND, & 93RD HIGHLANDERS.

2ND BRIGADE: 1ST & 2ND BATTALIONS 1ST ROYALS, *71ST HIGHLAND LIGHT INFANTRY, AND 72ND HIGHLANDERS.

NEAR KAMARA CHURCH.

NUMBER OF GRAVES—35.

(1.) THO^S HOLDER
42ND ROYAL HIGH^{DS}
10TH APRIL 1856

(2.) ARCH^D ROSS
42ND ROYAL HIGH^{DS}
2nd MARCH 1856

(3.) ALEX^R HOOD
42ND ROYAL HIGH^{DS}
7 JAN^y 1856

(4.) ALEX^R MUNRO
42ND ROYAL HIGH^{DS}
2nd MAY 1856

(5.) A. M^CLEAN
79TH
HIGHLANDERS
DIED 2nd APRIL 1856

(6.) T. HAY L^T
1855

(7.) M^W HILL. L^T
1855

(8.) A^R LEE. L^T
1st APRIL
1855

(9.) R^t WEIR
79TH
HIGHL^{RS}
1854

(10.) DAVID PATRICK
72nd HIGHLANDERS
31ST OCT. 1855

(11.) DE^{IS} DESMOND
79TH
26TH FEB^{RY}
1855

(12.) ihs
To the Memory of
F. A. GRANT
Lieutenant
79th Cameron Highlanders
October 1st 1854
ST. JOHN. XI. 25. 26.

(13.) (Monument.)
TO THE MEMORY
OF THE
OFFICERS AND MEN
HIGHLAND DIVISION
WHO DIED AT KAMARA
1855-6

(14.) A. CRUICKSHANKS
42ND ROYAL HIGH^{DS}
10TH MARCH 1856

(15.) A. MAYS. L^T
1856

(16.) TO THE
MEMORY
OF
CAPTAIN HENRY WHICHCOTE TURNER
OF THE 1st ROYAL REGIMENT
DIED MARCH 1st 1856

(17.) A^R RONALD
92.
HIGH^{RS} 9TH APRIL
1856

(18.) WILL^M WATSON
42nd ROYAL HIGH^{rs}
11TH DEC^R 1855

(19.) A^{LEX} REID
92ND
HIGHLANDERS
DIED 6TH D^{EC}
1855

(20.) J^{MS} M^CDONALD
92
HIGHLANDERS
D^D 15TH SEPT. 1855

---

* Yenikale; sailed for Kertch 22nd May 1855.

HIGHLAND DIVISION, KAMARA.

(21.) J. THOMSON
92ND HIGHLANDERS
16TH DECR 1855

(22.) DAID MGAHALE
92 HIGHLANDERS
DIED 19 DER 1855

(23.) P. PAXTON
92 HIGHRS 3 JANY 1856

(24.) ALEX HUNTER
92 HIGHLANDERS
7TH DECR 1855

(25.) WILLM GIBSON
42ND ROYAL HIGHDS
11TH JANY 1856

(26.) JOHN HOLMES
79TH
4TH JANY 1856

(27.) WILLM MATHEWS
42ND ROYAL HIGHRS
10TH DECR 1855

(28.) MATHW TANNER
42ND ROYAL HIGHDRS
11TH DECR 1855

(29.) PR SMITH
42ND ROYAL HIGHRS
28TH DECR 1855

(30) G. ROBERTSON
79TH HIGHLANDERS
11TH MARCH 1856

(31.) G. D. W. SCOTT
DIED 27TH NOVR 1855

(32.) G. MCINTOSH
79TH HIGHLANDERS
1855

(33.) JMS DUNSMORE
92ND HIGHLANDERS
DIED 24TH NOV 1855

(34.) G. WHITLOCK
L. T. 12TH MAY 1856

(35.) JOHN ROSS L. T
DIED 13TH FEBRY 1856

(36.) ROBT WHITELAW
24TH JANY 1856
AGED 10 DAYS

93RD HIGHLANDERS' CAMP.

NUMBER OF GRAVES—10.

(1.) SACRED TO THE MEMORY OF GEORGE KING BAND 93rd Highlanders DIED 12th December 1855 — A Soldiers Grave less often sought than found Erected By A Friend *(Wood.)*

72ND HIGHLANDERS' CAMP.

NUMBER OF GRAVES—2.

(1.) SACRED to the MEMORY OF ML WATERS WHO DEPARTED THIS LIFE ON THE 1ST APRIL 1856

(2.) SACRED To the MEMORY of PATRICK MC BREARTY Who Departed this Life on the 30th December 1855

(3.) *(Front.)* 1856
(Right.) I H S 72nd or Duke of Albany's own HIGHLANDERS 1855 1856
(Left.) Militum respice, cineres
(Rear.) SOLDIERS of the 72d HIGHLANDERS who were killed or died during the Siege are buried near SEVASTOPOL in the Cemetry of the GUards

1ST ROYALS CAMP.

NUMBER OF GRAVES—13.

(23.) TO THE Memory of Pte G. Miles 1ST Battn 1st Royals Died 5th Decr 1855 AGED 19 *(Wood.)*

(2.) To The Memory of Pte W. Fletcher 1st Battn 1st Royals Died 17th Novr 1855 Aged 30 *(Wood.)*

(3.) Pt WILLIAM CLARK 2nd Batt 1st Royal Regt Died 11th Decr 1855 Aged 39 Years *(Wood.)*

(4.) Pt JOHN BROWN 2nd Batt 1st Royal Regt. Died 6th April 1856 Aged 25 Years *(Wood.)*

(5.) Pte JAMES NEWMAN 2nd Battn 1st Royal Regt. Died 19th April 1856 Aged 23 Years *(Wood.)*

(6.) Pt EDWARD CASTLES 2nd Batt 1st Royal Regt. Died 29th April 1856 Aged 28 Years *(Wood.)*

(7.) Pt FRANCIS NOLAN 2nd Batt 1st Royal Regt Died 25th Decr 1855 Aged 21 Years *(Wood.)*

(8.) Pt ROBERT ADCOCK 2nd Batt 1st Royal Regt Died 8th Decr 1855 Aged 24 Years *(Wood.)*

(9.) Pt WILLIAM BASS 2nd Batt 1st Royal Regt Died 14th Jany 1856 Aged 20 Years *(Wood.)*

(10.) Pt Thos Cordry 1st Battn Royals Died 25th March 1856 Aged 29 Yrs *(Wood.)*

(11.) 1st Battn Royals GEORGE POWELL DIED 7TH FEBY 1856 Aged 19 YEARS *(Wood.)*

(12.) TO THE MEMORY OF Mary Anne Wife of Sergeant Mathew PHENIX 1ST Battn Royals DIED 2nd of Novr 1855 Age 25 Years
I know that my Redeemer liveth and that he shall stand at the latter day upon the earth And though after my skin worms destroy this body yet in my flesh shall I see God whom I shall see for myself and mine eyes shall behold and not another
Job. X 18 25 26 27 *(Wood.)*

(13.) THOMAS DEMPSTER 1st BATTN ROYALS DIED NOVR 7TH 1855 AGE 20 *(Wood.)*

CATHCART'S HILL.

NUMBER OF GRAVES AND MONUMENTS } 99

(1.)   IN MEMORY OF   *(Granite.)*
ARTHUR. JOHN. LAYARD
CAPTⁿ IN
HER B Mˢ 38ᵀᴴ REGIMENT OF Foot
BORN, 18 JULY, 1819
DIED 7 AUGT. 1855
R. I. P.

A. MACDONALD
SCULP
ABERDEEN

(2.)   SACRED
TO THE
MEMORY
OF
CAPTⁿ Wᵐ Hʸ TOOLE
OF THE 46ᵀᴴ REGIMENT
WHO DIED AT ALMA ON THE 21ˢᵗ SEPTʳ.
1854

(3.)   THIS STONE   *(Granite.)*
IS. LAID OVER THE REMAINS OF
FRANK JOHN CURTIS
(FOURTH SON OF
*CHARLES BERWICK CURTIS ESQʳᴱ
OF LONDON).
LIEUTENANT IN
HER BRITANNIC MAJESTY'S
46ᵀᴴ REGIMENT OF FOOT
WHO FELL STRUCK BY A CANNON BALL
WHILE ON DUTY IN THE TRENCHES
BEFORE SEBASTOPOL
AT 10 P.M MAY 2ᴺᴰ 1855
AGED 23.

†

SOUS CETTE PIERRE REPOSENT
LES RESTES MORTELS DE
FRANK JOHN CURTIS
(QUATRIEME FILS DE
CHARLES BERWICK CURTIS ESQʳᴱ
DE LONDRES)
LIEUTENANT
AU 46ᴱ RÉGIMENT D'INFANTERIE
DE SA MAJESTÉ BRITANNIQUE
QUI DE SERVICE DANS LES TRANCHÉES
DEVANT SÉBASTOPOL
TOMBA FRAPPÉ À 10 HEURES DU SOIR,
LE 2 MAI 1855
A L'AGE DE 23 ANS.

M. W. JOHNSON, NEW ROAD, LONDON

LIEUᵀ FRANK JOHN CURTIS
46ᵗʰ REGᵀ

(4.)   SACRED
TO THE MEMORY OF
MAJOR SAMUEL PHILIP TOWNSEND
ROYAL BRITISH ARTILLERY
WHO FELL AT INKERMANN ON THE 5ᵀᴴ
OF NOVEMBER 1854 IN COMMAND
OF A BATTERY OF 9 POUNDERS ATTACHED
TO THE 4ᵗʰ DIVISION UNDER
MAJOR GENʳˡ SIR. G. CATHCART

Τίς ημᾶς χωρισει αποτῆς αγαπης
Του χριστου ; Θλίψις ; ἠστενοκωριαῆ
διωγμος ; ἥμαχαιρα ;
Ἀλλέν τουτοις πᾶ σινῦπερνιχωμεν.
διατου αγαπησαντος ημας
Επιστο ληπρος Ρομαιους Κεφ. η.
ROMANS. CHAP. 8ᵀᴴ 35ᵀᴴ 37ᵀᴴ VERS.

(Foot.)
S. P. T. 1854

(5.)   *(Top.)*   *(Black Slate.)*
(Crest.)
BENEATH THIS STONE
LIE THE MORTAL REMAINS OF
SIR ROBERT LYDSTON NEWMAN,
OF MAMHEAD
IN THE COUNTY OF DEVON ENGLAND BARONET
CAPTAIN IN THE BRITISH GRENADIER GUARDS
WHO WAS KILLED AT THE BATTLE OF INKERMANN
ON THE 5ᵀᴴ OF NOVEMBER, 1854,
IN THE THIRTY FOURTH YEAR OF HIS AGE
Sᵀ LUKE XII. 4. 5. Sᵀ MATTHEW. XXIV. 44.

THIS MONUMENT IS ERECTED TO HIS
MEMORY AS A TRIBUTE OF AFFECTION BY
HIS SURVIVING BROTHERS AND SISTERS

(Left Face.)

" ВЕЛИКОБРИТАНСКОЙ СЛУЖБЫ, ГВАРДЕЙСКАГО ГРЕНАДЕРСКАГО КОРПУСА КАПИТАНА, РОДИВШАГОСЯ ВЪ АНГЛІИ."

СЕЙ ПАМЯТНИКЪ ВОЗДВИГНУТЪ БРАТЬЯМИ И СЕСТРАМИ УСОПШАГО ВЪ ЗНАКЪ КЪ НЕМУИХЪ ЛЮБВИ.

ВЪ ПОМѢСТЬѢ МАМГЕДЪ ВЪ ГРАФСТВѢ ДЕВОНЪ И УБИТАГО ВЪ СРАЖЕНІИ ПРИ ИНКЕРМАНѢ

НА 34 М ГОДУ ОТЪ РОЖДЕНІЯ

24ᵒᴳᴼ ОКТЯБРЯ
5ᴳᴼ НОЯБРЯ 1854 ГОДА.

НЬЮМАНЪ.

ЗДѢСЬ ПОКОИТСЯ ПРАХЪ
БАРОНЕТА СРЪ РОБЕРТА ЛИДСТОНА.

(6.) †   *(Head.)*
Sacred to the Memory of
A. C. F. Fitzroy
Captain Royal Artillery
Who died on the 11ᵗʰ Septʳ 1855
of a wound recᵈ in the trenches
before Sebastopol 8ᵗʰ Septʳ
1855

(Back.)
ERECTED BY HIS FRIENDS
& BROTHER OFFICERS

(Slab.)
CAPTAIN A. C. L. FITZROY
ROYAL ARTILLERY
WOUNDED 8ᵀᴴ SEPT
DIED 10ᵀᴴ SEPT. 1856

(Foot.)
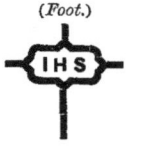

(7.) †   *(Marble.)*
WILLIAM KERR
Lieut 30ᵗʰ Regiment
Born 28ᵗʰ March 1831
Killed at the storming of the
REDAN
Septʳ 8ᵗʰ 1855
"God is our refuge and strength."
Psalm 46. v. 1.

ВИЛЬЯМЪ КЕРРЪ
ЛѢЙТЕНАНТЪ 30ᴳᴼ ПОЛКА
РОДИЛСЯ 28ᴳᴼ МАРТА 1831
РЕДАНУ,
8ᴳᴼ СЕНТЯБРЯ 1856 ГОДА
БГЪ НАМЪ ПРИКѢЖИЩЕИ СИЛА
ҮАЛОМ ХМ͠Ѕ

(8.)   IHS
SACRED
TO THE MEMORY OF
Colonel The Honᵇˡᵉ F. G. HOOD
GRENADIER GUARDS
KILLED 18ᵗʰ OCTOBER 1854.
AND
‡ CAPTAIN A. E. ROWLEY
GRENADIER GUARDS
KILLED 16ᵗʰ OCTOBER 1854

(9.)   SACRED
TO THE
MEMORY
OF
LIEUᵀ JOHN HORNDON MESSENGER
OF THE 46ᵀᴴ REGᵀ
WHO WAS KILLED WHILE ON DUTY
AS ACTING ENGINEER
BY THE EXPLOSION OF A MINE
ON THE 15ᵀᴴ JANʸ
1856

(10.)   SACRED
to the
memory
of

LIEUᵀ COˡ EDWARD PAKENHAM
GRENADIER GUARDS
WHO FELL AT INKERMANN
NOVEMBER 5ᵀᴴ 1854

CAPTAIN THE HONᵇˡᴱ HENRY NEVILLE,
GRENADIER GUARDS
WHO FELL AT INKERMANN
NOVEMBER 5ᵀᴴ 1854

---

* Presented a Model of Cathcart's Hill to the United Service Institution, but at present it requires corrections and additions.
† Gravestones changed to their present positions on 2ⁿᵈ July 1856, by order of Capt. Hon. H. Keppel, R.N.   ‡ See No. 93 Tomb.

CATHCART'S HILL

KEY

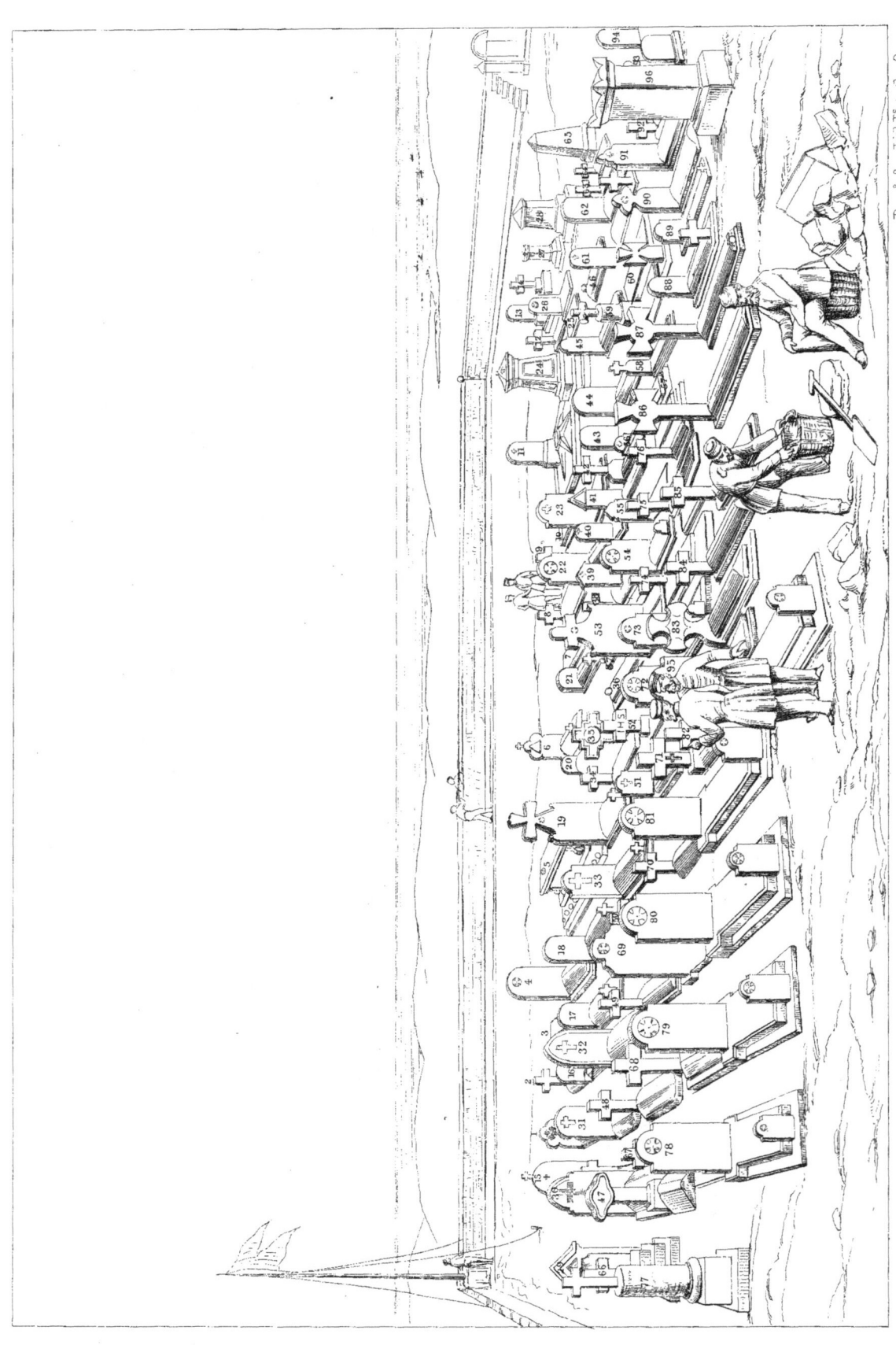

CATHCART'S HILL.

CATHCART'S HILL.

(11.)   (Marble.)

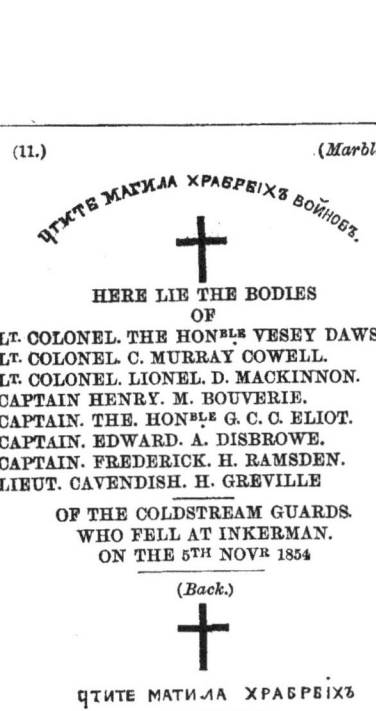

HERE LIE THE BODIES
OF
LT. COLONEL. THE HON^{BLE} VESEY DAWSON.
LT. COLONEL. C. MURRAY COWELL.
LT. COLONEL. LIONEL. D. MACKINNON.
CAPTAIN HENRY. M. BOUVERIE.
CAPTAIN. THE. HON^{BLE} G. C. C. ELIOT.
CAPTAIN. EDWARD. A. DISBROWE.
CAPTAIN. FREDERICK. H. RAMSDEN.
LIEUT. CAVENDISH. H. GREVILLE

OF THE COLDSTREAM GUARDS.
WHO FELL AT INKERMAN.
ON THE 5TH NOV^R 1854

(Back.)

✝

ΨΤИΤΕ ΜΑΤИΛΑ ΧΡΑБΡЫΙΧЪ
ВΟИΗΟΒЪ

(12.)
SACRED
TO THE MEMORY OF
CAPTAIN HYLTON JOLIFFE.
COLDSTREAM GUARDS
DIED 4th OCT^R
1854

(13.)   SACRED   (Marble.)
TO THE MEMORY OF
LIEUT. COLONEL
JAMES HUNTER BLAIR,
SCOTS FUSILIER GUARDS
MEMBER OF PARLIAMENT FOR THE
COUNTY OF AYR
WHO WAS KILLED AT
THE BATTLE OF INKERMAN.
5TH NOVEMBER 1854

(Foot.)   (Stone.)

✝

(14.)   THIS CROSS
WAS ERECTED BY
HIS BROTHER OFFICERS TO THE MEMORY OF
COLONEL AUGUSTUS COX
GRENADIER GUARDS
WHO AFTER SHARING IN THE VICTORY OF THE ALMA
MARCHED WITH HIS REGT TO BALAKLAVA
AND DIED
OF FATIGUE
A FEW HOURS
AFTER THE
CAPTURE OF
THAT STATION
SEPT^R 26
1854

(15.)   (Marble.)

✝

SACRED TO THE MEMORY
OF
W. P. COPPINGER
SUB, INSPECTOR OF IRISH CONSTABULARY
AND SERVING WITH THE COMMISSARIAT
IN THE CRIMEA
DIED 11TH AUGUST 1855
AGED 29 YEARS

THIS STONE WAS ERECTED TO HIS
MEMORY BY HIS BROTHER OFFIC^{RS}
OF THE CONSTABULARY

(Foot.)

W. P. C.

(16.)   SACRED TO THE MEMORY
OF
JOHN AUCHMUTY
CAPTAIN 57TH REGIMENT
DIED BALACLAVA NOV^R 13TH 1854

GEORGE UDNEY HAGUE
LIEUT 57TH REGIMENT
WOUNDED NOV^R 5TH
DIED AT SEA NOV^R 11TH 1854

D'ARCY CURWEN
LIEUT. 57TH REGT
DIED IN CAMP OCT^R 1855

(Foot.)
✝
I. H. S

(17.)   (Marble.)
SACRED TO THE MEMORY OF
LIEUTENANT
GEORGE MITCHELL
57th Regiment
who died in Camp on the 28th
of a wound received in the
trenches
MARCH 18TH 1855

(Foot.)   (Stone.)
✝
I H S

(18.)   (Marble.)
SACRED TO THE MEMORY
OF
JAMES FRANKLYN BLAND
Captain 57th Regiment
who died in Camp on the 8th
of a wound received in Action
NOVEMBER 5TH 1854

(Foot.)
✝
I H S

(19.)

HERE
Lieth the
Mortal Remains
of Captain
EDWARD STANLEY
57th Regt Killed at the
BATTLE of InKerman
5th Novr 1854
To Whose Memory
this Stone Is Erected, by
the Men of his Company.
"CAST DOWN BUT Not
DESTROYED 2. Cor. 49.

(Foot.)
✝
I H S

(20.)   (Marble.)
SACRED TO THE MEMORY
OF
JAMES COLLINS ASHWIN
LIEUT 57TH REGIMENT
KILLED IN ACTION
JUNE 18TH 1855

(Foot.)   (Stone.)
✝
I H S

(21.)   (Marble.)
SACRED TO THE MEMORY
OF
GEORGE HERMAN NORMAN
CAPTAIN 57TH REGIMENT
WOUNDED JUNE 18TH
DIED IN CAMP JUNE 30TH
1855.

(Foot.)   (Stone.)
✝
I H S

(22.)   (Marble.)
✝
SACRED
TO THE MEMORY OF
LT. Col. W. H. L. D. CUDDY
OF H.B.M. 55th REGT OF FOOT
WHO WAS KILLED 8TH SEPT^R 1855
WHILST GALLANTLY LEADING HIS REGT
IN THE ASSAULT ON THE GREAT REDAN
OF SEVASTOPOL
REQUIESCAT IN PACE

(23.)
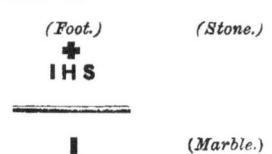

LIEUT. LEA BIRCH
DIED 8TH OCTOBER 1854.
CAPTAIN, H, T, BUTLER.
KILLED AT THE BATTLE OF INKERMAN
5TH NOVEMBER 1854
AND
ASSISTANT SURGEON J. J. NORRIS
DIED 22ND NOV^R 1854
ALL OF THE 55TH REGT OF FOOT.
THIS STONE IS ERECTED
BY THE OFFICERS OF THE 55" REGT
AS, A, TRIBUTE OF RESPECT TO THE
MEMORY, AND OF SINCERE GRIEF
FOR THEIR LOSS

(Back.)
ALSO
IN MEMORY OF
MAJOR J. B. ROSE
AND
CAPTAIN. J. G. SCHAW.
H. M. 55TH REGT
KILLED AT THE BATTLE OF THE ALMA
20TH SEPT^R 1854
AND BURIED ON THE FIELD

CATHCART'S HILL.

(24.) (MONUMENT.)
(Front.)

✝

SACRED
TO THE MEMORY
OF
THE OFFICERS. N. C. OFFICERS
& MEN OF
THE ROYAL ARTILLERY.
WHO WERE KILLED IN ACTION
OR HAVE DIED DURING THE
EASTERN CAMPAIGN.
THIS MONUMENT
IS ERECTED BY THE OFFICERS
OF THE REGIMENT
SERVING IN THE CRIMEA.
A. D. 1856.

(Right.)
KILLED
BRIGR. GENL. F. STRANGWAYS
5TH NOVR 1854.
MAJOR. S. P. TOWNSEND.
5TH NOVR 1854.
CAPTAINS. A. OLDFIELD.
17TH AUGST 1855.
A. DEW. 20TH SEPTR 1854.
S. CHILDERS. 23RD OCTR 1854.
A. GORDON. 6TH JULY. 1854.
E. G. SNOW. 6TH SEPTR 1855.
LIEUTs. E. LUCE 11TH APRIL. 1855.
R. COCKERELL. 20TH SEPTR 1854.
R. WALSHAM. 20TH SEPTR 1854.
R. MITCHELL. 12TH APRIL 1855.
D. A. COMSYS G. YELLON.
15TH NOVR 1855.
W. HAYTOR. 8TH SEP. 1855

(Rear.)
DIED OF WOUNDS.
CAPTN. A. C. L. FITZROY.
10TH SEPTR 1855.
LIEUT. T. DAWSON.
11TH DECR 1855.
1467
NON COMSD OFFICERS.
AND MEN.

(Left.)
DIED
LT. COLL. E. HARRISON.
12TH AUGST 1855.
MAJORS G. R. LEVINGE.
2ND AUGST 1854.
W. SWINTON. 2ND JANY 1855.
CAPTNS H. PATTON.
7TH SEPTR 1854
W. GUILLE. 28TH OCTR 1854.
T. SAVAGE. 22ND JUNE. 1855.
LIEUTS. H. SINGER. 4TH OCTR 1854.
E. McLACHLAN. 29TH NOVR 1854.
SIR. G. YOUNG. BARTT.
22ND OCTR 1855.
E. MARSHALL. 29TH NOVR 1855.
ASST. COMSY. H. WRIGHT.
15TH AUGST 1854.

(25.) G. H. H. GREATHEAD
1ST LIEUT. OF. H. M. S BRITANNIA
HE FELL
MORTALLY WOUNDED WHEN GALLANTLY DOING
HIS DUTY IN THE 21 GUN BATTERY
ON THE 20TH OCTOBER 1854

(26.) (Marble.)

✝

SACRED
TO THE MEMORY OF
CHARLES THOMAS KING ESQRE
CAPTAIN IN. H. M. 32nd REGT.
WHO DIED OF CHOLERA AT
BALACLAVA
ON THE 28TH MAY 1855
WHEN ORDERLY OFFICER TO
F. M. THE LORD RAGLAN G.C.B
DARMANIN MALTA

(27.) (MONUMENT.)
(Front.)
18TH
ROYAL. IRISH.
REGIMENT.

(Left.)
LIEUTENANT.
W. J. MEURANT.
KILLED.
18TH JUNE. 1855.
AT. THE. ASSAULT.
OF. THE.
CREEK. BATTERY.

(Right.)
DIED
ENS. E. D. RICARD
5TH MAY. 1856.
3. SERJEANTS.
77 RANK. AND. FILE.

(Rear.)
KILLED AND DIED
OF
THEIR WOUNDS.
3. SERJEANTS
1. DRUMMER.
85. RANK. AND. FILE

(28.) (MONUMENT.)
(Front.)

✝

XLIV
SACRED
TO THE MEMORY OF
CAPTAINS
BOWES FENWICK
HONBLE C. W. H. AGAR
W. H. MANSFIELD
AND
F. W. T CAULFIELD
ALL OF THE 44TH REGT
AND WHO DIED OF
WOUNDS RECEIVED ON THE
18TH JUNE 1855
THEIR REMAINS ARE
BURIED ON 3D DIVN HILL
800 YARDS WEST
FROM THIS SPOT.

(Right.)
ALSO
TO THE MEMORY OF
LIEUT R. FITZ. RD EYRE
AND
DR JAMES THOMSON
OF THE 44TH REGT
WHO DIED AT BALAKLAVA
IN SEPR 1854.

(Rear.)
ALSO
TO THE MEMORY OF
18 SERJEANTS
12 DRUMMERS
420 RANK AND FILE
WHO WERE KILLED,
OR DIED OF WOUNDS,
OR DISEASE
DURING THE WAR.

(29.)

✝

SACRED
TO THE MEMORY
OF
LT COLL TYLER
62D REGT
WHO DIED AT BALAKLAVA
HOSPITAL ON THE
23D OCTOBER
1855
FROM THE EFFECTS OF A
WOUND RECEIVED AT
THE ASSAULT ON THE
REDAN
ON THE 8TH SEPTR
1855

(30.) SACRED TO THE MEMORY OF

LIEUT C. J. WHITE 62ND
REGT WHO WAS KILLED
IN THE TRENCHES ON
THE 2ND OF MAY
1855

(31.)* SACRED TO THE MEMORY OF

CAPT R. A. COX AND
LT L. BLAKISTON
62D REGT
Who fell in the assault
of the Redan
on the 8th September
1855

(32.)†

✝

< SACRED >
TO
THE MEMORY OF
LIEUTT COLL R. A. SHEARMAN.
MAJOR W. F. DICKSON AND
CAPTN J. B. FORSTER 62ND
REGT WHO FELL IN THE
ATTACK ON THE QUARRIES
ON THE MORNING OF THE
8TH OF JUNE
1855

---

* Over 2 Graves. † Over 3 Graves.

CATHCART'S HILL.

(33.)

SACRED TO THE MEMORY
of
G. C. W. CURTOIS
Lieut. 63rd Regiment
Who Was Killed at The
Battle of Inkerman
5th November
* 1854 *

Beloved and Regretted By
His Brother Officers.

(Foot.)

(34.)
HERE LIES
THE BODY
OF
RICHARD J. THORLEY STONE LIEUT
55th REGT WHO FELL WHILE GALLAN-
-TLY LEADING HIS PARTY AT THE
ATTACK ON THE
QUARRIES ON THE
7th JUNE 1855
AGED 18 YEARS

(Foot.)

(35.)   (Portland Stone.)
SACRED
TO
THE MEMORY
OF
LIEUTENANT HENRY FRANCIS
EDEN HURT OF THE 21ST OR ROYAL
BRITISH FUSILIERS WHO
FELL AT INKERMAN ON THE
5TH NOVEMBER A.D. 1854
THIS STONE IS ERECTED BY
HIS BROTHER OFFICERS

(36.)   1 GRAVE.

(37.)   1 GRAVE.

(38.)
IN MEMORY
OF
LIEUT
C. H. EVANS
H.M. 55TH REGT DIED 6TH AUGUST 1855.
OF A WOUND RECD IN THE TRENCHES
BEFORE SEBASTOPOL AGED
19 YEARS
SINCERELY
REGRETTED
BY HIS
BROTHER
OFFICERS

(39.)

SACRED TO THE MEMORY OF
COLONEL H. C. COBBE, C.B.
4TH THE KING'S OWN REGIMENT
WHO DIED AUGUST 6TH 1856
OF WOUND RECEIVED WHEN
IN COMMAND OF THE TRENCHES
LEFT ATTACK, JUNE 18TH 1855
DEEPLY REGRETTED
BY HIS BROTHER OFFICERS

Полковнику Коббе 4го пѣхотнаго полка, умерь 6го Августа 1855 отъ раны по лученной вотра ншей, во вовре мя командованія Аншскои Лівои атакои 8ѣ Іюня 1855

(40.)

SACRED TO THE MEMORY OF
MAJOR GENERAL
SIR JOHN CAMPBELL
BART KILLED IN ACTION
June 18th 1855

(41.)   SACRED   (Marble.)
To the memory of
Brigadier General
Fox Strangways
Killed in action 5th Novr 1854

Посвящено Памяти Бригадіраго Генерала Королевскои Коннои Артиллеріи Рокгер Странгвеиса убить 4/5 Ноябр 1854

(Back.)

Бригадный Генералъ Ѳомасъ Фоксъ Странгвейсъ Кавалеръ Св Анны, котоpь ть получилъ отъ импера тора Все-россій ска Александ ра въ знакъ отличи те его служ бы шведскому оружію, оказанный при Лейпцигскомъ-же 1813., и который взялъ импер отъ оро мъ своего сертука.. шведскаго ордена Л Ш тш и зо Л Ш тож падали швeдскои, которые были даны Цеcаревичамъ Шведскимъ при собств-енной ска о благосклон-ности, за его мужествомъ при Лейпцигскомъ же 1813 года

(42.)   (Slab.)

SACRED TO THE MEMORY
of
the Honble
SIR GEORGE CATHCART, K.C.B
LIEUT GENL COMMANDING THE
4th Division of the British Army in the
CRIMEA
BORN 1794. KILLED 5" Novr 1854
AT THE BATTLE OF
INKERMAN.

He served with the Russian Army in
the Years 1813 and 1814. and was Aide-de-Camp
to the Duke of Wellington at Waterloo—
He was appointed in 1852
Governor of the Cape of Good Hope
from which place he had just returned.

o—o—o

ГЕНЕРАЛЪ-ЛЕЙТЕНАНТЪ КАТКАРТЪ, СЫНЪ ГЕНЕРА ЛА ГРАФА МАШКАРТА БЫВШИХЪ АНГЛІЙСКИМЪ ПОСЛАННИКОМЪ ВЪ ПЕТЕРСБУРГѢ, СЛУЖИЛЪ ВЪ ПРИШТАБѢ ОТЦА ЕГО ВЪ 1313 И 1814 ГОДАХЪ. БЫЛ АДЪЮТА НТОМЪ РУССКАГО ИМПРОТИВЪ ФРАНЦУЗОВЪ. ВЪ СРАЖЕНІЯХЪ С ДУВЕЛЛ ИТА. ДУВЕЛЛ ИТА. ВЪ 1852 ГО ДУ БЫЛЪ ВЕЛИТ. ОНАТРИ ВАТЕРЛО ОКОМ СРАЖЕНІИ ЛЕВЪ 1815 ГЪ. НАЗНАЧЕНЪ ЗАНТЛ ТИСКИМ ПРАВИТЕ ЛЬСТВОМЪ ВОЕННЫМЪ ГУБЕРНАТОРОМ МЫСА ДОБРЫЙ НАДЕ Ж ДЫ ОТЪ. КУДА ОПОСНЕУ Л ЪКОН ТОВЕРПУЛЪ ВЪ РЯДАХЪ ПРИ НЯ ТЪ ИЗ Я ДИВИЗИИ СЕЙ АРМІИ

This Tomb was placed here
by the Officers and men of the
4TH DIVISION.

(43.)   (Marble.)

SACRED TO THE MEMORY OF
Brigadier General
THOMAS LEIGH GOLDIE
Commanding 1st Brigade
of the
4th Division of the British Army
And
Lieut Colonel of the 57th Regiment
WHO FELL AT INKERMAN
Nov. 5th 1854.

(Foot.)

(44.)   (Marble.)

SACRED TO THE MEMORY
OF
LIEUT. COLONEL
THOMAS SHADFORTH
COMMANDING 57TH REGIMENT
KILLED IN ACTION
JUNE 18TH 1855.

(Foot.)

(45.)   (Portland Stone.)

SACRED
TO THE MEMORY, OF
LIEUT HENRY TRYON
RIFLE BRIGADE
KILLED IN ACTION
ON THE 20th NOVEMBER
1854.

(Foot.)

(46.)   1 GRAVE.

(47.)

SACRED
✻ To The ✻
Memory
of
Capt A. W. FrASer 63rd Regt
who departed this Life
8th Decr
1855
May he Rest
in
Peace

(48.)

IN
Memory
of
CAPTAIN BINGHAM MULLER
2nd Battn Royal Regiment
KILLED IN THE ATTACK ON THE
QUARRIES ON THE 7TH JUNE 1855
THIS STONE IS ERECTED BY HIS
BROTHER
OFFICERS

R I P

(49.)

SACRED
TO THE
MEMORY
of
Bt MAJOR
G. N. HARRISON
63RD REGt
Killed
7th July
1855

(50.)

IN
MEMORY
OF
LIEUTT. WILLIAM BELLEW.
2ND BATTN ROYAL REGIMENT.
WHO DIED ON THE 16TH JUNE 1855.
OF WOUNDS RECEIVED IN THE ATTACK.
ON THE QUARRIES ON THE 7TH JUNE.

THIS STONE
IS ERECTED
BY HIS
BROTHER
OFFICERS

R I P

(51.)   (Marble.)

SACRED
TO THE MEMORY OF

LIEUT COL. E. S. T. SWYNY WHO
FELL ON THE 5TH NOVR '54 WHEN IN
COMD OF THE 63RD REGT AT THE
BATTLE OF INKERMAN.——ALSO
IN MEMORY OF LIEUT. G. C. W.
CURTOIS, ENSN H. T. TWYSDEN,
AND G. H. CLUTTERBUCK WHO
FELL IN THE SAME BATTLE—
THE TWO LAST WHILST CAR-
-RYING THE COLORS OF THE REG.
ALSO IN MEMORY OF Bt MAJOR
G.N.HARRISON WHO WAS KILLED
WHILST ON DUTY AT THE TREN
-CHES ON THE 7 JULY 1855.

(Foot.)

(52.)

IHS
BENEATH
REPOSES ALL THAT WAS MORTAL OF
THE
REVD. GERARD STRICKLAND
CATHOLIC CHAPLAIN OF THE
BRITISH ARMY IN THE EAST
HE DIED ON THE 22ND APRIL 1856
OF A MALIGNANT FEVER CAUGHT
WHILST VOLUNTARILY ATTENDING
THE SICK IN THE FRENCH HOSPITAL

MAY HIS PURE SPIRIT REST IN PEACE
AMEN

THIS SIMPLE MONUMENT WAS ERECTED
BY THE CATHOLIC OFFICERS AND SOLDIERS
OF THE 4TH DIVISION IN TESTIMONY OF THEIR
GRATITUDE FOR HIS SERVICES AMONG THEM
AND OF ADMIRATION OF HIS NOBLE
QUALITIES AND GREAT ZEAL

(53.)

⊕
Памятникъ

Капитану
Ну Брей Агарѣ Картрейту
по бата Мока Штуцзер пои
бригади убитъ при Инкерманѣ
5 Ноября 1854г.

TO THE MEMORY OF
AUBREY, AGAR, CARTWRIGHT ESQR
Captn In H.M. 1st Battn
Rifle, Brigade Killed at Inkerman
Novr 5th 1854.

EGLI IMPLORA, ETERNA, QUIETE

(Foot.)

(54.)   (Marble.)

IN MEMORY OF
CAPTN R. LLOYD EDWARDS
68th LIGHT INFANTRY
WHO WAS KILLED DURING
A SORTIE ON THE TRENCHES
BEFORE SEBASTOPOL
ON THE 11th MAY. 1855

(Foot.)

✝

(55.)

SACRED

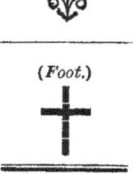

TO THE MEMORY
OF
CAPTN E. B. MAUNSELL
39TH REGT
KILLED IN THE TRENCHES
BEFORE SEBASTOPOL
ON THE 10TH JULY 1855.

ERECTED BY HIS BROTHER OFFICERS
IN TOKEN OF THEIR ESTEEM.

(Foot.)
+
E. B. M.

(Back.)

Чтите сию мои и ли
благо слое ле нимъ тѣ
которые у мератъ
въ Господѣ

CATHCART'S HILL.

(56.)   (Marble.)

SACRED TO THE MEMORY
OF
CAPTAIN ROWLAND AYNSWORTH FRAZER
42nd ROYAL HIGHLANDERS
KILLED IN THE TRENCHES
BEFORE SEBASTOPOL
16th JULY 1855.
ERECTED BY HIS BROTHER OFFICERS

(Foot.)

(57.)

XLI
SACRED TO THE MEMORY
OF
LT COLL J. EMAN, C.B
CAPTNS E. EVERY & J. LOCKHART
WHO FELL IN THE ASSAULT ON THE REDAN
8TH SEPTR 1855
Also
LT HARRIOT DIED OF WOUNDS
8TH DECR 1854
Died OF Sickness
SURGN ANDERSON 3rd JANY 1855
CAPTN JOHNSTON 9TH OCTR

(58.)   (Head.)

SACRED
TO THE MEMORY OF
CAPTAIN
DUNCOMBE BUCKLEY
SCOTS FUSILIER GUARDS
KILLED IN THE TRENCHES
6TH SEPTR
1855

(Slab.)
SACRED
TO THE MEMORY OF
DUNCOMBE FREDERICK BATT
BUCKLEY,
LIEUT. AND CAPTAIN IN THE
SCOTS FUSILIER GUARDS
WHO WAS KILLED IN THE TRENCHES
BEFORE SEVASTOPOL
6TH SEPTEMBER 1855.

ПОСВЯЩЕН О ПАМЯТИ
ДУНКОМБА ФРНДЕРИКА БАТЪ
БУКЛЕЯ
КАПИТАНА ШОТЛАНСКОЙ ГВАРДЕЙСКОЙ
ПѢХОТЫ
ПАДШАГО, ВЪ ТРАНШЕЯХЪ ПЕРЕДЪ
СЕВАСТОПОЛЕМЪ
6 СЕНТЯБРЯ
25 АВГУСТА 1855.

G. MAILE
NEW-ROAD LONDON

(59.)   STONE PILLAR.
(Front.)
TO
LIEUT COLL C. F. SEYMOUR
SCO FUSR GUARDS
KILLED IN ACTION
NOVR 5TH 1854

I H S

(Back.)

Σοῦτες
Ἐισωσοῦ να
εσωσικη

ΰβδιχ υε
ποκο
α τη ε ρε τηα χι

(Slab.)   (Marble.)
Beneath this stone lie the remains
of
LIEUTT COLL CHARLES FRANCIS SEYMOUR
of the Scots Fusilier Guards
Assistant Adjutant Genral of the Fourth Division
who fell at the Battle of Inkermann
Nov 5th 1854
By the side of his General
THE HONBLE SIR GEORGE CATHCART
on whose Staff he had long served
Aged 35 years

ВЪ ПАМЯТИ Б М Ч-
ХІ ЕСТВЕННАГО ПАДШАГО
ВЪ ЛПОЩ СПОРОВЪ

(Foot.)   (Marble.)
G. F. S
Ætat 35
FOY POUR DEVOIR

(60.)
SACRED
TO THE MEMORY OF
HUGH FITZHARDING DRUMMOND
BREVET-MAJOR & ADJUTANT
1ST BATTALION
SCOTS FUSILIER GUARDS
KILLED IN THE TRENCHES
BEFORE SEBASTOPOL
BY THE EXPLOSION OF A SHELL
ON THE 13TH AUGUST. 1855.
AGED 25 YEARS.

THIS STONE IS ERECTED
BY HIS SORROWING BROTHER OFFICERS
AS A TOKEN OF THEIR AFFECTION.

G. MAILE
NEW ROAD LONDON

(61.)

IN MEMORY
OF
Captain Richard Leigh Lye
20TH REGT
WHO DIED IN THIS CAMP
AGED 33
ON 10TH DECEMBER 1854.

(62.)   ПАМЯТНИКЪ
Поручику
А В. ТОЛФРЕЮ
ребята Мо на Штурерной:
Бригадиз би Л М Лоби Мни
треа жае Мтиъ споли
Умери при Лагерѣ
XXVII Ноября
1854 го года

Sacred to the memory of
A. W. GODFREY
Lieutenant 1ST Battn Rifle
Brigade Who died in Camp.
Novr 27 1854.
Beloved and Regretted by
All Who knew him.

(63.)   SACRED   (Marble.)
TO THE
MEMORY OF
Capta George Rochfort
49TH REGT
WHO WAS KILLED IN THE TRENCHES
DURING THE ATTACK
ON THE REDAN
ON THE
8TH SEPTR 1855

(64.)   Sacred   (Marble.)
TO THE
MEMORY OF
Lieut Christopher Michell
49TH REGT
WHO DIED ON THE 14TH SEPTEMBER 1855
OF WOUNDS RECEIVED
DURING THE ATTACK
ON
THE REDAN

(65.)   MONUMENT.
(Front.)
ERECTED BY THE OFFICERS
NON COMMISSIONED
OFFICERS AND MEN OF THE
1ST BTN RIFLE BRIGADE
TO THE MEMORY
OF THEIR COMRADES
7 OFFICERS 1 SERGT MAJOR
4 COLOR SERGEANTS
16 SERGEANTS
27 CORPORALS 4 BUGLERS
416 PRIVATES
WHO LOST THEIR LIVES IN THE
EASTERN CAMPAIGNS
1854, 55 & 56

(Right.)
KILLED
CAPTN A. A. CARTWRIGHT
5TH NOVR 1854
LIEUT H. TRYON
20TH NOVR 1854

(Rear.)
DIED OF WOUNDS
MAJOR. E. ROOPER
10TH NOVR 1854
LIEUT E. A. P. BOILEAU
1ST AUGUST 1855

(Left.)
DIED OF CHOLERA
LT. COL. S. BECKWITH
25TH SEPTR 1854
LIEUTT A. W. GODFREY
27TH NOVR 1854
ASSIST. SURGEON. J. A. SHORROCK
21ST SEPT. 1854

CATHCART'S HILL.

(66.)
SACRED
TO THE
MEMORY
OF
QUARTERMASTER. W. STILLWELL
OF THE BUFFS
WHO DIED IN CAMP
12 JUNE 1855

(67.)
To the
MEMORY
of
CAPTAIN CHARLES CORNWALLIS
ROSS. the BUFFS
who was killed in the trenches
before
SEBASTOPOL
31st August
1855

(68.)
IN MEMORY
OF
LIEUT JAS. B. DENNIS
"The Buffs"
WHO DIED 4TH OCTR
OF WOUNDS RECEIVED
IN THE TRENCHES BEFORE
SEBASTOPOL
19TH AUGST
1855

(69.) (Marble.)
SACRED TO THE MEMORY OF
STEPHEN REMNANT CHAPMAN
MAJOR XXTH REGT
ASSISTANT ENGINEER
DURING THE SIEGE OF
SEBASTOPOL
DIED 20TH SEPTEMBER 1855
FROM THE EFFECTS OF A WOUND
RECEIVED ON THE 8TH
AGED 30 YEARS

(70.)
SACRED
TO THE
MEMORY
OF
LIET F. PARR. H.M. XXth REGT
DIED
MARCH 25th 1855. AGED 19 YRS.

(71.)
SACRED
to the
MEMORY
of
J. H. CLUTTERBUCK
ENS 63rd REGT

(72.) (Marble)
SACRED
TO THE MEMORY OF
JOHN CROSBY VAUGHAN ESQRE
CAPTAIN IN HER MAJESTY'S
38th REGIMENT
WHO DIED, JUNE 16th 1855
OF A WOUND RECEIVED
IN THE TRENCHES
AGED 25 YEARS

(Foot.)

(73.) (Marble.)
IN MEMORY OF
LIEUT F. GROTE BARKER
68th LIGHT INFANTRY
KILLED AT THE BATTLE OF
INKERMAN
ON THE 5th NOVEMBER. 1854

(Foot.)

(74.) (Head.)

(Slab.)
SACRED
TO THE MEMORY OF
WALTER SIMPSON ESQRE
SURGEON 17TH REGT DIED
IN CAMP BEFORE SEBASTOPOL
31ST MAY. 1855.

(75.) (Head.)

(Slab.)
SACRED
TO
THE MEMORY OF
CAPTN J. L CROKER
17th Regt
WHO FELL IN ACTION
18TH JUNE 1855.

(76.)
SACRED
TO THE
MEMORY
OF
LIEUT S. J. SEAGRAM
17TH REGT
WHO DIED IN CAMP
ON THE 11TH OF MARCH
1856

(77.) *
SACRED
TO
THE MEMORY OF
CAPTAIN BOWLES
10TH HUSSARS
WHO DIED
IN THE CRIMEA
A.D. 1855

(78.) (Marble.)
IN MEMORY OF
LIEUT. JAMES MARSHALL
68th LIGHT INFANTRY
WHO WAS KILLED
IN THE TRENCHES
BEFORE SEBASTOPOL
ON THE 8th JUNE. 1855

(Foot.)

(79.) (Marble.)
IN MEMORY OF
ASST. SURGN. J. F. O'LEARY
68th LIGHT INFANTRY
KILLED IN THE TRENCHES
BEFORE SEBASTOPOL
ON THE 17th OCTOBER. 1854

(Foot.)

(80.) (Marble.)
IN MEMORY OF
LIEUT. HARRY E. SMYTH
68th LIGHT INFANTRY
WHO DIED AT BALACLAVA
ON THE 14th MARCH. 1855

(Foot.)

(81.) (Marble.)
IN MEMORY OF
MAJOR. HENEAGE. G. WYNNE
68th LIGHT INFANTRY
KILLED AT THE BATTLE OF
INKERMAN
ON THE 5th NOVEMBER 1854

(Foot.)

---

* This Officer died at Vernoutka, and was buried there under a tree, on the bark of which were cut his name, rank, age, and date of decease.

CATHCART'S HILL.

(82.)
SACRED
to the
MEMORY
OF
H. T. TWYSDEN. ESQ
ENS. 63rd REGt.

(83.)
TO THE
MEMORY
OF
LIEUT. OWEN. G. SAUNDERS. DAVIES
38th Regt
who fell in Action on the 18th June 1855
Erected
BY HIS BROTHER OFFICERS AS A TESTIMONY
of their
high
esteem

(84.)
SACRED
TO THE
MEMORY
OF
W. H. DOWLING Esqre
Lieut XX Regt
who was killed at Inkerman
5th November
1854

(85.)
SACRED
to the
MEMORY
of
Brevit Major THOMAS DAVIS
95th Regiment
who died in Camp before
Sebastapol
5th April 1855
Generally Beloved
And
Respected

(86.) (Marble.)
IN
MEMORY
OF
ACTING STAFF ASST. SURGEON
HARRY HARRISON
ATTACHED TO
95TH REGT.
who died in
Camp before
SEBASTOPOL
of Fever
contracted in the
discharge of his
Duties
ERECTED BY
the Officers of
95TH REGT.

(87.) (Marble.)
IN
MEMORY
OF
CAPTN. LIONEL FRASER
95TH REGT.
Who died from
a wound received
in the Trenches before
SEBASTOPOL
1ST SEPTR 1855

(88.) (Head.)
✝
SACRED
TO
THE MEMORY OF
CAPTAIN C. ANDERSON
OF THE 31ST REGIMENT
WHO WAS KILLED
IN THE TRENCHES
ON THE 5TH SEPTEMBER
1855
THIS STONE IS ERECTED
BY HIS BROTHER OFFICERS

(Foot.)
(Front.)
SACRED
TO THE
MEMORY OF
CAPTAIN C. ANDERSON 31ST REGT. WHO
WAS KILLED IN THE TRENCHES WHILST
ACTING AS ASSISTANT ENGINEER
ON THE
5TH SEPTEMBER 1855.

(Back.)
ERECTED BY THE
OFFICERS OF ROYAL ENGINEERS AS
A TOKEN OF THEIR ESTEEM.

(89.)
✝
SACRED
TO
THE MEMORY OF
CAPTAIN F. SIMES. ATTREE
OF THE 31ST REGIMENT
WHO WAS KILLED
IN THE TRENCHES
ON THE 8TH SEPTEMBER 1855
AGED 27 YEARS
THIS STONE IS ERECTED BY
HIS BROTHER OFFICERS BY
WHOM HE WAS BELOVED AND
RESPECTED

(Foot.)
IHS

(90.)
SACRED TO THE MEMORY
of
CAPTAIN
J. C. N. STEVENSON
30TH REGIMENT
Killed in Action 8TH Septr
1855
ERECTED BY HIS BROTHER
OFFICERS

(91.)
SACRED
IHS
to the memory
of
LIEUTENANT COLONEL
JAMES BRODIE PATTULLO. C.B
30th Regiment. Who died of WOUNDS
received on the 8th of September. 1855
at the Assault on the Great Redan

This Monument was erected to him
by his Brother Officers

(92.) (Head) (Portland Stone.)
ihs

(Foot.) (Portland Stone.)
✝
Richd Grenville Deane
Ensign 30th Regt
Fell Septr 8 1855
Aged 18 Years

Jesu, mercy;

(93.)
IHS
* A. E. ROWLEY
LIEUT AND CAPTAIN
GRENAdIER GUARdS
KILLED OcToBER 16
1854
ST JOHN XI 25, 26

(94.) (Portland Stone.)
SACRED TO THE MEMORY OF
✝
† VALENTINE BENNETT ESQRE
LIEUT IN THE 33RD REGT.
WHO FELL BEFORE SEBASTOPOL IN
THE ATTACK ON THE REDAN
OF THE 18TH JUNE 1855
AGED 27

HE ASKED LIFE OF THEE & THOU HAST
GIVEN HIM LENGTH OF DAYS FOR
EVER AND EVER Psalm xx. 5
✝
MAY HE REST IN PEACE

---

* The Stone designated, happening to be lying about, was placed over this grave just previous to the evacuation of the Crimea, but does not properly belong to it—*vide* No. 8 Tomb, page 44.

† Although a Monument is placed here to this Officer, he was not buried on the spot (*vide* Tomb 22, page 3), nor were some others—viz. Captains Layard, King, &c. (Tombs 1 and 26, 15 and 2, pages 44 and 46, 37 and 42). The remains of several Officers were also sent home at the request of their friends—viz. those of Captain Pechell, 77th Regiment, Tomb 36, Page 9; and Brigadier-General Tylden, R.E., who died of cholera, 22nd Sept. 1854, and was first buried at Alma; also Lieut. Dawson, R.A., who died at the Castle Hospital, Balaklava, of wounds received at the Inkermann explosion, 15th Nov. 1855. The bodies of Capt. Crofton, 77th, and Lieut.-Colonel Alexander, R.E., were removed to their present resting-places (*vide* Tombs 33 and 2, pages 8 and 16); and those of eight Officers of the Coldstream Guards (Tomb 11, page 45) conveyed from Inkermann.

CATHCART'S HILL—MALAKOFF—YENIKALE.

(95.) *(Marble.)*

TO THE MEMORY OF
CAPT. WILLIAM FREDERICK. A. ROOKE
47th REGIMENT
MAJOR OF BRIGADE 2nd BRIGADE 2nd DIVISION
OF WESTWOOD HOUSE, ESSEX,
WHO DIED OCTOBER 1st 1855
AGED 30 YEARS
OF A WOUND RECEIVED AT THE ATTACK
UPON THE REDAN SEPR. 8

This stone was erected by his brother Officers

(Foot.)

(96.) MONUMENT.
(Front.)

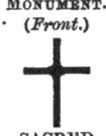

SACRED
TO
the MEMORY of
the
Officers XXX Regt
who fell or Died
in the Campaign
in the Crimea
1854 & 1855.

(Right.)
Lieut F. LUXMORE,
Killed at Alma 20th Sepr 1854
Captn A. W. CONOLLY
and Lieut A. GIBSON.
Killed at Inkerman 5th Novr 1854
Lieut J. D. ROSSLEWIN.
Died of wounds at Inkerman 7th Novr 1854. and
Engn J. THOMPSON.
at Balaklava 10th Novr 1854
Lieut & Adjt J. FORBES
Died of wounds 1st Sepr 1855
Ensn R. G. DEANE
Killed at the Assault of the Redan 8th Sepr 1855.

(Left.)
LT Col. J. B. PATTULLO
Died of wounds 9th Sepr 1855

Captn J. C. N. STEVENSON
Killed in Action 8th Sepr
& LIEUT W. KERR
23rd Sepr 1855.

Ensn W. Y. JOHNSTONE
Died of Cholera at the Belbec on the 25th Sepr

LT Col. W. F. HOEY
at Balaklava on the 29th Sepr 1854 &

Ensn T. M. FITZPATRICK
in Camp before Sebastopol 26th June 1855.

(Rear.)

THIS
Monument was
ERECTED
by
their Brother Officers
April 1856

Cathcart's Hill Cemetery was originally a square earthwork, afterwards converted into the 4th Division Burial Ground, but eventually, in cases where it was practicable, most Officers were buried there, with the exception of those belonging to the Cavalry, Royal Engineers, Light Division, and, we might almost add, the Artillery and Navy.

MALAKOFF.

(Wooden Cross.)

8
SEPTEMBRE
1855

Unis pour la Victoire.   Du Soldat c'est la Gloire
Réunis par la Mort.   Des Braves c'est le Sort

YENIKALE.
NEAR CHURCH

NUMBER OF TOMBSTONES—5.

(1.)
J. H. GILBORNE
Assist. Surgeon
*71 H. L. I
Died Janry 23rd 1856
Aged 22 Years
erected by his regiment.

(2.)

IN MEMORY OF
ROBERT BOXALL, Esqre
Surgeon
Anglo - Turkish
Contingent

Erected by his Sister
1856

(3.)

ROBERT HUNTER
MAJOR
71 H. L. I.
died Octr 30th 1855
Aged 40 years

* Arrived at Yenikale from before Sebastopol 24th May 1855; Embarked at Kertch for Malta 22nd June 1855.

E. Walker, lith.

Turkish Cemetery

London, Published by Ackermann & Co 106 Strand W.C.

SCUTARI.

British Burial Ground

Day & Son, Lith.rs to The Queen.

SCUTARI.

NUMBER OF GRAVES AND PITS—743.

LEFT OF BURIAL GROUND
(LOOKING FROM THE SEA.)

(1.) Sacred *(Marble.)*
TO THE MEMORY OF
ANN CLIFFORD
DIED 29TH SEPTR 1854
AGED 31 YRS
The above is a tribute of esteem
to a devoted Wife, from an
affectionate Husband
of the 50th Queen's own Regiment.

(2.) *(Front.)* *(Marble.)*
WILLIAM FREDERICK VISCOUNT CHEWTON

(Back.)
(Coronet.)
SACRED
TO THE MEMORY OF
WILLIAM FREDERICK VISCOUNT CHEWTON
ELDEST SON OF THE EARL WALDEGRAVE
CAPTN SCOTS FUSILIER GUARDS
WHO DIED AT SCUTARI THE 8TH OF OCTOBER 1854
AGED 38
OF WOUNDS RECEIVED IN ACTION
WHILST GALLANTLY LEADING ON HIS MEN
AT THE MEMORABLE
BATTLE OF THE ALMA
20TH SEPTEMBER 1854
THIS TABLET IS ERECTED
BY HIS SORROWING WIDOW

(3.) SACRED *(Marble.)*
TO
THE MEMORY OF
LIEUTENANT
T. W. WOLLOCOMBE
47th REGIMENT
Who died at Scutari on the 7th Octr 1854
of Wounds received at the Battle of the
ALMA

(4.) SACRED
TO
THE MEMORY
OF
MARY. F. S. FINNERTY
47th REGIMENT
Who died at Scutari
7th SEPTEMBER 1855
AGED 6 MONTHS

(5.) *(Marble.)*
Æ XXIII

HARRY GEORGE TEESDALE LIEUT ROYAL ENGINEERS SON OF COL. H. G. TEESDALE R.H.A. WOUNDED AT ALMA DIED AT SCUTARI OCT. XII. MDCCCLIV

(6.) SACRED
To the MEMORY of
Honble GREY NEVILLE
5th Dragoon Guards
Youngest Son of Lord
Braybrooke
DIED at Scutari Novr 1854
Of Wounds Received at
Balaklava 25th Octr
1854 AGED 24 YEARS
Surviving by only Six days
his Brother The Honble HENRY
NEVILLE Grenadier Guards
Killed at Inkerman 5th Novr
1854.—To the dear Memory of
those so loved and early
lost their Sorrowing Family
inscribe this STONE

(7.) ✝ *(Marble.)*

SACRED
TO THE MEMORY
OF
LIEUT J. HOLFORD
M.M. 28TH REGIMENT
DIED 29TH NOVEMBER 1854

ERECTED BY A FRIEND.

(8.) Sacred *(Marble.)*
TO THE MEMORY OF
LT and ADJT ARTHUR DILLON MAULE
88TH CONAT RANGERS
Who died at Scutari 14th Novbr /54
From the effects of Wounds received
In the Trenches before Sebastopol
ON THE 26TH OCTOBR 54
This Monument
is Erected by his Brother Officers
As a mark of their Esteem
and affection

(9.) S M AUG F C WEBB CAPT XVII LANCERS WOUNDED AT BALACLAVA OCTR 25TH DIED AT SCUTARI NOVTH 6 1854 AGED XXII

(10.) SACRED *(Marble.)*
TO THE MEMORY OF
LIEUT COLONEL HARRY SMITH
68TH LIGHT INFANTRY
WHO DIED AT SCUTARI ON THE 28TH
NOVEMBER, 1854, OF A WOUND RECEIVED
AT THE BATTLE OF INKERMANN

(11.) Erected *(Marble.)*
As a mark of respect & esteem
by his Brother Officers to the
Memory of the Lt Coln George
Ainslie 21st Royal British
Fusiliers who died at Scutari
on the 14th Novr 1854 Age 45 Years
from a wound received when
leading on the right wing of
his Regt. at the Battle of Inkermn
on the 5th November 1855

(12.) SAC RED *(Marble.)*
TO The Memory of
TOOSEY WILLIAMS
ROYAL SCOTS GREYS
Who DIED Novr 23rd
1854
I Am Thine Save Me
PSAm cxix. 94
From His Sincere Friend
C. H. LINDSAY
Grenr Guards

(13.) SACRED *(Marble.)*
TO THE MEMORY OF
DAVID ANDERSON
STAFF ASSISTANT SURGEON
NATIVE OF DUMFRIES
Who died
at Scutari of Cholera
on the 4th November 1854
AGED   YEARS

(14.) IN MEMORY OF *(Marble.)*
CAPTAIN ARTHUR THISTLETHWAYTE
SCOTS FUSILIER GUARDS
WHO EXPIRED AT
SCUTARI BARRACK HOSPITAL
THE 26th of NOVEMBER 1854
BELOVED AND RESPECTED

(15.) S. M. *(Marble.)*
R. H. PAYNE CRAWFARD
CAPTAIN H. B. M. XC REG
DIED AT SCUTARI
FEB 24 1855

(16.) SACRED *(Marble.)*
TO THE MEMORY OF
STAFF SURGEON G. HUME READE
WHO DEPARTED THIS LIFE
the 28th NOVr 1854
AGED 61 YEARS

This Monument is Erected By His
Afflicted Wife and Children

SCUTARI.

(17.) Sacred
To the MEMORY of
THOMAS· KYD. MORGAN
Lieutenant H M 63rd Reg^t
Second Son of James Morgan
of the City of Edinburgh
IN SCOTLAND
Who DIED at Scutari 11th Dec^r
1854 of Wounds received
in the Battle of
INKERMANN
AGED 19

ERECTED
by an affectionate Mother
in Commemoration of a most
dearly beloved Son

(18.) Sacred (Marble.)
To the memory of
Lt Colonel J. G Champion 95th Reg^t
who died at Scutari Hospital on the
30th November, 1854 from a wound received
while gallantly commanding his Regim^t
at the Battle of Inkerman on the 5th Ins^t

He ever proved himself a thorough Gentle-
man and brave Soldier.

(19.) SACRED (Marble.)
TO
THE MEMORY
OF
GEORGE HENRY HUGHES
CAPTAIN
23rd ROYAL WELSH FUSILIERS
Who was compelled to retire from
the fatigues of the Siege of
SEBASTOPOL
by illness of which he died at
Constantinople
11th DECEMBER 1854
AGED 28 Years
THIS STONE IS ERECTED BY HIS
BROTHER OFFICERS

(20.) SACRED
TO THE MEMORY
OF
LIEU^T HUGH CHARLES HARRIOTT
41ST REGT
who died at Scutari on the
8TH DECEMBER 1854
of a Wound received when Command-
ing the Light Company of his
Regiment in the Action of the
26TH OCTOBER 1854
BEFORE SEBASTOPOL
AGED YEARS
ERECTED BY HIS BROTHER OFFICERS

(21.) SACRED (Marble.)
TO THE MEMORY OF THOMAS MATTHEW HOPKINS
1ST OFFICER OF THE STEAM SHIP ADELAIDE
DIED 18st MARCH 1855 OF FEVER TAKEN WHILST
IN DISCHARGE OF HIS DUTY ON A VOYAGE FROM
THE CRIMEA
WITH INVALIDS
AGED 35 Y^{RS}

(22.) SACRED (Marble.)
TO
The MEMORY Of
Joseph Long 4th Comp^y
Royal Sappers & Miners
Who DIED March 21st 1855
AGED 25 YEARS
I Am Thine Save Me

Erected by a Comrade

(23.) SACRED (Marble.)
To the
Memory of
JAMES INGLIS COCHRAN
of the Commissariat Staff
who Died
on the
20th Dec^r
1855
Aged 23 y^{rs}

(24.) HARVEY LUDLOW (Marble.)
F. R. C. S.
DIED
4 APRIL 1855
AGED 28

(25.) SOPHIA BARNES (Marble.)
NURSE
4 APRIL 1855

(26.) Sophia Walford (Marble.)
Matron
Barrack hospital
Scutari
Entered into rest
30th Aug. 1855
Aged 46
She hath done what she could

(27.) SACRED TO THE MEMORY
OF R. SIMONS—AGE 22
ACT SURGEON WHO DIED OF
FEVER AT SCUTARI APRIL 28
1855.

(28.) DR. JAMES. A. WISHART
STAFF SURGEON
DIED 25TH MAY 1855
AGED 33
WITH CHRIST WHICH IS FAR BETTER P^H 121, 23
THY BROTHER SHALL RISE AGAIN JOHN 11, 23
ERECTED BY HIS SISTER

(29.) (Marble.)
TO THE MEMORY OF
NATHANIEL EVANSON HARRISON
L^T COLONEL COMM^G R.A
4TH DIVISION
OF THE BRITISH ARMY BEFORE SEBASTOPOL
DIED 12TH AUGUST 1855 AGED 42 YEARS
DEEPLY REGRETTED BY ALL WHO KNEW HIS
MANLY AND CHRISTIAN CHARACTER
AND BY THE SERVICE TO WHICH HE BELONGED
FIGHT THE GOOD FIGHT
1ST TIMOTHY. 6 CH. 12 V.

(30.) (Marble.)
The dead
Shall be raised
Reverend
henry John Whitfield
June 18. 1855

(31.) CAP^N F BELSON R.E
DIED
14 AUG^T 1855
AGED
28 YEARS

(32.) LIEU^T WILLIAM
MEREDYTH SOMERVILLE
R.E
Died at Scutari
3rd Sepr 1855 aged 20
His Illness was
Contracted in the
Trenches before
Sebastopol

(33.) SACRED TO THE MEMORY
OF
CHARLES HENRY BECK
LIEU^T 23D ROYAL WELSH FUSILIERS
WHO DIED 29TH SEPT^R 1855
OF WOUNDS RECEIVED 8TH SEPT^R 1855
AT THE ASSAULT ON THE REDAN
SEBASTOPOL
AGED 19 YEARS

THIS STONE IS PLACED
BY HIS BROTHER OFFICERS

(34.)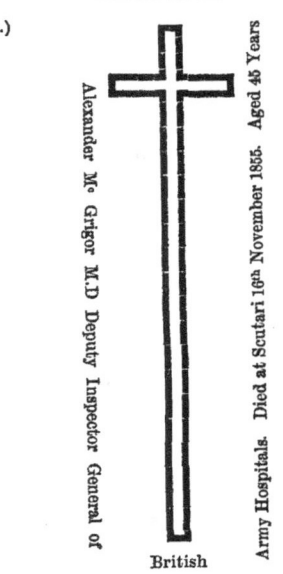
Alexander Mc Grigor M.D Deputy Inspector General of Army Hospitals. Died at Scutari 16th November 1855. Aged 45 Years
British

(35.) SACRED
TO THE MEMORY OF
TERENCE H. WALL
ASS^T SURGEON OF
H. M. S LEOPARD
DIED AT CONSTANTINOPLE
DEC^R 16TH 1855
A TRIBUTE OF FRIENDSHIP

(36.) SACRED TO THE MEMORY
of
HENRY CROFTON SINGER LIEU^T R.A
AGED 26 YEARS
WHO WAS KILLED IN A COLLISION
AT SEA OCTOBER 2nd 1854
ON HIS RETURN FROM THE CRIMEA
INVALIDED
THIS MONUMENT IS ERECTED BY
HIS FATHER JOSEPH HENDERSON SINGER
BISHOP of MEATH

(37.) SACRED
TO
THE MEMORY OF
W. L. MACNISH
LIEU^T 93^d HIGHLANDERS
Who Was Drowned
at
Scutarie May 19th 1854
THIS TABLET
WAS ERECTED
By his Brother OFFICERS

SCUTARI.

(38.)   SACRED   (*Wood.*)
TO THE MEMORY OF
SUSAN Mc DERMOTT WIFE
TO G. J. Mc DERMOTT 88TH REGT
WHO DEPARTED THIS LIFE SEPT 28TH
1854 AT SCUTARI BKS AGED 27 YEARS

(39.)   SACRED   (*Wood.*)
To The
MEMORY
of
George Coombs
Late Fireman
P. O & Coy Steam Ship
RIPON
died 22nd Decemr 1854
Aged 23 Years
May he rest in peace

(40.)   SACRED   (*Marble.*)
TO THE MEMORY OF
MAJOR. J. B. SHARPE 20TH REGIMENT
WHO DIED AT SCUTARI
28TH DECR 1854
OF WOUNDS RECEIVED AT THE
BATTLE OF INKERMAN

(41.)   MAJR C. S. GLAZBROOK
49TH REGT OF FOOT
DIED AT SCUTARI
THE 18th DECEMBER 1854
OF WOUNDS RECEIVED
BEFORE SEBASTOPOL
ON THE 17TH NOVr 1854

(42.)   Sacred to the Memory
OF
LUCAS WARD ESQRE
PURVEYOR TO THE FORCES
WHO DIED
AT
SCUTARI JANy 1ST 1855
AFTER SERVING HIS COUNTRY 46 YEARS
ALSO
To the Memory of
JANE WARD
WIFE OF THE ABOVE
WHO DIED AT THE SAME PLACE
JANy 3RD 1855
THIS MONUMENT WAS ERECTED BY
THE MEMBERS OF HIS DEPARTMENT AS
A TRIBUTE OF ESTEEM AND RESPECT
FOR AN OLD AND FAITHFUL PUBLIC OFFICER

(43.)   To the Memory of
CAPTAIN JOHN WARREN 55TH REGT
Born 23rd June 1831 at Fort St George
East India Died 22nd December 1854
on Board the Steamer Victoria
off Constantinople—He was present
at the Battles of ALMA 20th Septr 1854
where he was wounded. INKERMAN
on the 26th Octr & again on the 5th Nov/54
On all these occasions he distinguished
himself—His Death was the result of
Fever brought on by over exertion after
the last Battle of INKERMAN when
doing duty as Adjutt of his Regiment

(44.)
DEDICATED BY HIS BROTHER OFFICERS
TO THE MEMORY OF
WILLIAM PITCAIRN CAMPBELL
AGED 30
MAJOR 23RD ROYAL WELSH FUSILIERS
WOUNDED ON THE ALMA
HE WAS APPOINTED A STAFF OFFICER AT SCUTARI
AND DIED THERE OF FEVER MARCH 22ND 1855
A CHRISTIAN SOLDIER
FINDING COMFORT IN DEATH FROM THESE ASSURING
WORDS OF THE SAVIOUR IN WHOM HE TRUSTED

COME UNTO ME ALL YE THAT LABOUR AND ARE
HEAVY LADEN AND I WILL GIVE YOU REST
MAT 11TH CHAP. 28TH VERSE

(45.)   SACRED   (*Marble.*)
TO THE MEMORY OF
WILLIAM RICHARD NEWPORT CAMPBELL
CAPTAIN 5TH DRAGOON GUARDS
WHO DIED AT SCUTARI
ON THE 23RD DECEMBER 1854
HAVING SERVED IN THE ACTIONS OF PUNNIAR
SOBRAON, CHILLIANWALLAH, GOOJERAT
AND BALACLAVA
HE FELL A V VICTIM TO
THE HARDSHIPS AND PRIVATIONS
OF THE CRIMEAN CAMPAIGN

THIS TABLET
IS ERECTED BY HIS SORROWING MOTHER
T. GAFFIN
REGENT ST. LONDON

(46.) SACRED TO THE MEMORY OF
MAJOR ROBERT WILLIAM COLVILL
LATE OF HER MAJESTY'S 97TH REGIMENT
YIELDING TO THE SEVERITY
OF A WINTER CAMPAIGN
WITH THE ALLIED ARMY BEFORE
SEVASTOPOL
HE DIED ON THE PASSAGE FROM
BALAKLAVA TO THE HOSPITAL AT SCUTARI
ON THE 2ND JANUARY 1855
AGED 42 YEARS
CHEERFULLY TERMINATING HIS LIFE
IN HIS COUNTRY'S SERVICE

A BEREAVED AND SORROWING SISTER
HAS ERECTED THIS TOMB AS A FAINT
MEMORIAL OF HIS PRIVATE WORTH
AND EXCELLENCE

(47.)   SACRED
TO THE MEMORY OF
ASST SURGEON ALEXANDER STRUTHERS M.D
DIED AT SCUTARI 20 JANUARY

(48.)   SACRED
TO THE MEMORY
OF
FREDERICK. A. MACARTNEY
Staff Asst Surgeon
WHO DIED AT SCUTARI
FEBRUARY 12th 1855
AGED 22 YEARS
Jesus Saith I Am The Resurrection and
The Life. He that Believeth in me though
He were dead, yet Shall he Live.

(49.)   In Memory
of
John Grabnam
Asst Surgeon 71st Regt
who died at
Scutari
February 16th A.D. 1855
Aged 24 Years

(50.)   S. M
REVD GEOR HENRY PROCTOR
CHAPLAIN H. M. F
SON OF GEOR PROCTOR D.D
RECTOR OF HADLEY
WHO DIED AT SCUTARI
MARCH 10TH 1855
AGED 34 YEARS
HIS PARENTS HAVE PLACED
THIS STONE

(51.)   SACRED
TO THE MEMORY OF
V. MACKESY ESQR 63RD REGT
SON OF J. L. MACKESEY M.D OF
WATERFORD WHO DIED
ON THE 7TH MARCH 1855
AGED 24 YEARS
HE WAS A ZEALOUS SOLDIER
AND DEEPLY REGRETTED BY THE
OFFICERS AND MEN OF HIS CORPS

(52.)   IN MEMORY OF
EDMUND SIDNEY MASON ESQRE M.D
ASSISTANT SURGEON 13TH REGT LIGHT INFTY
ONLY SON OF EDMUND SIDNEY MASON ESQRE
LATE OF MERTON HALL WIGTONSHIRE WHO DIED
IN THE HOSPITAL AT SCUTARI WHILST ACTIVELY
AND FAITHFULLY DISCHARGING HIS TOO
ARDUOUS PROFESSIONAL DUTIES
FEBRUARY 8TH
1855

(53.)   SACRED
TO THE MEMORY
of
PRIVATE JOHN BRUCE
13 Light Dragoons
WHO
Departed This Life
The 9TH OF MARCH 1855
Aged 33 Years
ERECTED
By His Affectionate Wife

(54.)   (*Marble.*)
(IRON RAILING ROUND GRAVE.)
(*Head.*)
TO THE MEMORY OF
THE HONBLE JOHN WILLIAM
HELY HUTCHINSON
CAPTN 13TH LIGHT DRAGOONS
WHO DIED AT SCUTARI
JULY 2ND 1855 AGED 25
THIS STONE IS ERECTED BY
HIS BROTHER OFFICERS

(*Foot.*)
"HE THAT BELIEVETH IN THE SON
HATH LIFE EVERLASTING"
JOHN-3-36

(55.)

ARTHUR FERDINAND
PLATT
49TH REGt
11th August 1855
Aged 20

(56.)   John Herring Whitwell
of Peterborough England

Born Mar. 15. 1832
Died Sept. 2. 1855

SCUTARI.

(57.) In memory of
Henry Arthur Wight Esq'
Lieut 6th Dragoon Guards
Eldest Son of the late
Arthur Wight Esq'
Major 23rd Regt B.N.I
of Brabonf Manor, near Guildford
Surrey. On his passage to England
For the recovery of his health
He was too ill to proceed, and
He departed this life
On the 23rd September 1855
Aged 19
In Scutari Hospital
His loss is deeply
Lamented by his family
And friends.

(58.) To the Memory of
Mary Marks
Nurse
died at the Palace Hospital
Scutari
Oct 8 1855
aged 47

(59.) (Broken Column.)
(Top.)
MAJOR
Lv. LETTGAu
CaPT. A. HACKE
DR. F. KEITEL
Lieut. P. GOBEL
Ens F. ZISCHKA

E. Serj: FLEMMING. Jgr GÄNSLER
C. GESTERDING. A. LUDWIG.
G. SPIELKER. G. KOCH. A. HESSE
F. EGGERT. W. FREESE. G. ENGELL

G. FEYROHR. H. KÖHLER
C. STOBBEy. W. KNuTH
H. POHMOLLER
H MEYER

(Bottom.)
F. KOCH
W. MÜHLENBERG

H. VAuKATH. L. RÄTZER
H. BARTELS — C. RuHLICH
F. WARCKENTHIN. F. GOLLIN
G. HEILMANN. L. BURCKHARDT
—●—
GESTORBEN-ZU-SCUTARI
1855.

(Rear.)
ERRICHTET
ZUR
ERINNERuNG
ANDIE
SEIT. DER. EINSCHIFFuNG
VON. ENGLAND. GESTORBENEN
KAMERADEN
VOM
1sten Jager = Corps
B. G. L

(60.) SACRED (Wood.)
TO THE MEMORY OF
JAMES SMITH
CARPENTER
WHO DEPARTED THIS
LIFE
IN HIS 22D YEAR
NOV. 23D 1855
A Tribute of Friendship

(61.) *Died at Palace Hospital
* CHARLOTTE MOORE
Hyder Pasha 22nd Novr. 1855

(62.)
✝
FANNY Y. A. M. BIRT
Died Sept 2nd 1855
aged 3 years

(63.) SACRED (Wood.)
TO
The MEMORY Of
Pt Michael Walsh 33rd Regt
DIED 11th Jany 1855
AGED
29 YEARS

(64.) SACRED
TO THE MEMORY
OF ALFRED HENRY CHERRY ESQr.
VETy SURGEON ROYAL DRAGOONS
WHO DIED AT SCUTARI
ON THE 7TH MARCH 1856
AGED 30 YEARS

(65.) IN (Wood.)
MEMORY
OF
JOHN PATTISON
ENGINEER, STEAM
TRNSPORT, ANDES
WHO DIED OF TYPHUS
FEVER IN THE
HOSPITAL OF SCUTARI
DEC 30TH 1855
AGED 37 YEARS

(66.) † (Front,)
To the Memory
of
Lieut. Montagu Wigley Bell
Lieut. Josiah Holford and
Quarter Master Samuel Spence
Who died during the Campaigns
of 1854 and 1855
This Cross is Erected
By Their
Brother Officers
of H. B. M.'s
Twenty-eigth Regiment
1856.

(Rear.)
Also
To the Memory
of the
Non Commissioned Officers
And Privates of H. B. M's
Twenty-eigth Regiment
Who died during the Campaigns
of 1854 and 1855
Before Sebastopol
May they rest in Peace
1856.

RIGHT OF BURIAL GROUND
(LOOKING FROM THE SEA.)

(67.) WILLIAM MURTA (Wood.)
92ND REGT.

(68.)
✝
SACRED
TO THE MEMORY OF
TRUMPET MAJOR FRANCIS JOHNSON
12TH ROYAL LANCERS
WHO DEPARTED THIS LIFE
ON THE 22ND DECR 1855
IN THE 35TH YEAR OF HIS AGE
THIS STONE WAS ERECTED BY
THE NON. COMMISSIONED OFFICERS
OF THE 13TH LIGHT DRAGOONS
AS A MARK OF
RESPECT

(69.) SACRED
TO THE MEMORY OF
CAPTAIN H. E. SMITH
OF THE SHIP CHALMERS
WHO DEPARTED THIS LIFE
21ST JUNE 1855
AGED 51 YEARS
THE LORD GAVE, AND
THE LORD HATH TAKEN
AWAY BLESSED BE THE
NAME OF THE LORD

(70.) SACRED
TO
THE MEMORY OF
CHARLES PLATT
LATE STEWARD
OF THE HAREM HOSPITAL
DIED
22ND MAY 1855

AGED 29 YEARS

PREPARE TO MEET THY GOD

(Foot.)
C. P
22ND MAY 1855

(71.) IN ✠ RI
Sacred
To The Memory of
"Henry Abernethy"
Stoker "Great Britain" Steam Ship
Who departed this life 17th July 1855
Aged 50 Years
May he rest in peace
His Shipmates last token of Friendship

(72.) SACRED
TO
THE MEMORY
of
SERJT J. COOPER
33rd REGT WHO DEPED
THIS LIFE 19TH JULY
1855 IN THE 26TH YEAR
OF SHIS AGE
E
STAY POPLE AS YOU PASS BY,

AS YOU ARE NOW—SO ONCE WAS
I, AND AS I AM NOW, SO, WILL
YOU BE, PREPARE FOR DEATH,
AND FOLLOW ME,
THIS TOMB IS ERECTED BY HIS
BROTHER NON COMD OFFICERS.
AS A MARK OF ESTEEM & RESPECT
TOWARDS HIM
D, A, T

---

* Widow of Lt. Col. Moore, 6th (Inniskilling) Dragoons, who lost his life by fire in the "Europa" Transport.
† Placed after the evacuation of the Crimea and Scutari by the British troops.

SCUTARI.

(73.) FELIM PATRICK BYRNE
BORN IN THE
CONNAUGHT RANGERS
DIED AUGUST 16TH 1855
AGED 7 MONTHS
REQUIESCANT IN PACE

(74.) Sacred to the Memory
of
P. Frederick Litchfield 49th Regt
Who departed this life on 2 April 1855
Aged 27 Years
This Tablet was erected
by his beloved and affec-
-tionate Wife

(75.) SACRED
TO
THE MEMORY OF
SERJT JOHN BAILES
33RD REGIMENT
WHO DIED AT THE GENL HOSPL
16TH NOVR 1855
AGED 39 YEARS

BLESSED ARE THE DEAD
THAT DIE IN THE LORD

(76.)

SACRED
TO THE MEMORY
OF ALEXR. HAMILTON SERGT R.A
WHO DIED OF CHOLERA ON THE 20TH
OF NOVEMBER 1855
AGED 31 YEARS
BELOVED BY ALL WHO KNEW HIM
THIS STONE WAS ERECTED
BY HIS AFFECTIONATE WIFE WHO IS
LEFT TO LAMENT HIS LOSS

AT LEFT OF BURIAL GROUND
(LOOKING FROM THE SEA.)

Pieces of wood designating the persons interred were in some cases temporarily placed at the head of the Graves for the purpose of marking the spot, in the expectation of proper tombstones being erected at a future period.—The following were still standing on the 15th of July, 1856.

(A.) A Russian Offr.
(B.) A RUSSIAN GENL
(C.) A RUSSIAN OFFR
(D.) LIEUT HOUGHTON—11 H—
(E.) A Russian Officer
(F.) A RUSSIAN OFFR
(G.) DR BROWN
(H.) A WOMAN
(J.) MAJOR SORELL 81ST REGT
(K.) MR WM PEAKE ORD DEPT
(L.) DR COMPTON
(M.) * A RUSSIAN GENL
(N.) DR MACKEY
(O.) W. SAUNDERS DEPT PROVT MARL
(P.) A CARPENTER
(Q.) MR BROWN COMY DEPT
(R.) REVD MR LEE
    (*Underneath in Pencil*)
    Thomas Onien
(S.) TO THE MEMORY OF STAFF ASST SURGEON
    H. W. WOOD
(T.) ENS VON CISKA. GERMAN LEGION
(U.) MISS M. CLOUGH
(V.) DOCTOR MAYNE
(W.) LIEUT †(Goebel) GERMAN LEGION
(X.) JAMES †(Goeken) COMMISTRIAT CLERK
(Y.) SACRED TO THE MEMORY OF
    DISPENSER J. BEVERIDGE
(Z.) DOCTOR KEITEL GERMAN LEGION
(Z¹.) CHARLOTTE BARKER
    DAUGHTER OF W. B. BARKER
    LAND TRANSPORT CORPS

ON FIELD OF INGOUR, GEORGIA
(220 YARDS FROM LEFT BANK OF RIVER)

CAPTAIN
‡ FREDERICK HENRY DYMOCK
95TH REGIMENT
Aide-de-Camp To
Lieut. Col. Simmons R.E
Qceen's Commissioner
with the Turkish Army under
His Highness Omar Pasha
KILLED IN ACTION
6TH NOVR 1855

---

* Tombstone subsequently erected.   † Written in pencil.
‡ This Officer was buried the same day between two trees, a canopy of hanging vines overhead.

E. Walker, lith.

London, Published by Ackermann & C° 106 Strand W.C.

Day & Son, Lith's to The Queen

MODELS OF PRINCIPAL MONUMENTS IN THE CRIMEA AND AT SCUTARI.
MADE OF INKERMANN STONE, AND PRESENTED TO HER MAJESTY THE QUEEN AT OSBORNE.
Scale ½ inch to a Foot, except N°s 3, 10, & 14, which are 1 inch

	N°	Page		N°	Page		N°	Page		N°	Page
1	Battle of Balaklava	—	41	8	18th Royal Irish	27	46	15	Royal Marines (Light Infantry)	1	39	22	Major Genl Sir J. Campbell, Bart.	40	47
2	Royal Artillery	24	46	9	Royal Sappers & Miners	18, 17	16	44th Regiment	28, 46	23	Redan Obelisk	—	30
3	Capt. Sir F. Newman, Bart.	5, 44	10	Lieut Somerville, R.E.	32, 54	17	Land Transpt & Army Works Corps	3, 31	24	1st Brigade, Light Division	1	1
4	90th Light Infantry		11	Lt Genl Honble Sir G. Cathcart K.C.B	42, 47	18	Brigr Genl Fox Strangways R.A.	41, 47	25	8. Officers Coldstream Guards.	11, 45
5			12			19			26		

No. 14.—Average Strength of the several Divisions (before Sebastopol) of the British Army during the months specified below.

	November, 1854.	December, 1854.	January, 1855.	February, 1855.	March, 1855.
1st Division	5511	5692	5909	5197	4550
2nd Ditto	4389	4794	4545	4468	4985
3rd Ditto	1830	4650	5056	5923	6650
4th Ditto	5100	5200	4412	3900	4010
Light Ditto	4385	5174	5196	5090	5688
Siege Train	1022	977	1428	1088	1700
Heavy Cavalry	812	733	1080	1006	1044
Light Cavalry	740	665	657	709	721
Royal Horse Artillery	400	360	350	350	370

No. 15.—Return of the Names, Rank, and Regiment (or Corps), of all Officers who remained from the first Landing until they Died or Fell in Action.

(Allies first Landed in the Crimea 14th Sept. 1854.)

NAMES.	Rank.	Regiments or Corps.	Cause and Date of Death.
Raglan, Lord, G.C.B.	Field Marshal	Royal Horse Gds	Died of disease, 28 June 1855. Commander of the Forces.
Estcourt, J.	Major Gen.	Unattached	Died, 24 June 1855. Adjutant General.
Cathcart, Hon. Sir G., K.C.B.	Lieut. General	ditto	Killed, 5 Nov. 1854. Commanded 4th Division.
Cust, H.	Captain	Coldstream Gds.	Killed, 20 Sept. 1854. Aide-de-camp to Major General Bentinck.
Seymour, C.	Lieut. Colonel	Scots Fusil. Gds.	Killed, 5 Nov. 1854. Assist. Adjt. Gen. 4th Division.
Allix, W.	Captain	1st Royal Reg.	Killed, 5 Nov. 1854. Aide-de-camp to Lieut. General Sir De Lacy Evans.
Turner, H.	ditto	ditto	Died of disease, 1 Mar. 1856.
Yea, L.	Brevet Col.	7th Fusiliers	Killed, 18 June 1855. Commanded 1st Brigade Light Division.
Sharpe, J.	Brevet Major	20th Regiment	Died of wounds, 28 Dec. 1854. Major of Brigade.
Chapman, S.	Captain	ditto	Died, 20 Sept. 1855. Assist. Engineer.
Campbell, W.	ditto	23d R. W. Fusil.	Died of disease at Scutari, 22 Mar. 1855. Dep. Assist. Quartermaster General at Scutari.
Marsh, H. S. St. V.	Lieutenant	33rd Regiment	Killed, 24 June 1855. Assist. Engineer.
Campbell, Sir John, Bart.	Major Gen.	38th Regiment	Killed, 18 June 1855. Commanded 1st Brig. 4th Div.
Layard, A.	Captain	ditto	Died of disease, 7 Aug. 1855. Dep. Assist. Quartermaster General 2nd Division.
Johnstone, W.	ditto	41st Regiment	Died of disease, 10 Oct. 1855. Provost Marshal.
Rooke, W.	ditto	47th Regiment	Died of wounds, 1 Oct. 1855. Major of Brigade.
Adams, H., C.B.	Major Gen.	49th Regiment	Died of wounds, 17 Dec. 1854. Commanded a Brigade 2nd Division.
Glazbrook, C.	Captain	ditto	Died of wounds, 18 Dec. 1854. Dep. Assist. Quartermaster General 2nd Division.
Butler, H.	ditto	55th Regiment	Killed, 5 Nov. 1854. Ditto.
Goldie, T. L.	Brigadier Gen	57th Regiment	Killed, 5 Nov. 1854. Commanded 1st Brig. 4th Div.
Wellesley, E.	Brevet Major	73rd Regiment	Killed, 20 Sept. 1854. Assist. Quartermaster Gen. Head Quarters.
Charteris, Hon. W.	Lieutenant	92d Highlanders	Killed, 25 Oct. 1854. Extra Aide-de-camp to Major General Earl of Lucan.
Strangways, Fox	Brigadier Gen	Royal Artillery	Killed, 5 Nov. 1854. Commanded Royal Artillery.
Tylden, W.	ditto	Royal Engineers	Died of disease, 22 Sept. 1854. Commanded Royal Eng.
Nolan, J.	Captain	15th Hussars	Killed, 25 Oct. 1854. Aide-de-camp to Major General Sir R. Airey.
Halkett, J.	Major	4th Lt Dragoons	Killed, 25 Oct. 1854.
Sparke, H.	Lieutenant	ditto	Ditto, ditto.
Longmore, C.	Captain	8th Hussars	Died of disease, 3 Sept. 1855.
Lockwood, G.	ditto	ditto	Killed, 25 Oct. 1854.
FitzGibbon, Visct.	Lieutenant	ditto	Ditto, ditto.
Cresswell, W.	Captain	11th Hussars	Died of disease, 19 Sept. 1854.
Annesley, Hon. R.	Lieutenant	ditto	Ditto, 28 " "
Houghton, G.	ditto	ditto	Ditto, 22 Oct. "
Oldham, J.	Captain	13th Lt Dragoons	Killed, 25 Oct. 1854.
Goad, T.	ditto	ditto	Ditto, ditto.
Irwin, T.	Adjutant	ditto	Died of disease, 26 Sept. 1854.
Montgomery, H.	Cornet	ditto	Killed, 25 Oct. 1854.
Foster, C.	Quartermastr	ditto	Died of disease, 25 Jan. 1855.
Willett, A.	Major	17th Lancers	Died of disease, 22 Oct. 1854.
Winter, J.	Captain	ditto	Killed, 25 Oct. 1854.
Webb, A.	ditto	ditto	Died of wounds, 6 Nov. 1854.
Thomson, J.	Lieutenant	ditto	Killed, 25 Oct. 1854.
Clevland, A.	Cornet	ditto	Died of wounds, 6 Nov. 1854.
Townsend, S.	Major	Royal Artillery	Killed, 5 Nov. 1854.
Swinton, W.	ditto	ditto	Died, 2 Jan. 1855.
Dew, A.	Captain	ditto	Killed, 20 Sept. 1854.
Guille, W.	Lieutenant	ditto	Died, 28 Oct. 1854.
Singer, H.	Lieutenant	ditto	Ditto 2 " "
Walsham, R.	ditto	ditto	Killed, 20 Sept. 1854.
Cockerell, R.	ditto	ditto	Ditto, ditto.

No. 15.—Return of the Names, Rank, and Regiment (or Corps), of all Officers who remained from the first Landing until they Died or Fell in Action.—*(continued.)*

NAMES.	Rank.	Regiments or Corps.	Cause and Date of Death.
Alexander, C.	Lieut. Colonel	Royal Engineers	Died, 19 Oct. 1854.
Tylden, R.	Brevet Col.	ditto	Died of wounds, 2 Aug. 1855.
Craigie, A.	Captain	ditto	Killed, 13 March 1855.
Inglis, W.	ditto	ditto	Lost in the *Prince*, 14 Nov. 1854.
Murray, J.	Lieutenant	ditto	Killed, 18 June 1855.
Baynes, C.	ditto	ditto	Died of wounds, 7 May 1855.
Teesdale, H.	ditto	ditto	Ditto, 12 Oct. 1854.
Graves, T.	ditto	ditto	Killed, 18 June 1855.
Hood, Hon. F.	Brevet Col.	Grenadier Gds., 3rd Battalion.	Killed, 18 Oct. 1854.
Cox, A.	Lieut. Colonel	ditto	Died of disease, 26 Sept. 1854.
Pakenham, E.	ditto	ditto	Killed, 5 Nov. 1854.
Rowley, A.	Captain	ditto	Ditto, 16 Oct. "
Neville, Hon. H.	ditto	ditto	Ditto, 5 Nov. "
Newman, Sir R., Bt.	ditto	ditto	Ditto, ditto.
Huthwaite, F.	Surgeon	ditto	Died of wounds, 30 Sept. 1854.
Dawson, Hon. T.	Lieut. Colonel	Coldstream Gds. 1st Battalion.	Killed, 5 Nov. 1854.
Cowell, J.	ditto	ditto	Died of wounds, 6 Nov. 1854.
Elliot, Hon. G.	Captain	ditto	Killed, 5 Nov. 1854.
Bouverie, H.	ditto	ditto	Ditto, ditto.
Ramsden, F.	ditto	ditto	Died of wounds, 5 Nov. 1854.
Drummond, Hon. R.	ditto	ditto	Died of disease, 1 Oct. 1855.
Disbrowe, E.	Lieutenant	ditto	Died of wounds, 6 Nov. 1854.
Greville, C.	ditto	ditto	Killed, 5 Nov. 1854.
Drummond, H.	Major & Adjt.	Scots Fusil. Gds. 1st Battalion.	Ditto, 13 Aug. 1855.
Buckley, D.	Captain	ditto	Ditto, 6 Sept. 1855.
Chewton, Viscount	ditto	ditto	Died of wounds, 8 Oct. 1854.
Cobbe, H.	Brevet Col.	4th (K. O.) Reg.	Ditto, 6 Aug. 1855.
Arnold, W.	Captain	ditto	Ditto, 5 May 1855, while a prisoner of war.
Leahy, J.	Quartermastr	ditto	Died of disease, 18 Sept. 1855.
Mills, F.	Lieut. Colonel	7th Royal Fusil.	Died of wounds, 18 Aug. 1855.
Monck, Hon. W.	Captain	ditto	Killed, 20 Sept. 1854.
Hare, Hon. C.	ditto	ditto	Died of wounds, 22 Sept. 1854.
Molesworth, J.	Lieutenant	ditto	Died of disease, 5 Oct. 1854.
Hobson, J.	Adjutant	ditto	Killed, 18 June 1855.
Langham, J.	Assist. Surg.	ditto	Died of disease, 4 Feb. 1855.
Unett, T.	Lieut. Colonel	19th Regiment	Died of wounds, 14 Sept. 1855.
Godfrey, P.	Captain	ditto	Ditto, 13 " "
Ker, J.	ditto	ditto	Ditto, 7 Nov. 1854.
Wardlaw, R.	Lieutenant	ditto	Killed, 20 Sept. 1854.
Stockwell, G.	Ensign	ditto	Ditto, ditto.
Lye, R.	Captain	20th Regiment	Died of disease, 10 Dec. 1854.
Dowling, W.	Lieutenant	ditto	Killed, 5 Nov. 1854.
Parr, F.	ditto	ditto	Died of disease, 25 Mar. 1856.
Kekewich, L.	ditto	ditto	Ditto, 16 Feb. 1855.
Ainslie, F.	Lieut. Colonel	21st Fusiliers	Died of wounds, 14 Nov. 1854.
Hurt, W.	Lieutenant	ditto	Ditto, 6 " "
Chester, H.	Lieut. Colonel	23rd R.W. Fusil.	Killed, 20 Sept. 1854.
Evans, F.	Captain	ditto	Ditto, ditto.
Wynn, A.	ditto	ditto	Ditto, ditto.
Hughes, G.	ditto	ditto	Died of disease, 11 Dec. 1854.
Poole, W.	ditto	ditto	Died of wounds, 24 Sept. 1855.
Conolly, J.	ditto	ditto	Killed, 20 Sept. 1854.
Applewhaite, A.	Lieut. & Adjt.	ditto	Died of wounds, 22 Sept. 1854.
Dyneley, D.	Lieutenant	ditto	Ditto, 9 Sept. 1855.
Radcliffe, F.	ditto	ditto	Killed, 20 Sept. 1854.
Young, Sir W., Bart.	ditto	ditto	Ditto, ditto.
Anstruther, H.	ditto	ditto	Ditto, ditto.
Butler, J.	ditto	ditto	Ditto, ditto.
Holford, J.	ditto	28th Regiment	Died of disease, 29 Nov. 1854.
Bell, M.	ditto	ditto	Ditto, 7 Jan. 1855.
Spence, S.	Quartermastr	ditto	Ditto, 7 Nov. 1854.
Hoey, W.	Lieut. Colonel	30th Regiment	Ditto, 29 Sept. 1854.
Patullo, P.	ditto	ditto	Died of wounds, 9 " 1855.
Connolly, A.	Captain	ditto	Ditto, 6 Nov. 1854.
Luxmoore, F.	Lieutenant	ditto	Killed, 20 Sept. 1854.
Gibson, A.	ditto	ditto	Ditto, 5 Nov. "
Ross-Lewin, J.	ditto	ditto	Died of wounds, 7 Nov. 1854.
Johnston, W.	Ensign	ditto	Died of disease, 25 Sept. "
Blake, J.	Lieut. Colonel	33rd Regiment	Ditto, 23 Aug. 1855.
Gough, T.	ditto	ditto	Died of disease, 18 Sept. "
Burke, H.	Captain	ditto	Died of disease, 18 Jan. "
Montagu, F.	Lieutenant	ditto	Killed, 20 Sept. 1854.
Worthington, W.	ditto	ditto	Ditto, ditto.
Bennett, V.	ditto	ditto	Ditto, 18 June 1855.
Thorold, H.	ditto	ditto	Ditto, 5 Nov. 1854.
M'Grath, P.	Paymaster	ditto	Died of disease, 9 Feb. 1855.
Vaughan, J.	Captain	38th Regiment	Died of wounds, 16 June "
Davies, O.	Lieutenant	ditto	Killed, 18 June 1855.
Eman, J.	Lieut. Colonel	41st Regiment	Died of wounds, 10 Sept. 1855.
Carpenter, G.	ditto	ditto	Ditto, 6 Nov. 1854.
Swaby, J.	Lieutenant	ditto	Killed, 5 Nov. 1854.
Stirling, J.	ditto	ditto	Ditto, ditto.
Harriott, H.	ditto	ditto	Ditto, 8 Dec. 1854.
Taylor, A.	ditto	ditto	Killed, 5 Nov. 1854.
Anderson, W.	Surgeon	ditto	Died of disease, 3 Jan. 1855.
Lamont, J.	Assist. Surg.	ditto	Ditto, 5 " "
Cunninghame, R.	Captain	42d Highlanders	Ditto, 5 Sept. "
Fraser, G.	ditto	ditto	Killed, 16 July 1855.
Fenwick, B.	ditto	44th Regiment	Died of wounds, 20 June 1855
Agar, Hon. C.	ditto	ditto	Ditto, 18 " "

APPENDIX.

No. 13.—RETURN showing the state of each Regiment, &c., on its Embarkation for Active Service in the East, its subsequent Increase and Decrease, and Strength on the 1st of April, 1856.

Date of Embarkation of Head Quarters.	CORPS.	Strength on Embarkation.		Reinforcements.		TOTAL.		DECREASE.								Strength of each Regiment on 1st of April, 1856.	
								Died in the East.		Invalided Home.		Prisoners of War and Deserters.		TOTAL.			
		Officers.	Non-commissioned Officers and Men.	Officers.	Non-commissioned Officers and Men.	Officers.	Non-commissioned Officers and Men.	Officers.	Non-commissioned Officers and Men.	Officers.	Non-commissioned Officers and Men.	Officers.	Non-commissioned Officers and Men. (Prisoners of War / Deserters)	Officers.	Non-commissioned Officers and Men.	Officers.	Non-commissioned Officers and Men.
July 28, 1855	1st Dragoon Guards	19	358	..	..	19	358	..	47	2	21	..	..	2	68	21	286
June 2, 1854	4th Ditto	20	297	10	262	30	559	..	103	6	55	..	3 / 3	6	164	26	392
May 27, "	5th Ditto	19	295	11	248	30	543	7	81	9	89	..	.. / 1	16	171	18	371
July 21, 1855	6th Ditto	19	354	4	1	23	355	2	24	9	34	..	..	11	58	11	301
May 10, 1854	1st Dragoons	19	294	10	279	29	573	1	89	14	60	..	.. / 1	15	149	15	416
July 25, "	2nd Ditto	18	299	10	272	28	571	2	89	11	75	..	.. / 2	13	166	15	404
July 18, "	4th Ditto	20	299	7	345	27	644	3	123	11	74	..	18 / 1	14	216	14	438
May 29, "	6th Ditto	19	295	12	336	31	631	1	102	11	71	..	.. / 4	12	177	21	430
May 2, "	8th Ditto	20	294	9	350	29	644	3	105	5	54	1	6 / 1	9	167	21	463
Jan. 31, 1855	10th Ditto (from Bombay)	26	672	15	223	41	895	2	62	11	85	..	17 / 1	13	165	28	743
May 15, 1854	11th Ditto	18	295	16	306	34	601	5	109	13	72	..	8 / ..	18	189	17	419
Feb. 22, 1855	12th Ditto (from Madras)	30	527	11	149	41	676	..	26	13	71	..	.. / 1	13	98	27	575
May 12, 1854	13th Ditto	20	295	11	288	31	583	6	102	13	89	..	13 / ..	19	204	14	387
April 25, 1854	17th Ditto	20	294	14	366	34	660	5	110	16	70	1	.. / 16	22	196	16	464
	Total Cavalry	287	4868	140	3425	427	8293	37	1172	144	920	2	65 / 31	183	2188	264	6089
From Mar. 19 to Aug. 9, 1854	Royal Artillery	120	3095	268	7628	388	10,723	23	1483	145	2117	..	..	168	3600	220	7123
From Feb. to May, 1854	Royal Sappers and Miners	3	403	92	1241	95	1644	20	241	31	157	..	.. / 4	51	402	44	1242
Feb. 22, 1854	Grenadier Guards, 3rd Bat.	32	946	41	1395	73	2341	8	784	34	430	..	.. / 3	42	1217	32	1162
Feb. 22, "	Coldstream " 1st Bat.	33	920	52	1148	85	2068	13	716	41	271	..	.. / 4	54	991	33	1088
Feb. 28, "	Scots Fusilier " 1st Bat.	30	932	37	1163	67	2095	5	656	24	332	..	6 / 1	29	995	38	1113
	Total Guards	95	2798	130	3706	225	6504	26	2156	99	1033	..	6 / 8	125	3203	103	3363
April 21, 1854	1st Foot 1st Battalion	30	911	28	659	58	1570	2	460	34	183	..	.. / 8	36	651	27	880
April 14, 1855	Ditto 2nd ditto	25	751	15	204	40	955	4	78	14	169	..	7 / 1	18	255	25	730
April 14, "	3rd Foot	24	673	34	419	58	1092	3	146	22	106	1	.. / 2	26	254	32	837
March 9, 1854	4th Ditto	32	911	23	624	55	1535	3	339	21	275	1	2 / 1	25	617	33	919
April 5, "	7th Ditto	30	911	43	969	73	1880	14	540	23	378	..	25 / 8	37	951	38	931
Nov. 19, "	9th Ditto	20	549	30	558	50	1107	3	137	18	153	..	.. / 1	21	291	31	725
June 7, 1855	13th Ditto	30	858	13	192	43	1050	..	87	7	141	..	.. / 2	7	230	36	865
Jan. 10, "	14th Ditto	22	671	23	506	45	1177	1	77	15	199	..	.. / 1	16	277	32	878
Dec. 2, 1854	17th Ditto	23	719	31	549	54	1268	3	181	24	192	..	.. / 1	27	374	31	886
Dec. 8, "	18th Ditto	30	821	30	435	60	1256	1	169	26	209	..	5 / ..	27	383	37	863
April 20, "	19th Ditto	31	913	32	683	63	1596	6	458	29	312	..	.. / 4	35	774	29	823
July 17, "	20th Ditto	30	961	41	508	71	1469	6	419	27	201	..	13 / ..	33	633	35	836
Aug. 15, "	21st Ditto	33	974	25	575	58	1549	2	372	25	224	..	49 / 3	27	648	33	903
April 4, "	23rd Ditto	31	911	41	1074	72	1985	22	700	21	345	1	46 / 2	44	1093	31	902
Feb. 22, "	28th Ditto	31	899	32	690	63	1589	1	317	19	232	..	8 / ..	20	557	41	804
May 1, "	30th Ditto	34	895	46	559	80	1454	16	406	37	300	..	1 / 5	53	712	27	753
May 15, 1855	31st Ditto	30	740	13	301	43	1041	2	114	13	133	..	.. / 2	15	249	30	884
March 1, 1854	33rd Ditto	33	915	35	689	68	1604	8	311	17	223	..	14 / ..	25	548	39	691
Nov. 22, "	34th Ditto	26	793	37	474	63	1267	8	270	25	279	..	5 / ..	33	554	35	743
April 26, "	38th Ditto	32	910	33	756	65	1666	2	486	23	260	..	9 / 8	25	763	36	901
Dec. 9, "	39th Ditto	24	660	23	527	47	1187	1	109	17	129	..	.. / 1	18	239	28	966
April 10, "	41st Ditto	28	869	32	575	60	1444	13	436	21	306	..	6 / ..	34	748	27	720
May 20, "	42nd Ditto	33	918	18	319	51	1237	2	265	16	136	..	2 / 18	20	403	32	847
March 10, "	44th Ditto	31	923	32	640	63	1563	6	449	25	250	..	11 / 1	31	711	33	849
Oct. 12, "	46th Ditto	33	963	22	492	55	1455	3	570	18	196	..	.. / 3	21	769	35	682
April 10, "	47th Ditto	29	889	26	549	55	1438	3	570	21	288	..	8 / ..	24	666	34	818
April 13, 1855	48th Ditto	25	802	23	142	48	944	..	73	12	94	..	.. / 3	12	170	32	827
April 9, 1854	49th Ditto	27	907	39	583	66	1490	9	391	27	256	..	3 / 4	36	654	33	839
Feb. 24, "	50th Ditto	31	910	32	508	63	1418	4	508	26	172	2	23 / 3	32	706	34	721
May 10, "	55th Ditto	31	892	33	611	64	1503	12	369	29	313	..	9 / 2	41	693	26	810
July 30, 1855	56th Ditto	32	861	8	57	40	918	..	38	6	32	..	.. / 1	6	71	35	841
Sept. 12, 1854	57th Ditto	19	742	35	585	54	1327	10	277	11	209	..	5 / 8	21	499	34	865
Nov. 3, "	62nd Ditto	20	546	27	533	47	1079	8	246	10	202	1	.. / 1	19	449	31	638
July 21, "	63rd Ditto	31	977	31	346	62	1323	8	458	26	200	..	4 / ..	34	663	33	708
Aug. 7, "	68th Ditto	28	841	22	480	50	1321	7	257	16	184	..	24 / 12	23	477	32	862
Jan. 26, 1855	71st Ditto	32	891	16	178	48	1069	3	94	8	67	..	2 / ..	11	163	38	900
May 22, "	72nd Ditto	30	607	10	321	40	928	1	100	13	84	..	1 / ..	14	185	29	763
March 10, 1854	77th Ditto	31	910	37	765	68	1675	15	467	24	321	..	20 / ..	39	808	32	878
May 4, "	79th Ditto	31	917	26	429	57	1346	6	354	22	171	..	11 / ..	28	536	33	816
Aug. 26, 1855	82nd Ditto	28	576	9	351	37	927	..	30	4	31	..	.. / ..	4	61	34	858
April 4, 1854	88th Ditto	32	911	33	1085	65	1996	11	466	22	444	..	8 / 7	33	925	33	1022
Dec. 2, "	89th Ditto	23	691	24	541	47	1232	4	230	12	199	1	.. / 5	17	434	29	836
Nov. 19, "	90th Ditto	32	814	23	458	55	1272	5	274	25	204	..	27 / 4	30	509	27	757
Aug. 29, 1855	92nd Ditto	16	491	9	210	25	701	..	9	2	11	..	.. / 2	2	20	30	635
Feb. 27, 1854	93rd Ditto	33	911	29	435	62	1346	7	307	22	234	1	1 / 2	30	544	31	787
April 6, "	95th Ditto	30	911	37	583	67	1494	10	557	30	289	..	.. / 7	40	853	28	636
Nov. 15, "	97th Ditto	28	889	36	588	64	1477	10	424	19	218	..	.. / 12	29	654	39	860
July 13, "	Rifle Brigade 1st Battalion	25	975	27	808	52	1783	6	453	14	359	..	.. / ..	20	812	34	977
Feb. 24, "	Ditto 2nd ditto	32	961	44	831	76	1792	9	498	35	318	..	.. / 5	44	821	31	967
	Total Infantry of the Line	1402	40,841	1368	25,954	2770	66,795	280	15,146	973	10,431	8	276 / 204	1261	26,057	1588	40,524
April & May, 1855	Land Transport Corps	28	505	125	6917	153	7422	2	466	15	202	..	1 / 6	17	675	163	6795
Oct. 11, 1855	BRITISH GERMAN LEGION. 1st Jager Battalion	36	895	6	..	42	895	2	30	..	21	..	.. / 72	2	123	48	854
Oct. 26, "	1st Light Infantry	36	938	..	..	36	938	..	2	..	..	..	.. / ..	..	2	39	923
Dec. 22, "	2nd Ditto	31	972	..	..	31	972	..	2	..	..	..	4 / ..	..	6	36	996
Dec. 24, "	3rd Ditto	29	810	..	..	29	810	..	3	..	20	..	3 / ..	..	26	35	965
	Total Brit. German Legion	132	3615	6	..	138	3615	2	37	..	41	..	.. / 79	2	157	158	3738
Nov. 16, 1855	BRITISH SWISS LEGION. 1st Reg. Light Infantry	52	1360	..	..	52	1360	..	2	..	..	..	.. / ..	..	4	52	1356
Feb. 9, 1856	2nd Ditto 1st Bat.	25	684	..	..	25	684	..	4	..	..	..	.. / ..	..	4	25	680
	Total British Swiss Legion	77	2044	..	..	77	2044	..	6	..	..	..	2 / ..	..	8	77	2036
	General Total of all Arms	2144	58,169	2129	48,871	4273	107,040	390	20,707	1407	14,901	10	348 / 334	1807	36,290	2617	70,910

APPENDIX.

No. 7.—RETURN of the Killed in Action and Died of Wounds of the British Army in the Crimea, distributed Regimentally.—(*continued.*)

CORPS.	Killed in Action.			Died of Wounds.			Date of Arrival in the East.
	Officers.	Non-commissioned Officers.	Drummers, and Rank and File.	Officers.	Non-commissioned Officers.	Drummers, and Rank and File.	
39th Ditto	1	..	3	..	1	6	Jan. 1, 1855
41st Ditto	6	6	104	3	3	32	April 15, 1854
42nd Ditto	1	..	21	..	2	6	June 9, "
44th Ditto	..	..	23	4	3	28	April 10, "
46th Ditto	1	1	19	..	..	12	Nov. 8, "
47th Ditto	..	3	81	2	1	35	April 19, "
48th Ditto	..	..	5	..	..	7	April 21, 1855
49th Ditto	4	5	84	3	5	114	Apr. 19 & 28, 1854
50th Ditto	1	2	34	1	..	20	April 15, 1854
55th Ditto	5	3	84	1	3	55	May 21, "
56th Ditto	..	..	5	..	..	3	Aug. 25, 1855
57th Ditto	3	11	49	5	4	17	Sept. 23, 1854
62nd Ditto	6	5	26	1	..	6	Nov. 12, "
63rd Ditto	4	..	17	..	1	47	Sept. 1, "
68th Ditto	5	..	32	1	..	19	Sept. 3, "
71st Ditto	..	..	..	..	..	..	{ Dec. 22, " Feb. 3, 1855 }
72nd Ditto	..	..	6	1	..	6	May 29, "
77th Ditto	5	7	68	..	1	333	April 17, 1854
79th Ditto	..	..	7	..	1	4	May 27, "
82nd Ditto	..	..	..	..	..	..	Sept. 2, 1855
88th Ditto	5	8	106	2	3	42	April 19, 1854
89th Ditto	1	..	4	..	..	9	Dec. 13, "
90th Ditto	3	4	40	1	1	47	Dec. 5, "
92nd Ditto	..	..	..	..	..	..	Sept. 15, 1855
93rd Ditto	..	..	8	1	1	10	April 11, 1854
95th Ditto	6	8	72	1	6	98	April 24, "
97th Ditto	7	6	61	1	2	40	Nov. 20, "
Rifle Brigade, 1st Battalion	2	8	44	2	4	42	July 30, "
Ditto, 2nd Batt.	4	9	82	1	5	51	April 30, "
Total Infantry	110	129	1929	68	77	1647	
Staff Officers	3	..	..	2	..	..	
General Total of all Arms	157	161	2437	86	85	1848	

No. 8.—RETURN showing the Total Number of Men of Lord Raglan's Army Sick during each Month, from the landing in Turkey.

MONTHS.	Total Sick or Wounded of all Arms during each Month.
1854.	
April	503
May	1,835
June	3,498
July	6,937
August	11,236
September	11,693
October	11,988
November	16,846
December	19,479
1855.	
January	23,076
To 17 February ....Crimea	9,284
To 25 " ....Scutari	6,725
To 17 " ....Abydos	385
To 25 " ....Gallipoli	70
To 20 " ....Smyrna	500
TOTAL to latest dates in February	16,964

No. 9.—STATEMENT showing the Total Number of Vessels which arrived at Scutari with Sick and Wounded from the Crimea between 18th of September, 1854, and 25th of February, 1855, with the Total Number of Officers and Men conveyed therein, and the Number of each Rank that died on the Passage.

No. of Vessels.	Number Conveyed.		Died on Passage.	
	Officers.	Men.	Officers.	Men.
78	316	17,067	6	924

No. 10.—RETURN showing the Number of Officers and Men in Hospital in the Crimea, at Scutari, and elsewhere, at the dates specified below, distinguishing the Sick from the Wounded.

Hospitals.	Last Dates.	Officers.	Men.	Of whom Wounded.
	1855.			
Crimea	February 10	69	4,945	59
Scutari	February 18	76	4,984	Not stated.
Varna	January 20	1	32	"
Abydos	February 10	..	264	"
Gallipoli	February 18	..	54	"
Smyrna	..	..	500	"
Totals		146	10,779	
Grand Total Officers and Men in Hospitals			10,625	

No. 11.—RETURN showing the Number of Officers and Men who died from Sickness at Varna or elsewhere, from date of landing in Turkey to 6th September (date of Embarkation for Crimea) 903

No. 12.—RETURN showing the following particulars concerning the late ARMY IN THE EAST.

REGIMENTS (by Brigades and Divisions) which composed the ARMY IN THE EAST.	Original Strength on joining the Army in Serjeants, Drummers, and Rank and File.	Number of Officers Killed.	Number of Officers Wounded.	Number of Non-commissioned Officers and Men Killed.	Number of Non-commissioned Officers and Men Wounded.	Total Killed and Wounded.
CAVALRY DIVISION.						
1st (Heavy) Brigade—						
1st Dragoon Guards	353	..	..	..	4	5
4th Ditto	295	..	3	2	12	17
5th Ditto	295	..	4	2	7	13
1st Dragoons	295	..	4	2	57	63
2nd Ditto	299	..	..	2	14	16
6th Ditto	279	..	..	2	14	16
2nd (Light) Brigade—						
6th Dragoon Guards	354	..	..	..	..	..
4th Light Dragoons	299	2	2	17	24	45
12th Lancers	514	..	..	..	..	..
13th Light Dragoons	295	3	3	11	31	48
3rd (Hussar) Brigade—						
8th Hussars	292	2	3	19	21	45
10th Ditto	658	..	..	..	4	4
11th Ditto	297	..	2	26	29	57
17th Lancers	294	2	5	32	34	73
Total Cavalry	4819	9	26	114	237	386
Royal Artillery	7032	11	30	121	632	794
Royal Sappers and Miners	403	9	13	32	86	140
FIRST DIVISION.						
1st Brigade—						
Grenadier Guards, 3rd Bat.	904	5	12	111	410	538
Coldstream " 1st Bat.	919	8	6	77	202	293
Scots Fusilier " 1st Bat.	935	2	23	85	336	446
2nd Brigade—						
9th Foot	586	..	2	14	83	99
13th Ditto	855	..	..	..	11	11
31st Ditto	742	2	1	14	84	101
56th Ditto	846	..	1	5	13	19
SECOND DIVISION.						
1st Brigade—						
3rd Foot	694	..	13	48	259	320
30th Ditto	692	3	19	105	364	491
55th Ditto	966	5	18	87	412	522
95th Ditto	911	6	21	80	361	468
2nd Brigade—						
41st Foot	863	6	13	110	426	555
47th Ditto	682	..	9	84	216	309
49th Ditto	898	4	10	89	325	428
62nd Ditto	574	6	7	31	121	165
82nd Ditto	561	..	..	..	..	..
THIRD DIVISION.						
1st Brigade—						
4th Foot	910	..	5	22	142	169
14th Ditto	689	..	..	9	46	55
39th Ditto	700	1	1	3	46	51
50th Ditto	912	1	4	36	67	108
89th Ditto	691	1	..	4	73	78
2nd Brigade—						
18th Foot	814	1	10	39	267	317
28th Ditto	889	..	9	24	89	122
38th Ditto	909	1	7	22	200	230
44th Ditto	923	..	8	23	156	187
FOURTH DIVISION.						
1st Brigade—						
17th Foot	720	1	5	21	134	161
20th Ditto	955	1	10	42	81	134
21st Ditto	978	..	10	34	100	144
57th Ditto	774	3	11	60	237	311
63rd Ditto	978	4	8	17	127	156
2nd Brigade—						
46th Foot	963	1	2	20	71	94
48th Ditto	851	..	2	5	60	67
68th Ditto	861	5	4	32	71	112
Rifle Brigade, 1st Battalion	975	2	5	52	212	271
HIGHLAND DIVISION.						
1st Brigade—						
42nd Foot	914	1	2	21	119	143
79th Ditto	916	..	2	7	55	64
92nd Ditto	491	..	..	..	..	..
93rd Ditto	911	1	2	8	95	106
2nd Brigade—						
1st Foot, 1st Battalion	911	1	2	15	79	97
Ditto, 2nd Battalion	796	1	8	19	146	174
71st Ditto	891	..	..	..	1	1
72nd Ditto	607	..	..	6	48	54
LIGHT DIVISION.						
1st Brigade—						
7th Foot	911	5	23	102	402	532
23rd Ditto	909	10	15	118	495	638
33rd Ditto	913	7	21	95	293	416
34th Ditto	597	5	18	71	375	469
Rifle Brigade, 2nd Battalion	962	4	15	91	569	679
2nd Brigade—						
19th Foot	912	1	20	73	502	596
77th Ditto	903	5	11	75	606	697
88th Ditto	910	5	16	114	400	535
90th Ditto	813	3	15	44	221	283
97th Ditto	889	7	9	67	198	281
Total Infantry	43,276	125	435	2331	10,406	13,297
Staff Officers	..	3	11	..	..	14
General Total of all Arms	55,530	157	515	2598	11,361	14,631

APPENDIX.

The accuracy of the following thirteen Returns may be relied upon, as they are, by permission, taken from the Work styled "Despatches and Papers relative to the Campaign in Turkey, Asia Minor, and the Crimea," compiled and arranged by Capt. F. SAYER, Deputy Assistant Quarter-Master-General to the Forces. London: Harrison, 59, Pall Mall.

No. 1.—RETURN showing the Total Number of Non-commissioned Officers and Men sent to the Crimea from the Commencement of the War to the end of March, 1856.

	Non-commissioned Officers, Trumpeters, Buglers & Drummers.	Farriers and Rank and File.		Men.
Cavalry	479	7,814	equal to	8,293
Artillery	443	10,280	"	10,723
Sappers and Miners	81	1,563	"	1,644
Infantry	4,001	69,298	"	73,299
Total embarked for the East to the end of March, 1856	5,004	88,955	"	93,959

In addition to the above, the following Battalions of the British German Legion and Swiss Legion embarked, and were stationed on the Bosphorus or at Smyrna, namely—

		Non-commissioned Officers, Buglers, and Drummers.	Rank and File.		Men.
British German Legion	1st Jäger Battalion	76	819	equal to	895
	1st Light Infantry	68	870	"	938
	2nd Ditto	73	899	"	972
	3rd Ditto	57	753	"	810
Total British German Legion		274	3,341	"	3,615
British Swiss Legion	1st Regt. Light Infantry	91	1,269	"	1,360
	2nd Ditto, 1st Battalion	48	636	"	684
Total British Swiss Legion		139	1,905	"	2,044

Grand Total embarked from England, the Mediterranean, or India, including Foreign Legions ... 99,618

No. 2.—GENERAL TOTAL of Troops *originally* embarked for the East under Lord Raglan.

Officers.	Serjeants.	Buglers, Trumpeters & Drummers.	Rank and File.	Grand Total.
933	1,257	432	23,473	26,095

No. 3.—TOTAL NUMBER of English Troops *present* at the Battle of Alma.

Cavalry	1,100
Artillery and Engineers	3,100
Infantry	22,600
Total	26,800

No. 4.—RETURN of the Total Number of Officers and Men in the Army who have been *Killed* in the Crimea up to the 1st of June, 1856, distinguishing Cavalry, Infantry, Artillery, Sappers and Miners, as well as Officers, Non-commissioned Officers, and Men.

	Officers.	Non-commissioned Officers.	Men.
Cavalry	8	10	104
Artillery	10	10	111
*Sappers and Miners	9	1	31
Infantry	119	140	2191
Staff	11	...	...
Total	157	161	2437
General Total			2755

No. 5.—STATEMENT showing the Total Strength and the Total Number *Killed* and *Wounded* of each Infantry Division of the British Army.

	Strength of each Division.	Officers, Non-commissioned Officers, and Men.
1st Division	11,011	1,507
2nd Division	12,455	3,258
3rd Division	13,132	1,317
4th Division	12,943	1,450
Highland Division	9,533	639
Light Division	17,211	5,126
Grand Total	76,285	13,297

No. 6.—STATEMENT OF CASUALTIES in the 1st Brigade Light Division, the Highland Brigade, and Brigade of Guards.

CASUALTIES IN FIRST BRIGADE LIGHT DIVISION.

REGIMENT.	Total Strength, including Reinforcements.		Number of Officers Killed.	Number of Non-commissioned Officers and Men Killed.	Number of Officers Wounded.	Number of Non-commissioned Officers and Men Wounded.	Total Killed and Wounded.
	Officers.	Men.					
7th	73	1880	5	102	23	402	532
23rd	72	1985	10	118	15	495	638
33rd	68	1604	7	95	21	293	416
	213	5469	22	315	†59	1190	1586

CASUALTIES IN THE HIGHLAND BRIGADE.

	Officers	Men					
42nd	51	1237	1	21	2	119	143
79th	57	1346	...	7	2	55	64
93rd	62	1346	1	8	2	95	106
	170	3929	2	36	‡6	259	303

CASUALTIES IN THE BRIGADE OF GUARDS.

	Officers	Men					
Grenadier Guards	73	2341	5	111	12	410	538
Coldstream Guards	85	2068	8	77	6	202	293
Scots Fusilier Guards	67	2095	2	85	23	336	446
	225	6504	15	273	§41	948	1277

No. 7.—RETURN of the Killed in Action and Died of Wounds of the British Army in the Crimea, distributed Regimentally, with the date of the Arrival of each Regiment in the East.

CORPS.	Killed in Action.			Died of Wounds.			Date of Arrival in the East.
	Officers.	Non-commissioned Officers.	Trumpeters or Drummers, and Rank and File.	Officers.	Non-commissioned Officers.	Trumpeters or Drummers, and Rank and File.	
1st Dragoon Guards	..	..	..	..	..	..	Aug. 10, 1855
4th Ditto	..	..	1	..	..	1	July 10, 1854
5th Ditto	..	..	2	1	..	..	June 13, "
6th Ditto	..	..	..	..	..	..	Aug. 14, 1855
1st Dragoons	..	..	2	..	..	1	June 24, 1854
2nd Ditto	..	..	2	..	..	6	Aug. 8, "
4th Ditto	2	3	14	..	..	2	Aug. 1, "
6th Ditto	..	..	2	..	1	..	July 7, "
8th Ditto	2	3	16	..	..	7	{ May 20, " / June 7, "
10th Ditto	..	..	..	..	..	..	April 17, 1855
11th Ditto	..	2	24	1	..	3	June 21, 1854
12th Ditto	..	..	..	..	..	..	May 9, 1855
13th Ditto	3	1	10	..	..	3	June 21, 1854
17th Ditto	2	1	31	2	..	2	May 24, "
Total Cavalry	9	10	104	4	1	25	
Royal Artillery	11	10	111	1	4	48	During May, 1854
Royal Sappers and Miners	9	1	31	6	1	22	April 18 & 24, 1854 / May 9, 1854
Grenadier Guards, 3rd Battalion	5	3	108	1	1	32	April 28, 1854
Coldstream Guards, 1st Battalion	8	3	74	2	..	51	April 29, "
Scots Fusilier Gds., 1st Battalion	2	5	80	2	1	23	April 28, "
Total Foot Gds.	15	11	262	5	2	106	
1st Foot, 1st Batt.	1	..	15	..	..	10	May 5, 1854
Ditto, 2nd Batt.	1	..	19	1	1	14	April 21, 1855
3rd Ditto	..	5	43	3	3	27	April 28, "
4th Ditto	..	..	22	2	..	16	April 15, 1854
7th Ditto	5	8	94	3	8	74	April 22, "
9th Ditto	..	..	14	1	..	6	Nov. 27, "
13th Ditto	..	..	..	..	..	..	June 30, 1855
14th Ditto	..	..	9	..	..	7	Feb. 1, "
17th Ditto	1	1	20	..	..	13	Dec. 15, 1854
18th Ditto	1	1	38	..	2	48	Dec. 26, "
19th Ditto	1	3	70	3	3	62	May 11, "
20th Ditto	1	2	40	2	2	39	Aug. 7, "
21st Ditto	..	1	33	2	1	11	Sept. 14, "
23rd Ditto	10	7	111	6	4	71	April 25, "
28th Ditto	..	1	23	..	..	18	April 16, "
30th Ditto	3	1	104	7	2	47	May 12, "
31st Ditto	2	2	12	1	..	11	May 22, 1855
33rd Ditto	7	6	89	1	1	20	April 14, 1854
34th Ditto	5	1	70	2	2	44	Dec. 9 "
38th Ditto	1	4	18	2	1	20	May 11 & 17, 1854

* Now Royal Engineers. † Of this number 10 died of wounds. ‡ Of this number 1 died of wounds. § Of this number 5 died of wounds.

INDEX

(NOT INCLUDING APPENDIX).

To make a List of all the Names mentioned in the foregoing pages would entail a labour almost equal to that of writing the Work itself over again, the Compilers, therefore, with regret find themselves under the necessity of leaving out the names of Non-Commissioned Officers, Petty Officers, Soldiers and Sailors.

NAME.	No.	Page	NAME.	No.	Page	NAME.	No.	Page
A.			Clutterbuck, J., Ensign	51	48	Glazbrook, C., Major	41	55
Agar, Hon. C., Captain	2	22	" "	71	50	Gobel, P., Lieutenant	59	56
" "	28	46	Cobbe, H., Colonel	39	47	" "	W	57
Ainslie, G., Lieutenant Colonel	11	53	Cochran, J., Commissariat Clerk	23	54	Godfrey, P., Captain	1	7
Air, H.	24	26	Cockerell, R., Lieutenant	5	27	" A., Lieutenant	62	49
Alexander, C., Lieutenant Colonel	2	16	" "	1	28	" "	65	49
" "	n.	51	" "	24	46	Goldie, T., Brigadier General	43	47
Allix, W., Captain	3	21	Coeken, J., Commissariat Clerk	X	57	Goodall, J., Esq.,	4	38
Alt, H., Lieutenant	37	4	Compton, Dr.	L	57	Goodenough, R., Lieutenant	15	7
Ancell, M., Assistant Surgeon	1	33	Colt, O., Lieutenant	10	1	Gordon, A., Captain	4	16
" "	5	33	Colvill, R., Major	46	55	" "	24	46
Anderson, C., Captain	88	51	Conolly, A., Captain	96	52	Gough, T., Lieutenant Colonel	18	2
" D., Staff Assistant Surgeon	13	53	" J., Captain	3	28	Grabnam, J., Assistant Surgeon	49	55
" W., Surgeon	1	39	Coppinger, W., Dep. Assist. Com. Gen.	15	45	Grant, F., Lieutenant	12	42
" "	57	49	Corbett, E., Captain	47	9	Graves, T., Lieutenant	13	16
Anstruther, H., Lieutenant	3	28	Cowell, J., Lieutenant Colonel	11	45	Greathead, G., Lieutenant	25	46
Applewhaite, A., Lieut. and Adjutant	3	28	Cox, A., Colonel	14	45	Greville, C., Lieutenant	11	45
Armstrong, A., Lieut. and Adjutant	3	29	" R., Captain	31	46	Grogan, H., Captain	48	9
Ashwin, J., Lieutenant	20	45	Craigie, A., Captain	11	16	Guille, W., Captain	6	21
Attree, F., Captain	89	51	Crawfurd, R., Captain	15	53	" "	24	46
Auchmuty, J., Captain	16	45	Crofton, E., Captain	33	8	Gyngell, G., Rev.	21	38
Austin, T.	5	37	" "	n.	51			
			" G., Captain	8	16	**H.**		
B.			Croker, J., Captain	75	50	Hacke, A., Captain	59	56
Bainbrigge, E., Lieutenant	10	16	Cuddy, W., Lieutenant Colonel	22	45	Hague, G., Lieutenant	16	45
Barbance, B., Madame	1	14	Curry, D., Lieutenant	1	39	Hammet, L., Commander	7	23
Barker, Charlotte	Z	57	Curtis, F., Lieutenant	3	44	Hammond, M., Captain	53	5
" F., Lieutenant	73	50	Curtois, G., Lieutenant	33	47	Handcock, Hon. H., Lieutenant Colonel	14	7
Barnes, Sophia	25	54	" "	51	48	Harriott, H., Lieutenant	57	49
Bassano, C., Staff Surgeon	3	38	Curwen, D., Lieutenant	16	45	" "	20	54
Bayford, Charlotte	59	5	Cuttler, A., Lieutenant	1	39	Harris, J., Lieutenant	32	27
Bayley, E., Major	47	9				Harrison, G., Major	49	48
" H., Assistant Commissary Gen.	13	37	**D.**			" "	51	48
Baynes, C., Lieutenant	17	16	D'Aeth, E., Lieutenant	12	23	" H., Staff Assistant Surgeon	1	29
Beauchamp, F., Lieutenant	4	1	Daly, Hon C., Major	1	20	" "	86	51
Beck, C., Lieutenant	33	54	Dalton, T., Major	1	29	" N., Lieutenant Colonel	24	46
Beckwith, H., Assistant Surgeon	1	28	Dashwood, W., Lieutenant	3	21	" "	29	54
" S., Lieutenant Colonel	65	49	Davies, O., Lieutenant	83	51	Hayter, W., Deputy Assistant Commis.	4	5
Bell, M., Lieutenant	2	20	Davis, T., Major	1	29	" "	24	46
" "	66	56	Dawson, J., Lieutenant	85	51	Henderson, R.	1	25
Bellew, W., Lieutenant	50	48	" "	24	46	Henry, C., Lieutenant Col. (Right Arm)	25	21
Belson, F., Captain	31	54	" "	n.	51	Henty, F., Purveyor	2	38
Bennett, V., Lieutenant	18	2	" G., Captain	16	16	Heyland, L., Lieutenant	18	2
" "	22	3	" H., Lieutenant	8	39	" "	23	3
" "	31	3	" Hon. T., Lieutenant Colonel	11	45	Hill, A., Lieutenant	1	19
" "	94	51	Deane, R., Lieutenant	92	51	Hobson, J., Lieutenant and Adjutant	14	2
Beveridge, J., Dispenser	Y	57	Dennis, J., Lieutenant	96	52	Hoey, W., Lieutenant Colonel	96	52
Birch, L., Lieutenant	23	45	Dermon, W., Lieut. and Adjutant	68	50	Holden, E., Lieutenant	5	6
Birt, Fanny	62	56	Dew, A., Captain	4	7	Holford, J., Lieutenant	7	53
Blair, J., Lieutenant Colonel	13	45	Dickson, W., Major	24	46	" "	66	56
Blake, F., Colonel	18	2	Disbrowe, E., Captain	32	46	Hood, Hon. F., Colonel	8	44
Blakiston, L., Lieutenant	31	46	Donovan, H., Lieutenant	11	45	Hooper, W.	26	38
Bland, J., Captain	18	45	Douglas, W., Lieutenant	18	2	Hopkins, T.	21	54
Boileau, C., Lieutenant	65	49	Dowdall, G., Captain	13	23	Houghton, G., Lieutenant	D	57
Bond, W., Lieutenant	4	21	Dowling, W., Lieutenant	1	29	Hughes, G., Captain	19	54
Borough, R., Lieutenant	2	1	Dowse, F., Lieutenant	84	51	Hunter, R., Major	3	52
Bouverie, H., Captain	11	45	Drake, Elizabeth	1	39	Hurt, F., Lieutenant	37	4
Bowles, C., Captain	77	50	Drummond, H., Brev. Major and Adj.	2	31	" H., Lieutenant	35	47
Boxall, R., Surgeon	2	52	Dyke, P., Lieutenant	60	49	" R.	8	37
Boxer, E., Rear Admiral	20	38	Dymock, F., Captain	1	42	Hutchinson, Hon. J., Captain	54	55
" S., Esq.	23	38	" "	1	29	Hutton, J., Captain	11	7
Braybrooke, W., Lieutenant	1	29	Dyneley, D., Lieut. and Adjutant	2	57	Hyndman, R., Lieutenant	43	13
Brett, T., Mrs.	5	20	" "	5	6			
Brown, ——, Commissariat Clerk	Q	57		6	6	**I.**		
" Dr.	G	57	**E.**			Inglis, W., Captain	3	16
" W., Surgeon	1	29	Eddington, J., Captain	1	29			
Browne, Hon. C., Captain	50	5	" E., Lieutenant	1	29	**J.**		
" B., Lieutenant	32	8	Edwards, R., Captain	54	48	Jackson, E.	3	39
Buckley, D., Captain	58	49	Egerton, T., Colonel	29	8	James, G.	4	31
Burke, H., Captain	18	2	Eliot, Hon. G., Captain	11	45	Jesse, W., Captain	5	16
" "	38	4	Eman, J., Lieutenant Colonel	57	49	Johnston, W., Captain	2	38
" "	6	39	Esplin, W.	7	27	" "	57	49
Butler, H., Captain	23	45	Estcourt, J., Major General	1	31	" W., Ensign	96	52
" J., Lieutenant	3	28	Evans, C., Lieutenant	38	47	Joliffe, H., Captain	12	45
" Mary, Sister	1	39	" F., Captain	3	28	Jordan, W., Lieutenant	40	4
Byrne, F.	73	57	Every, E., Captain	57	49			
			Eyre, R., Lieutenant	28	46	**K.**		
C.						Karslake, H., Acting Mate	1	15
Campbell, Sir John, Bart., Major Gen.	40	47	**F.**			Keitel, F., Dr.	59	56
" W., Major	44	55	Fäcks, I.	6	37	" "	Z	57
" W., Captain	45	55	Fenwick, B., Captain	28	22	Ker, J., Captain	1	7
Cane, C.	22	26	" "	28	46	Kerr, W., Lieutenant	7	44
Carpenter, G., Lieutenant Colonel	2	30	Finnerty, Mary	44	53	" "	96	52
Carter, J., Lieutenant	6	16	Fitzclarence, Hon. E., Lieutenant	47	4	Kidd, T., Lieutenant	5	28
Cartwright, A., Captain	53	48	Fitzpatrick, T., Ensign	96	52	King, C., Captain	2	42
" "	65	49	Fitzroy, A., Captain	6	44	" "	26	46
Cathcart, Hon. Sir G., Lieutenant Gen.	42	47	" "	24	46	" F., Captain	7	16
Cattley, C., Interpreter	2	31	Forbes, J., Lieutenant and Adjutant	96	52	Kingsley, J., Lieutenant	1	29
Caulfield, F., Captain	3	22	Forman, B., Captain	17	2	Knight, C., Lieutenant	35	9
" "	28	46	Forster, J., Captain	32	46			
Champion, J., Lieutenant Colonel	1	29	Fortune, W.	30	26	**L.**		
" "	18	54	Foster, C., Quartermaster	4	32	Lamont, J., Assistant Surgeon	2	30
Chapman, S., Major	69	50	Fraser, L., Captain	1	29	Lawrence, H., Lieutenant	37	4
Cherry, A., Veterinary Surgeon	64	56	" "	87	51	Layard, A., Captain	15	37
Chester, H., Lieutenant Colonel	3	28	" A., Captain	47	48	" "	1	44
Chewton, Viscount, Captain	2	53	" R., Captain	56	49	Lee, Mr., Rev.	R	57
Childers, S., Captain	4	21	Freeman, J., Captain	2	39	Lempriere, A., Captain	30	8
" "	24	46				Lettgan, L., Major	59	56
Christie, P., Captain	3	25	**G.**			Levinge, C., Major	24	46
Clayton, F., Lieutenant	37	4	Gaynor, J., Lieutenant	5	25	Lockhart, J., Captain	57	49
Clifford, Ann	1	53	Gilborne, J., Assistant Surgeon	1	52	Longmore, J., Assistant Surgeon	9	7
Clough, M., Miss	U	57	Gilby, B., Major	31	8	Lowry, T., Lieutenant	14	16

INDEX.

NAME.	No.	Page
Luce, E., Lieutenant	9	16
" "	24	46
Ludlow, H., Staff Assistant Surgeon	24	54
Luxmore, F., Lieutenant	96	52
Lye, R., Captain	61	49
M.		
Macartney, C., Surgeon	25	8
" F., Staff Assistant Surgeon	48	55
Macdonald, J., Major	1	20
" J., Quartermaster	14	18
Mackesy, V., Lieutenant	51	55
Mackey, Dr.	N	57
Mackinnon, L., Lieutenant Colonel	11	45
Maclachlan, D., Lieutenant	7	21
" "	24	46
Macnish, W., Lieutenant	37	54
Maine, A., Lieutenant	27	8
Malcolm, L., Lieutenant	56	5
Mansfield, W., Captain	2	22
" "	28	46
Marks, Mary	58	56
Marsh, H., Lieutenant and Adjutant	18	2
" "	24	3
Marshall, J., Captain	7	32
" E., Lieutenant	2	5
" "	24	46
" J., Lieutenant	78	50
Mason, E., Assistant Surgeon	52	55
Maule, A., Lieutenant and Adjutant	8	53
Maunsell, E., Captain	55	48
Mayne, Dr.	V	57
McDermott, Susan	38	55
McGrath, P., Paymaster	18	2
McGregor, D., Lieutenant and Adjutant	12	7
McGrigor, A., Deputy Inspector General of Hospitals	34	54
Messenger, J., Lieutenant	9	44
Meurant, J., Lieutenant	27	46
Michell, C., Lieutenant	64	49
Michie, F.	3	37
Mitchell, G., Lieutenant	17	45
" R., Lieutenant	12	16
" "	24	46
Mockler, G., Reverend	2	39
Möller, J., Major	2	21
Monk, W.	10	37
Montagu, F., Lieutenant	18	2
" "	2	28
Moore, Charlotte	61	56
Morgan, T., Lieutenant	17	54
Morris, R., Mate	3	23
Muller, B., Captain	48	48
Murray, J., Lieutenant	15	16
N.		
Neville, Hon. H., Captain	10	44
" G., Cornet	6	53
Newman, Sir R., Bart., Captain	5	44
Nicholls, J., Dep. Ordnance Storekeeper	4	37
Nicholson, J., Captain	26	8
Nickels, S.	34	27
Norman, G., Captain	21	45
Norris, J., Assistant Surgeon	23	45
Norton, E., Major	40	9
O.		
O'Connor, N., Staff Surgeon	1	38
Ogilvie, B., Colonel	1	31
O'Leary, J., Assistant Surgeon	79	50
Oldfield, A., Captain	4	22
" "	24	46
Ormond, J.	14	26
Owen, W., Lieutenant	3	6
P.		
Pakenham, E., Lieutenant Colonel	10	44
Pamplin, Mary	2	32
Parker, W., Captain	34	8
Parr, F., Lieutenant	70	50
Pattison, J.	65	56
Patton, H., Captain	1	39
" "	24	46
Pattullo, J., Lieutenant Colonel	91	51
" "	96	52
Peake, W.	K	57
Pearson, G.	24	38
Pechell, W., Captain	36	9
" "	n.	51
Phenix, Mary	12	43

NAME.	No.	Page
Phipps, W., Ensign	1	7
Pine, C., Staff Surgeon	4	39
Platt, A., Ensign	55	55
" C.	70	56
Polhill, R., Lieutenant	1	29
Poole, W., Captain	5	6
Powell, C., Major	2	29
Preston, H., Captain	51	10
" G., Lieutenant	5	7
" H., Lieutenant	46	9
Proctor, G., Reverend	50	55
Purdy, B.	33	27
R.		
Radcliffe, F., Lieutenant	3	28
Raglan, Lord, Field Marshal		31
Ramsay, N., Lieutenant	45	4
Ramsden, F., Captain	11	45
Ranken, G., Major	1	10
Reade, G., Staff Surgeon	16	53
Renwick, W., Assistant Surgeon	1	39
Ricard, E., Ensign	3	21
" "	27	46
Richards, E., Captain	2	30
" J., Lieutenant	1	39
Ritchie, F.	8	25
" D.	13	26
Robinson, J., Captain	12	2
" "	37	4
Rochfort, G., Captain	63	49
Rooke, W., Captain	95	52
Rooper, E., Major	65	49
Rose, J., Major	23	45
Ross, C., Captain	67	50
Ross-Lewin, J., Lieutenant	96	52
Roto, G.	2	37
Rowley, A., Captain	8	44
" "	93	51
Ryder, H., Lieutenant	52	5
S.		
Sambell, M., Naval Instructor	25	38
Saunders, W.	0	57
Savage, J., Captain	2	28
" "	24	46
Sawell, J.	10	32
Schaw, J., Captain	23	45
Seagram, L., Lieutenant	76	50
Seymour, C., Lieutenant Colonel	59	49
Shadforth, T., Lieutenant Colonel	44	48
Sharpe, J., Major	40	55
Shearman, R., Lieutenant Colonel	32	46
Sheehan, D., Reverend	44	9
Sheil, J., Rev.	8	14
Shiffner, J., Captain	37	4
Shorrock, J., Assistant Surgeon	65	49
Simons, R., Acting Surgeon	27	54
Simpson, W., Surgeon	74	50
" R.	1	27
Singer, H., Lieutenant	24	46
" "	36	54
Smith, F., Surgeon	1	29
" "	7	39
" F., Captain	1	22
" J.	5	27
" J.	14	37
" H., Lieutenant Colonel	10	53
" H.	69	56
Smyth, H., Lieutenant	80	50
Snow, E., Captain	5	22
" "	24	46
Somerville, R., Lieutenant	5	6
" W., Lieutenant	32	54
Sorell, H., Major	J	57
Spalding, H., Mate	15	24
Spence, S., Quartermaster	1	21
" "	66	56
Spry, W., Sister	2	39
Stanley, E., Captain	19	45
Starrett, Margaret	1	30
Stevenson, J., Captain	90	51
" "	96	52
Stillwell, W., Quartermaster	30	12
" "	66	50
Stirling, J., Lieutenant	2	30
Stockwell, G., Ensign	1	7
Stone, R., Lieutenant	34	47
Stowe, W., Esq.	19	38
Strangways, Fox, Brigadier General	24	46
" "	41	47

NAME.	No.	Page
Strickland, G., Rev.	52	48
Struthers, A., Assistant Surgeon	47	55
Sumfleth, H.	4	25
Swaby, J., Lieutenant	2	30
Swift, A., Lieutenant	51	10
Swinton, W., Major	3	22
" "	24	46
Swyny, E., Lieutenant Colonel	51	48
T.		
Taule, Mary	9	37
Taylor, A., Lieutenant	2	30
Teesdale, H., Lieutenant	5	53
Thistlethwayte, A., Captain	14	53
" H., Lieutenant	18	2
Thompson, J., Ensign	96	52
" J.	16	37
Thomson, J., Assistant Surgeon	28	46
Thorold, H., Lieutenant	18	2
" "	31	3
" "	61	5
Thurlbeck, J.	1	24
Toole, W., Captain	2	44
Townsend, S., Major	4	44
" "	24	46
Tryon, H., Lieutenant	45	48
" "	65	49
Turner, H., Captain	16	42
Twyford, S., Lieutenant	14	24
Twysden, H., Ensign	82	51
" "	51	48
Tylden, W., Brigadier General	n.	51
Tyler, L., Lieutenant Colonel	29	46
U.		
Unett, T., Lieutenant Colonel	1	7
" "	16	7
V.		
Vaughan, H., Captain	51	10
" J., Captain	72	50
Vicars, H., Captain	3	7
W.		
Walford, Sophia	26	54
Wall, T., Assistant Surgeon	35	54
Walmesley, R., Lieutenant	37	9
Walsham, R., Lieutenant	24	46
Ward, L., Purveyor	42	55
" Jane	42	55
Wardlaw, R., Lieutenant	1	7
Warren, J., Captain	43	55
Webb, A., Captain	9	53
" E., Lieutenant	47	9
Welsford, A., Major	13	7
Whoble, R., Rev.	5	39
White, R., Lieutenant	30	46
" J., Assistant Surgeon	33	12
Whitfield, H., Rev.	30	54
Whitwell, J.	56	55
Wight, H., Lieutenant	57	56
Williams, T., Captain	12	53
Willias, G.	1	31
Willington, S.	16	2
Wilmer, H., Lieutenant	51	10
Wishart, J., Staff Surgeon	28	54
Witham, C., Lieutenant	1	39
Wollocombe, T., Lieutenant	3	53
Wood, H., Staff, Assistant Surgeon	8	57
Woodford, E., Lieutenant	20	2
Worthington, W., Lieutenant	18	2
Wray, J., Captain	47	9
Wright, W., Lieutenant	11	1
" H., Assistant Commissary	24	46
Wynn, A., Captain	3	28
Wynne, H., Major	81	50
Y.		
Yea, L., Colonel	15	2
Yellon, G., Deputy Assistant Commis.	1	5
Young, Sir W., Bart., Lieutenant	3	28
" Sir G., Bart., Lieutenant	24	46
" A., Lieutenant	19	26
Z.		
Zischka, F., Ensign	59	56
" "	T	57

APPENDIX.

No. 15.—Return of the Names, Rank, and Regiment (or Corps), of all Officers who remained from the first Landing until they Died or Fell in Action.—(continued.)

NAMES.	Rank.	Regiments or Corps.	Cause and Date of Death.
Caulfield, F.	Captain	44th Regiment	Died of wounds, 19 June 1855.
Eyre, R.	Lieutenant	ditto	Died of disease, 15 Oct. 1854.
Thomson, J.	Assist. Surg.	ditto	Ditto, 5 " "
O'Toole, W.	Captain	46th Regiment	Ditto, 21 Sept. "
Woolocombe, T.	Lieutenant	47th Regiment	Died of wounds, 7 Oct "
Powell, C.	Major	49th Regiment	Killed, 28 Oct. 1854.
Dalton, T.	ditto	ditto	Ditto, 5 Nov. "
Rochfort, G.	Captain	ditto	Ditto, 8 Sept. 1855.
Armstrong, A.	Lieut. & Adjt.	ditto	Ditto, 5 Nov. 1854.
Beckwith, H.	Assist. Surg.	ditto	Died of disease, 17 Oct. 1854.
Möller, J.	Major	50th Regiment	Died of wounds, 22 Dec. "
Dashwood, W.	Lieutenant	ditto	Killed, 5 Nov. 1854.
Cuddy, W.	Lieut. Colonel	55th Regiment	Ditto, 8 Sept. 1855.
Rose, J.	Major	ditto	Ditto, 20 Sept. 1854.
Schaw, J.	Captain	ditto	Ditto, ditto.
Warren, J.	Lieutenant	ditto	Died of disease, 22 Dec. 1854.
Birch, L.	ditto	ditto	Ditto, 8 Oct. "
Taylor, W.	ditto	ditto	Ditto, 20 Sept. "
Norris, J.	Assist. Surg.	ditto	Ditto, 22 Nov. "
Swiny, E.	Lieut. Colonel	63rd Regiment	Killed, 5 Nov. 1854.
Harrison, G.	Major	ditto	Ditto, 7 July 1855.
Curtois, G.	Lieutenant	ditto	Ditto, 5 Nov. 1854.
Morgan, T.	ditto	ditto	Died of disease, 11 Nov. 1854.
Mackesy, V.	ditto	ditto	Ditto. 7 Mar. 1856.
Tysden, H.	Ensign	ditto	Died of wounds, 9 Nov. 1854.
Clitterbuck, J.	ditto	ditto	Killed, 5 Nov. 1854.
Smyth, H.	Lieut. Colonel	68th Lt. Infantry	Died of wounds, 28 Nov. 1854.
Wynne, H.	Major	ditto	Killed, 5 Nov. 1854.
Edwards, R.	Captain	ditto	Ditto, 11 May 1855.
Marshall, J.	Lieutenant	ditto	Ditto, 8 June "
Barker, F.	ditto	ditto	Ditto, 5 Nov. 1854.
Smyth, H.	ditto	ditto	Died of disease, 14 Mar. 1855.
O'Leary, J.	Assist. Surg.	ditto	Killed, 17 Oct. 1854.
Egerton, T.	Brevet Col.	77th Regiment	Ditto, 20 Apr. 1855.
Lempriere, A.	Captain	ditto	Ditto, 19 " "
Gilby, B.	Major	ditto	Died of disease, 23 July 1855
Crofton, E.	Captain	ditto	Ditto, 27 Sept. 1854.
Nicholson, J.	ditto	ditto	Killed, 5 Nov. 1854.
Maine, A.	Lieutenant	ditto	Died of disease, 21 Nov. 1854.
Walmesley, R.	ditto	ditto	Ditto, 4 Oct. "
Alder, F.	ditto	ditto	Ditto, 6 " "
Macartney, C.	Surgeon	ditto	Died of wounds, 11 Apr. 1855.
Maitland, A.	Captain	79th Highlandrs	Died of disease, 7 Oct. 1854.
Grant, F.	Lieutenant	ditto	Ditto, 1 " "
Hill, A.	ditto	22nd Regiment	Died of disease, 21 June 1855. Attached to 79th Highldrs.
Norton, E.	Major	88th C. Rangers	Died of disease, 20 May 1855.
Bayley, E.	ditto	ditto	Died of wounds, 8 June "
Wray, J.	Captain	ditto	Killed, 7 June 1855.
Grogan, H.	ditto	ditto	Ditto, 8 Sept. "
Webb, E.	Lieutenant	ditto	Ditto, 7 June "
Maule, A.	Adjutant	ditto	Died of wounds, 14 Nov. 1854.
Banner, R.	Major	93d Highlanders	Died of disease, 6 Oct. 1854.
M'Gowan, J.	ditto	ditto	Died of wounds while a prisoner of war, 14 Aug. 1855.
Abercromby, R.	Lieutenant	ditto	Killed, 20 Sept. 1855.
Wemyss, J.	ditto	ditto	Died of disease, 13 June 1855.
Champion, J.	Major	95th Regiment	Died of wounds, 30 Nov. 1854
Davis, T.	ditto	ditto	Died of disease, 5 April 1855.
Dowdall, G.	Captain	ditto	⎫
Eddington, J.	ditto	ditto	⎬ Killed, 20 Sept. 1854.
Polhill, R.	Lieutenant	ditto	⎪
Eddington, E.	ditto	ditto	⎪
Kingsley, J.	Adjutant	ditto	⎭
Smith, F.	Assist. Surg.	ditto	Died of disease, 9 Feb. 1855.
Braybrooke, W.	Lieutenant	Ceylon Rifles (attached to 95th Regt).	Killed, 20 Sept. 1854.
Beckwith, T.	Lieut. Colonel	Rifle Brigade—1st Battalion	Died of disease, 25 Sept. 1854
Roper, E.	Major	ditto	Died of wounds, 10 Nov. "
Cartwright, A.	Captain	ditto	Killed, 5 Nov. 1854.
Tyon, H.	ditto	ditto	Ditto, 20 " "
Godfrey, A.	ditto	ditto	Died of disease, 27 Nov. 1854.
Sorrock, J.	Assist. Surg.	ditto	Ditto, 21 Sept. "
Hammond, M.	Captain	Rifle Brigade—2nd Battalion	Killed, 8 Sept. 1855.
Freeman, E.	ditto	ditto	Ditto, 18 June "
Malcolm, L.	Lieutenant	ditto	Ditto, 5 Nov. 1854.
Gwer, Lord F.	Ensign	ditto	Died of disease, 6 Oct. 1854.
Mitchell, J.	Surg., 1st cl.	Staff	Ditto, 24 Sept. "
Pie, C.	ditto ditto	ditto	Ditto, 6 Mar. 1855.
Mackey, P.	ditto 2nd cl.	ditto	Ditto, 5 Oct. 1854.
Bowne, W.	Assist. Surg.	ditto	Ditto, 26 Nov. "
Rid, A.	ditto	ditto	Ditto, 5 Oct. "

No. 16. — Return shewing the Names, Rank, and Regiment (or Corps) of all Officers who, arriving at any period after the first Landing, Died or Fell in Action, with the Date of their Arrival, and of their Death.

NAME.	Rank.	Regiment or Corps.	Date of Arrival.	Date of Death.	Remarks.
Forbes, John, Adjutant at Varna	Lieut.	30th Foot	Mar. 1855	1 Sept. 1855	Died of wounds ⎫ STAFF.
Anderson, C., Assist. Eng.	Captain	31st "	14 Apr. "	5 " "	Killed
Campbell, W.	ditto	5th Drag. Gds.	Oct. 1854	23 Dec. 1854	Disease
Sidebottom, G.	ditto	ditto	ditto	21 July 1855	On board ship
Neville, Hon. G.	Cornet	ditto	ditto	11 Nov. 1854	Wounds
Petre, O.	Lieut.	6th Drag. Gds	26 May 1855	25 " 1855	Disease
Wight, H.	ditto	ditto	9 July "	23 Sept. "	ditto
Williams, T.	Captain	2nd Dragoons	23 Sept. 1854	23 Nov. 1854	ditto
Boyd, W.	ditto	ditto	ditto	12 Sept. 1855	ditto
Freeman, J.	ditto	ditto	ditto	29 " 1854	ditto
Marshall, J.	ditto	4th Lt. Drag.	6 July 1855	30 " 1855	ditto
Dawson, H.	Lieut.	6th Dragoons	30 Sept. 1854	5 Oct. 1854	ditto
Bowles, C.	Captain	10th Hussars	17 April 1855	25 June 1855	ditto
Siddell, T.	Vet. Surg.	ditto	ditto	30 " "	ditto
Ancell, M.	Asst. Surg.	11th Hussars	7 April "	10 Aug. "	ditto
Hutchinson, Hon. J.	Captain	13th Lt. Drag.	21 May "	2 July "	ditto
Gavin, W.	Vet. Surg.	17th Lancers	20 Feb. "	9 June "	ditto
Harrison, N.	Lieut. Col.	Royl. Artillery	July "	14 Aug. "	ditto
Oldfield, A.	Captain	ditto	Dec. 1854	17 " "	Killed
Fitzroy, A.	ditto	ditto	July 1855	10 Sept. "	Wounds
Childers, S.	ditto	ditto	Oct. 1854	23 Oct. 1854	Killed
Gordon, A.	ditto	ditto	Mar. 1855	5 July 1855	ditto
Snow, E.	ditto	ditto	May "	6 Sept. "	ditto
Savage, J.	ditto	ditto	ditto	22 June "	Disease
Luce, E.	Lieut.	ditto	Mar. "	11 April "	Killed
Temple, F.	ditto	ditto	June "	June 1856	On board ship
Young, Sir G., Bart.	ditto	ditto	Sept. 1854	22 Oct. 1854	Disease
Maclachlan, D.	ditto	ditto	ditto	29 Nov. "	ditto
Mitchell, R.	ditto	ditto	Mar. 1855	14 April 1855	Killed
Marshall, E.	ditto	ditto	July "	29 Nov. "	Disease
Dawson, J.	ditto	ditto	" "	11 Dec. "	Wounds (accidentally)
Yellon, G.	Dep. Asst. Commry	ditto	..	15 Nov. "	Killed (accidentally)
Hayter, W.	ditto	ditto	" "	8 Sept. "	Killed
Jesse, W.	Captain	Royl. Enginrs.	June "	18 June 1855	Killed
King, F.	ditto	ditto	Dec. 1854	22 April "	Wounds
Dawson, G.	ditto	ditto	June 1855	7 June "	Killed
Crofton, G.	ditto	ditto	Dec. 1854	15 April "	Wounds
Belson, F.	ditto	ditto	Feb. 1855	14 Aug. "	Disease
Bainbrigge, E.	Lieut.	ditto	Mar. "	4 April "	Killed
Ranken, G.	Major	ditto	Aug. "	28 Feb. 1856	Killed (accidentally)
Carter, J.	Lieut.	ditto	Feb. "	2 May 1855	Killed
Lowry, T.	ditto	ditto	Dec. 1854	7 June "	ditto
Somerville, W.	ditto	ditto	June 1855	3 Sept. "	Disease
Davies, F.	Lieut.	Grenadier Gds	Nov. 1854	10 Nov. 1854	Wounds
Mackinnon, L.	Captain	Coldstrm Gds.	Oct. "	5 Nov. "	ditto
Jolliffe, H.	ditto	ditto	14 Sept. "	4 Oct. "	Disease
Blair, J.	Lieut. Col.	Scots Fus. Gds	18 Oct. "	6 Nov. "	Wounds
Muller, B.	Captain	1st Royl. Regt. 2nd Batt.	22 April 1855	7 June 1855	Killed
Bellew, W.	Lieut.	ditto	ditto	16 " "	Wounds
Ross, C.	Captain	3rd Buffs	1 May "	31 Aug. "	Missing
Dennis, J.	Lieut.	ditto	ditto	4 Oct. "	Wounds
Hyndman, R.	ditto	ditto	ditto	7 " "	Disease
Stillwell, W.	Quartermaster	ditto	ditto	12 June "	ditto
Browne, Hon. C.	Captain	7th Royal Fus.	25 Jan. "	22 Mar. "	Killed
Fitzclarence, Hon. E.	Lieut.	ditto	20 May "	23 July "	Wounds
Wright, W.	ditto	ditto	ditto	8 Sept. "	Killed
Colt, O.	ditto	ditto	7 July "	ditto "	Wounds
Beauchamp, F.	ditto	ditto	12 " "	2 Oct. "	ditto
Dent, T.	ditto	9th Regiment	27 Nov. 1854	5 Jan. "	Found dead on the road
Smith, F.	ditto	ditto	ditto	20 June "	Wounds
Le Blanc, E.	Surgeon	ditto	8 Jan. 1855	17 Mar. "	Shot by a French sentry
Townsend, H.	Captain	14th Regiment	20 Aug. "	29 Nov. "	At Therapia
Renwick, W.	Asst. Surg.	ditto	17 Nov. 1854	2 Mar. "	Disease
Croker, J.	Captain	17th Regiment	17 Dec. "	18 June "	Killed
Seagram, L.	Lieut.	ditto	24 " 1855	11 Mar. 1856	Disease
Simpson, W.	Surgeon	ditto	17 " 1854	31 May 1855	ditto
Meurant, J.	Lieut.	18th Roy. Irish	20 Feb. 1855	18 June "	Killed
Owen, F.	ditto	23rd R. Welsh Fusiliers	24 " "	30 " "	Wounds
Somerville, R.	ditto	ditto	20 Jan. "	8 Sept. "	Killed
Holden, E.	ditto	ditto	12 July "	9 " "	Wounds
Beck, C.	ditto	ditto	31 Aug. "	29 " "	ditto
Stevenson, J.	Captain	30th Regiment	12 July "	10 " "	ditto
Thompson, J.	Ensign	ditto	Nov. 1854	10 Nov. 1854	ditto
Kerr, W.	Lieut.	ditto	20 May 1855	23 Sept. 1855	ditto
Fitzpatrick, T.	Ensign	ditto	25 " "	26 June "	Disease
Deane, R.	ditto	ditto	1 Sept. "	8 Sept. "	Killed

APPENDIX.

No. 16.—RETURN shewing the Names, Rank, and Regiment (or Corps) of all OFFICERS, who, arriving at any period after the first Landing, Died or Fell in action, with the date of their Arrival, and of their Death.—(continued.)

NAME.	Rank.	Regiment or Corps.	Date of Arrival.	Date of Death.	Remarks.
Attree, F.	Captain	31st Regiment	22 May 1855	8 Sept. 1855	Killed
King, T.	ditto	32nd Regiment		28 May "	Disease
Heyland, L.	Lieut.	33rd Regiment	2 Dec. 1854	18 June "	Killed
Donovan, H.	ditto	ditto	27 Sept. "	8 Sept. "	ditto
Shiffner, J.	Captain	34th Regiment	9 Dec. "	18 June "	ditto
Robinson, J.	ditto	ditto	ditto	ditto	ditto
Hurt, F.	Lieut.	ditto	ditto	ditto	ditto
Jordan, W.	ditto	ditto	22 Jan. 1855	22 Mar. "	ditto
Lawrence, H.	ditto	ditto	Feb. "	8 June "	ditto
Clayton, R.	Ensign	ditto	9 Dec. 1854	12 July "	Wounds
Alt, H.	ditto	ditto	22 Jan. 1855	18 June "	ditto
Ramsay, N.	ditto	ditto	24 Feb. "	22 July "	Disease
Maunsell, E.	Captain	39th Regiment	10 Feb. "	10 " "	Killed
Richards, E.	ditto	41st Regiment	Oct. 1854	6 Nov. 1854	Wounds
Every, E.	ditto	ditto	6 Sept. 1855	8 Sept. 1855	Killed
Taylor, A.	Lieut.	ditto	Oct. 1854	5 Nov. 1854	ditto
Lockhart, J.	ditto	ditto	30 May 1855	8 Sept. 1855	ditto
Fitzgerald, L	Ensign	ditto	16 Nov. "	24 Dec. "	Wounds (promoted from ranks)
Mansfield, W.	Captain	44th Regiment	1 June "	28 June "	Wounds
Curtis, F.	Lieut.	46th Regiment	8 Nov. 1854	2 May "	Killed
Messenger, J.	ditto	ditto	15 Jan. 1855	15 Jan. 1856	Killed (by the explosion of a mine on the road)
Gaynor, J.	ditto	47th Regiment	" "	27 Aug. 1855	Disease (on board ship)
Michell, C.	Ensign	49th Regiment	15 June "	14 Sept. "	Wounds
Platt, A.	ditto	ditto	ditto	11 Dec. "	Disease
Bond, W.	Lieut.	50th Regiment	22 Nov. 1854	8 Dec. 1854	ditto
Stone, R.	ditto	55th Regiment	5 May 1855	7 June 1855	Killed
Evans, C.	ditto	ditto	16 June "	6 Aug. "	Wounds
Shadforth, T.	Brev. Col.	57th Regiment	8 Nov. 1854	18 June "	Killed
Stanley, E.	Captain	ditto	23 Sept. "	5 Nov. 1854	Wounds
Auchmuty, J.	ditto	ditto	ditto	13 " "	Disease
Bland, J.	ditto	ditto	ditto	8 " "	Wounds
Norman, G.	Lieut.	ditto	ditto	30 June 1855	ditto
Hague, G.	ditto	ditto	ditto	11 Nov. 1854	ditto
Ashwin, E.	ditto	ditto	5 Feb. 1855	18 June 1855	Killed
Curwen, D.	ditto	ditto	6 Sept. "	7 Oct. "	Disease
Mitchell, G.	Ensign	ditto	15 Nov. 1854	28 Mar. "	Wounds
Shearman, R.	Lieut. Col.	62nd Regiment	13 " "	8 June "	ditto
Tyler, L.	ditto	ditto	ditto	23 Oct. "	ditto
Forster, J.	Captain	ditto	ditto	8 June "	Killed
Dickson, W.	ditto	ditto	Dec. "	ditto	ditto
Cox, R.	ditto	ditto	22 Aug. 1855	8 Sept. "	ditto
Kilvington, F.	ditto	ditto	13 Nov. 1854		Disease
Blakiston, L.	Lieut.	ditto	ditto	8 Sept. 1855	Killed
White, G.	ditto	ditto	22 Jan. 1855	2 May "	Wounds
Fraser, A.W.	Captain	63rd Regiment	8 Nov. 1854	8 Dec. "	Disease
Hunter, R.	Major	71st Highland Lt. Infantry	7 Feb. 1855	30 Oct. "	ditto
Northey, W.	Lieut.	ditto	13 " "	29 May "	ditto
Gilborne, J.	Asst. Surg.	ditto	2 Nov. "	23 Jan. 1856	ditto
Macdonald, J.	Quartermaster	72nd Highlanders	13 June "	16 Sept. 1855	Wounds
Pechell, W.	Captain	77th Regiment	8 Nov. 1854	3 " "	Killed
Parker, W.	ditto	ditto	10 Aug. 1855	8 " "	ditto
Browne, B.	Ensign	ditto	18 Oct. "	15 Dec. "	Disease
Knight, C.	ditto	ditto	29 Nov. 1854	2 Oct. "	ditto
Corbett, E.	Captain	88th Connght Rangers	" "	7 June "	Killed
Preston, H.	Lieut.	ditto	22 Jan. 1855	14 April "	ditto
Grogan, H.	ditto	ditto	17 Oct. 1854	8 Sept. "	ditto
Macdonald, J.	Major	89th Regiment	19 Dec. "	15 Jan. "	Disease
Daly, Hon. C.	ditto	ditto	ditto	29 Dec. 1854	ditto
Hill, A.	Captain	ditto	ditto	31 Mar. 1855	Wounds (prisoner of war)
Darby, C.	ditto	ditto	ditto	..	Died at sea
Longfield, J.	Lieut.	ditto	ditto	20 Oct. "	Disease
Crawfurd, R.	Captain	90th Lt. Infty	5 Dec. 1854	24 Feb. 1855	Disease
Vaughan, H.	ditto	ditto	19 May 1855	12 Sept. "	Wounds
Preston, H.	ditto	ditto	5 Dec. 1854	8 " "	Killed
Swift, A.	Lieut.	ditto	10 Aug. 1855	ditto	ditto
Wilmer, H.	ditto	ditto	3 Sept. "	ditto	ditto
Ball, E.	ditto	93rd Highlanders	2 Dec. 1854	9 June "	Disease
Kirby, F.	ditto	ditto	ditto	16 Feb. "	ditto
Fraser, L.	Captain	95th Regiment	22 Aug. 1855	1 Sept. "	ditto
Handcock, Hon. H.	Lieut. Col.	97th Regiment	20 Nov. 1854	9 Sept. "	Wounds
Welsford, A.	Major	ditto	ditto	8 " "	Killed
Hutton, J.	Captain	ditto	ditto	ditto	ditto
Vicars, H.	ditto	ditto	ditto	22 Mar. "	ditto
M'Gregor, D.	Lieut.	ditto	ditto	8 Sept. "	ditto
Rambottom, H	ditto	ditto	ditto	5 Jan. "	Suffocated in his tent by charcoal
Goodenough R	ditto	ditto	28 Nov. "	20 Sept. "	Wounds
Preston, G.	ditto	ditto	10 Aug. 1855	31 Aug. "	Killed
Derman, W.	Adjutant	ditto	20 Nov. 1854	18 " "	ditto
Woodford, E.	Lieut.	Rifle Brigade, 2nd Batt.	20 May 1855	30 June "	Wounds
Cary, L.	ditto	ditto	22 April "	..	ditto (at Malta)
Borough, R.	ditto	ditto	5 Sept. "	13 Nov. "	Disease
Dyke, P.	Ensign	ditto	20 Jan. "	19 April "	ditto
Ryder, H.	ditto	ditto	22 April "	8 Sept. "	Killed
Spence, T.	Dep. Insp. Genl. of Hospitals	Staff	11 Nov. 1854	14 Nov. 1854	Lost in the Prince
Bassano, C.	Surgeon 1st class	ditto	12 Oct. 1855	1 Feb. 1856	Disease
O'Connor, N.	ditto	ditto	13 " "	7 June "	ditto
Macartney, F.	Asst. Surg.	ditto	8 Nov. 1854	12 Feb. 1855	ditto
Boyle, E.	ditto	ditto	13 " 1855	8 Dec. "	ditto
White, J.	Actg. Asst. Surgeon	ditto	7 Jan. "	3 July "	ditto
Longmore, J.	ditto	ditto	11 July "	21 Aug. "	ditto
Mitchell, T.	ditto	ditto	14 " "	29 Dec. "	ditto
Bayley, H.	Asst. Com. General	ditto	2 June "	24 July "	ditto
Coppinger, W.	Actg. Dep. Asst. Com. General	ditto	Oct. 1854	11 Aug. "	ditto
Tronton, —	ditto	ditto	ditto	2 Nov. 1854	ditto
Nicholls, J.	Deputy Ordnance Storekeeper	ditto	" 1855	3 " 1855	ditto

ROYAL NAVAL BRIGADE.

No. 17.—RETURN shewing the Names, Rank, and Ship of all OFFICERS of the Royal Naval Brigade Killed at the Siege of Sebastopol.

Rank.	Name.	Ship.	Date of Death.
Commander	L. Hammet	H. M. S. Albion	17 Aug. 1855
Lieutenant	Thomas O. Kidd	ditto	18 June "
Ditto	G. Greathead	H. M. S. Britannia	20 Oct. 1854
Ditto	Hon. C. B. H. Ruthven	" London	22 " "
Ditto	Samuel Twyford	" "	9 Apr. 1855
Mate	H. J. Spalding	" "	21 Jan. "
Lieutenant	W. H. Douglas	" Queen	11 Apr. "
Acting Mate	H. Karslake	" Rodney	12 Nov. 1854

Total Loss of the Royal Naval Brigade, averaging 1200 Men and Officers—
Officers ...... 8 Killed ... 3 Died of Disease ... 30 Wounded
Men............ 116 " ... 41 " ... 431 "

[*Note.*]—RETURNS Nos. 15 and 16 are principally compiled from Returns called for by Mr. William Ewart, M.P., and ordered by the House of Commons to be printed, 17th March, 1857.—Officers who died at Varna, Scutari, &c., or on board ship, but who never landed in the Crimea, are not included in these Returns; nor are those Officers who died of wounds or disease after arriving at home from the Crimea.